Democratic Uprisings in the
New Middle East

Mark A. Boyer and Shareen Hertel, Series Editors

International Studies Intensives (ISI) is a book series that springs from the desire to keep students engaged in the world around them. Books in the series address a wide array of topics in the international studies field, all devoted to getting students involved in the ways in which international events affect their daily lives. ISI books focus on innovative topics and approaches to study that cover popular and scholarly debates and employ new methods for presenting theories and concepts to students and scholars alike. ISI books pack a lot of information into a small space—they are meant to offer an intensive introduction to subjects often left out of the curriculum. ISI books are relatively short, visually attractive, and affordably priced.

Titles in the Series

The Rules of the Game: A Primer on International Relations, Mark R. Amstutz

Development Redefined: How the Market Met Its Match, Robin Broad and John Cavanagh

Protecting the Global Environment, Gary C. Bryner

A Tale of Two Quagmires: Iraq, Vietnam, and the Hard Lessons of War, Kenneth J. Campbell

Celebrity Diplomacy, Andrew F. Cooper

Global Health in the 21st Century: The Globalization of Disease and Wellness,
Debra L. DeLaet and David E. DeLaet

Terminate Terrorism: Framing, Gaming, and Negotiating Conflicts, Karen A. Feste

Watching Human Rights, Mark Gibney

The Global Classroom: An Essential Guide to Study Abroad, Jeffrey S. Lantis and Jessica DuPlaga

Democratic Uprisings in the New Middle East: Youth, Technology, Human Rights,
and US Foreign Policy, Mahmood Monshipouri

Sixteen Million One: Understanding Civil War, Patrick M. Regan

People Count! Networked Individuals in Global Politics, James N. Rosenau

Paradoxes of Power: US Foreign Policy in a Changing World, David Skidmore

Global Democracy and the World Social Forums, Jackie Smith and Marina Karides et al.

Forthcoming in the Series

The Stealth Pandemic: Violence against Women, David L. Richards and Jillienne Haglund

The Global Political Economy of Food, Kimberly Weir

Spirits Talking: Conversations on Right and Wrong in the Affairs of States, Stephen D. Wrage

Global Democracy and the World Social Forums, Second Edition
Jackie Smith and Marina Karides et al.

International Relations as Negotiation, Brian R. Urlacher

Democratic Uprisings in the New Middle East

Youth, Technology, Human Rights, and US Foreign Policy

Mahmood Monshipouri

Paradigm Publishers
Boulder • London

Figures to accompany the text can be found on the book's website:
www.paradigmpublishers.com/Books/BookDetail.aspx?productID=321173

Copyright © 2014 by Paradigm Publishers

Published in the United States by Paradigm Publishers, 5589 Arapahoe Avenue, Boulder, CO 80303 USA.

Paradigm Publishers is the trade name of Birkenkamp & Company, LLC, Dean Birkenkamp, President and Publisher.

Library of Congress Cataloging-in-Publication Data

Monshipouri, Mahmood, 1952–
   Democratic uprisings in the new Middle East : youth, technology, human rights, and US foreign policy / Mahmood Monshipouri.
       pages cm. — (International studies intensives)
   Includes bibliographical references and index.
   ISBN 978-1-61205-135-2 (pbk. : alk. paper)
   1. Arab Spring, 2010– 2. Political participation—Middle East. 3. Youth—Political activity—Middle East. 4. Youth—Middle East—Social conditions. 5. Social media—Middle East. 6. United States—Relations—Middle East. 7. Middle East—Relations—United States. I. Title.
   JQ1850.A91.M66 2013
   909'.097492708312—dc23

                                                                                    2013012792

Printed and bound in the United States of America on acid-free paper that meets the standards of the American National Standard for Permanence of Paper for Printed Library Materials.

Typeset by Straight Creek Bookmakers.

18 17 16 15 14   1 2 3 4 5

CONTENTS

PREFACE

A sweeping wave of rebellion in the Middle East and North Africa (MENA) in 2011 has exposed the failure of conventional political processes as well as obsolete state institutions to produce substantive democratic change. Since 2011, a combination of civil disobedience, political activism and defiance, counterculture, and social networking has resulted in an unprecedented cascade of falling regimes across the region. Economic stagnation has unquestionably been a key driving force behind democratic uprisings—popularly known as the Arab Spring—in the MENA region. High rates of unemployment and underemployment, especially among educated and young people, have led to nationwide opposition movements, spurring the region's burgeoning calls for democratic change. In addition to economic dynamics, one of the most obvious flaws of the Arab governments has been the failure of their educational method to prepare their students for the modern, information-age global economy.

The young Arabs who sparked these revolts often bore the consequences of the failed educational and political order. Today, the entire region faces antigovernment protests and dissent by a generation frustrated with their inability to find employment and freely express their opinions. As these protest movements demonstrate, the authoritarian populist social contract has come apart after many decades of mismanagement, nepotism, corruption, and political repression. The resulting unemployment and demographic youth bulge have marked the emergence of a new identity among the young Arabs encapsulated in the political slogan *Ash-sha'b yurīd isqāt an-nizām:* "The people want the fall of the regime."

Yet, significantly missing from the flurry of coverage of the Arab Spring has been a more considered assessment of the role of emotion, solidarity, and online activism. There is little doubt that modern communication technologies have helped open up a new space for public debate, especially by providing marginalized classes with a more effective voice. In an age of instant communication, these technologies have made borders and boundaries disappear, invoking a broader sense of empathy and belonging to a groundswell of resistance against tyrannical regimes. The impetus for change has increasingly become a regional drive, galvanizing the people to act against authoritarianism and stagnation. Contrary to the view that modern technologies pose a menace to cultural norms and identities, these technologies have reignited the need for emotional solidarity, cultural bonds, and translocal identities.

Especially noteworthy is the extent to which these uprisings have been fueled by a demographic surge of young people unable to find employment and frustrated by the lack of freedom. Although modern technologies and social media may have brought new politics to the streets, organization on the ground trumps the enthusiasm of young protesters when it comes to shaping a country's political future. How to turn elections into democracy in these post-conflict societies continues to be a daunting task, especially in countries with a long-standing history of military involvement in politics.

This book is a systematic attempt to understand the extraordinary events of the 2011 Arab revolts and beyond—developments that have shaken the foundation of the region's autocratic regimes as never before—with a view toward understanding the role of youth; new media technologies; and the rising demand for open politics, open society, and human rights. While acknowledging the limits of social change via the Internet and social media, this volume investigates the emerging politics in the MENA region by examining these largely peaceful—but at times violent—protests against dictatorial regimes and their entrenched political practices and their aftermath in a number of the region's countries.

Structure of the Book

This book is organized around six chapters. The first chapter explores the modern technologies and competing views on the effectiveness with which such technologies can instigate, organize, and provoke anti-regime demonstrations, noting in particular possibilities and constraints facing social movements in different contexts. Chapter 2 offers a broad assessment of the impact of the expansion of educational opportunities and an increased population of young men and women unable to find work. Here we examine the previous status quo and analyze the development of new trends as a sense of rage and rebellion spreads across the MENA region. To systematically examine these trends, we look at demographics, youth unemployment, educational achievement, and the outpouring of emotions and reactions to upheavals.

Chapter 3 deals with the issues surrounding the political economy of revolt, youth, and cyberspace and the rising significance of human rights and moral ideals for the younger generation. This chapter illustrates how modern notions or movements—such as human rights, democracy, and social justice—have created more global connectedness and a sense of sympathy within and among younger generations all over the world. In the ensuing chapter, our focus shifts to emerging identities in connection with emotional identification, protests, and new media. We examine the rise of Iran's "Green Movement," the "April 6 Youth Movement" in Egypt, and the rising significance of the role of women in the Arab Spring. Special attention in this chapter is given to the influence that moral emotions— a collective sense of reducing harm, vulnerability, and the suffering of others—have in shaping the level and intensity of emotional identification and human sympathy between different societies and people.

Chapter 5 turns to US-Iran relations with a view toward examining the implications of rivalry between the two in the context of identities and perspectives. Arguing that Iran has always been a trendsetter for the MENA region, this chapter shows why Iran's reformist Green Movement is seen as a power prelude to the currently unfolding Arab Spring. More specifically, this chapter argues that the resurgence of Islamic groups via ballot box in the post–2011 Arab Spring has given the US-Iran rivalry a new twist. The book's final chapter examines the regional tensions in Libya, Bahrain, and Syria and their consequences for US foreign policy in the MENA region. While examining the implications of the Arab Spring for US foreign policy, we devote special attention to Turkey. As the terms of governance in the region are drastically—if not permanently—altered and support for old autocrats is no longer sustainable, diplomatic maneuvers and marginal adjustments alone are insufficient.

Note: Figures to accompany the text may be seen on the website for the book: www.paradigmpublishers.com/Books/BookDetail.aspx?productID=321173

Acknowledgments

In writing this book, I benefited immensely from the guidance provided by Professor Mohammad R. Salama of San Francisco State University. Without his assistance, my trips to Cairo would not have been productive or even possible. Professor Mayy ElHayawi, of Al Alsun University and the Arab Academy in Cairo, and her husband, Ahmed ElHayawi, were gracious hosts, and so was Mr. Attiya Shakran, undersecretary of the State Information Service, whose invaluable insights and generous assistance made my stay in Egypt highly educational and immensely pleasant. Professors Dan Tschirgi, Ibrahim El Nur, Bahgat Korany, and Khaled Fahmy, all from the American University in Cairo, granted me interviews that were tremendously helpful in gaining a better understanding of Egypt in the post-Mubarak era. Professors Yomma Saber, Mohammad Nasser, and Khaled El-Beltagy of Al Alsun University were equally generous with their time and ideas. Professors Omaima Abou-Bakr, Mohamed Kamal, Mai Mogib Mosad, and Abdul Monem Al Mashat from Cairo University also offered helpful insights on the complexities of the transitional period in Egypt that proved refreshingly candid.

I am especially grateful to Bahey eldin Hassan, the director of Cairo Institute for Human Rights Studies; Negad El Borai, attorney at law; Nawla Darwish, a feminist and human rights activist; Ahmed Mahar, the founder and the general coordinator of the April 6 Youth Movement in Egypt; and Ayman Al-Sayyad, the editor-in-chief of *Weghat Nazar,* for sharing with me their perspectives on the uprisings, human rights, and the prospects for open society. I am also greatly indebted to Mr. Ibrahim el-Gamal and Gehad El-Haddad, both affiliated with the Muslim Brotherhood, who helped me reach a better understanding of the way the Muslim Brotherhood organized its political and cultural activities, how it plans to put Egypt on the path to development, and why many Egyptians supported and continue to support the Freedom and Justice Party (FJP) that today represents the Muslim Brotherhood.

I am particularly indebted to Ambassador Mohamed Badr Eldin Zayed, chair of the State Information Service, and Ayman Mohamed Walash, an expert on the political and media affairs section of the State Information Service.

My conversations with two Cairo University students—Asmaa Tohamy, an undergraduate student of political science, and Mustafa Abu Zaid, a mass communication major—proved incredibly helpful to grasp a youthful perspective on the challenges Egyptians and their nation face. In addition to these interviews, I spoke with many people and diverse groups in Cairo's Tahrir Square and learned from their thoughts and reflections on what was occurring. I found Egyptians to be a highly cultured, exceptionally friendly, and incredibly proud people. I will not miss any future opportunity to travel to Egypt and learn from this great people and nation. The comments by Travis Trapp, Jonathon Whooley, Anthony Rodregous, Erich Wieger, Evan Ducharme, Steve Barr, and Ace Wiseman on this chapter are gratefully acknowledged. The final responsibility for the accuracy and intellectual worth of this manuscript remains mine.

Chapter 1
MODERN TECHNOLOGIES

Possibilities and Constraints

The protests in the Middle East and North Africa (MENA) in 2011 have exposed—among other things—the failure of unilateral attempts by regimes to renegotiate ruling bargains.[1] The old ruling bargains between the ruler and the ruled, whereby submission and acquiescence on the part of the people were rewarded by a regime's attempt to provide socioeconomic security and political stability—have irreparably collapsed. A combination of nonviolent protests, online communication and activism, and the organizational skill of the youth movement since 2011 has resulted in an unprecedented cascade of falling regimes across the region. It is not clear, however, whether these revolts—spearheaded by youth-driven demonstrations, aided by online social networks, and facilitated by the emancipatory potential of a digital world—will prevail over well-entrenched institutions, such as the army, vested interests of privileged classes, and traditional Islamist groups.

What is evident, however, is that these uprisings have been organized, instigated, and sustained by nonviolent and nonideological movements that seek concrete responses to their demands for freedom, dignity, employment, and social justice. The increasing demands for agency, representation, democracy, and other elements of the international human rights regime can be termed "secular" in orientation without denying the role that religious constructs may have played in some such protests. In fact, as one expert poignantly notes, the 2011 Arab Spring emphatically rebuked the notion that rights were irrelevant to non-Western societies.[2] If nothing else, these uprisings illustrated how human rights–influenced movements could open the door to both violent backlash and revolutionary possibilities and change.[3]

Although every nation in the MENA region is wrestling with existential identity issues, the contagion effect created by the regime changes in Tunisia, Egypt, and Libya indicates the rise of a heightened sense of pan-Arabism as evidenced by a significant degree of imagined community among Arabs everywhere.[4] Aside from the common elements that link these upheavals, such as demands for dignity, freedom, and social justice, they have diverged fundamentally from each other insofar as the nature of their government and society, as well as civilian-military relations, is concerned. These similarities and differences will most likely yield variable implications for what the future holds in each country. Some scholars have warned against the idea that the Tunisian, Egyptian, and Libyan uprisings all constituted a cohesive Arab revolt, reminding us that Tunisians will need to cope with the class divisions that have fueled the protests. Egyptians must reshape their institutions of government, and Libyans will need to recover from a bloody civil war.[5] While Egypt struggles with its lingering military rule, Tunisia and Libya ought to redefine the relationship between their rich capital cities and their underprivileged heartlands.[6]

Yemen's president Ali Abdullah Saleh became the fourth Arab leader to be removed from the political scene since the 2011 protests. Saleh stepped down after thirty-three years in power and eleven-month protests that brought the country to the brink of civil war. In exchange for immunity from prosecution, as part of the Gulf Cooperation Council–brokered agreement, Saleh ceded power to the new president, Abd Rabbuh Mansur Hadi, who faces many challenges, not the least of which are tackling widespread poverty and malnutrition, a secessionist movement in the south, rebellions across the country, and a fight against al-Qaeda elements present in Yemen. He will serve a two-year term and oversee the drafting of a new constitution in an attempt to pave the way for the new parliamentary and presidential elections in 2014.[7]

The sectarian discrimination and old ruling dynasty continue to cast a shadow of uncertainty over Bahrain, a tiny island state where Saudi Arabia and the United Arab Emirates provide security forces and where stability seems a distant possibility for many years to come. Likewise, Syria's Bashar al-Assad, a member of the minority Alawite who rules over the Sunni-majority country, faces a daunting task of restoring stability to a chaotic country whose leader has prompted even the Arab League, which has a history of neglecting, perhaps even excusing the follies of its members, to suspend its membership.[8]

There can be no doubt that economic conditions and grievances factored heavily into the eruption of protests and the ensuing developments.[9] Aside from economic stagnation, experts agree that perhaps one of the most obvious flaws of the Arab governments was the failure of their educational method to prepare their students for the modern, information-age global economy. For a very long time, much of the state's investment has been in the region's plentiful oil and gas resources, leaving the vast majority of the people—especially the youth—outside of such entrepreneurship that has largely benefited the autocratic regimes and their cronies. With low levels of direct foreign investment in human capital, Arab schools and universities have failed to prepare their youth for the modern economy. Additionally, endemic corruption and woefully inadequate legal systems have frightened away legitimate investors. As a result, foreign investment and development have been supplanted by those seeking to exploit the region alongside its crooked elite.[10]

The young Arabs who sparked these revolts often bore the consequences of the failed educational and political order. They struggled, as Rami G. Khouri notes, against "humiliation" and a lack of "legitimacy" caused by several decades of socioeconomic and political deprivation.[11] Experiencing a marked "youth bulge," the entire region faces antigovernment protests and dissent by a generation frustrated with their inability to find employment and freely express their opinions. These youth populations, who spearheaded the post-2009 election "Green Movement" in Iran amid alleged voting fraud, have been at the forefront of the "Jasmine Revolution" in Tunisia and the "Nile Revolution" in Egypt. The Western world, experts aptly note, must watch for cases where political regimes are immensely weak and the countries are distressingly fragmented. It is within this context that such youth bulges can produce extended civil conflict, political instability, and ultimately failed states. Yemen and Palestine are prime examples. Calls for change alongside youth unrest in Iran are equally worth watching.[12]

This book is a systematic attempt to understand the extraordinary events of the 2011 Arab revolts and beyond—developments that have shaken the foundation of the region's autocratic regimes as never before—with an eye toward understanding the role of youth activists and online communities in building shared meanings, bonds, and identities in today's open societies; dynamic and interactive social contexts; and global environments. Our central arguments are twofold: (1) social media and information and communication technologies (ICTs) have empowered younger generations to participate in and shape the public discourse over politics; but (2) what ultimately leads to political transformation and building trust and coalition can only be achieved through direct and bottom-up participation supported by stronger organizational foundations. While acknowledging the limits of social change via the Internet and social media, this book investigates traditional and new politics in the MENA region as well as Western governments' reactions to these uprisings.

Youth and Unemployment

Young Egyptians' most important contribution today seems to be constructing an identity alongside their vision of a twenty-first-century Egypt.[13] Some observers have dubbed these youth movements "Generation Freedom," which are well described by four attributes: *plentiful, pinched, plugged in*, and *proactive*.[14] Others have upended the developmental rationale and assumptions behind governments' repressive policies and programs. Marked by the slogan *Hiya thawrat karama* ("This is a revolution of honor and dignity"), these uprisings, which started in the streets of Sidi Bouzid in the poor highlands of Tunisia, following Mohamed Bouazizi's self-immolation, have discredited the governments' tired argument that freedom must give way to stability, and that stability is crucial for the sake of development.[15] Failure to reframe the debate in the post–Osama bin Laden era will severely stymie the progress toward achieving universal human rights standards throughout the world, especially at a time when it seems to have generated new and historic momentum in the MENA region.

The rise of social movements and demands for freedom in the MENA region—as reflected in the emergence of a real sense of hope and possibility among the younger generation—have provided a counter-narrative to terrorism and Islamic extremism. Today's youth in the Muslim world seem to be more interested in jobs and freedoms than in Islamic militants' agenda of using violence to topple autocratic regimes and wreak havoc on Western imperialism. One of the most formidable challenges facing the governments throughout the MENA region is undoubtedly youth unemployment. In one study, the Abu Dhabi–based Arab Monetary Fund (AMF), an Arab League affiliate, concluded that regional countries need to create at least 40 million jobs by 2020 to adequately tackle the unemployment problem.[16]

These popular uprisings—also known as the Arab Spring—that have thus far toppled autocratic leaders in Tunisia, Egypt, and Libya have been led mainly by Arab youths who sought jobs and greater political freedoms. The Arab youth have vehemently rejected US military interventions and policies in the MENA region. As Al Jazeera English's senior political analyst Marwan Bishara puts it, "They collectively rejected the choice between thuggish dictators and their cynical foreign powers, between repressive patriarchies and imported paternalism, between surrender and suicide. The Arab youth had opted for a third choice: freedom."[17]

The ensuing political and national outcries have placed a damper on the tourism industry, undermined economic growth, and mounted enormous pressure on the Arab governments to support their growing populations. The youth unemployment rate in the Middle East of 25 percent, according to an April 2011 International Monetary Fund (IMF) report, "exceeds that of any other region in the world." Joblessness, as the IMF report demonstrates, "is largely a youth phenomenon, with people between the ages of 15 and 24 accounting for 40 percent of all people without jobs in the region, and this figure rises to as much as 60 percent in Egypt and Syria."[18]

The MENA region has become a hotbed of anger, rebellion, and protests for an entire generation that feels disillusioned and disenfranchised. A cursory look at demographic factors shows that a substantial portion of the population in the region is below the age of thirty. The youth represents a great share of the labor force and places enormous pressure on the labor market. Worse yet, economic growth in the region cannot absorb the flow of youth entering the labor market. Moreover, private investments are flowing primarily to informal economic sectors that create few or poor-quality jobs. An inept educational system has provided graduates with training that fails to serve the needs of potential employers. Poor governance has hampered job creation by discouraging potential investors. Additionally, public institutions and policies are neither efficient enough to deal with labor-market reforms nor able to effectively carry out the macroeconomic strategies necessary to generate long-term growth.[19]

Between 2000 and 2010, approximately 7 million new jobs were created in the Gulf Cooperation Council (GCC) countries—Bahrain, Kuwait, Oman, Qatar, Saudi Arabia, and the United Arab Emirates—of which fewer than 2 million went to nationals, according to a report issued by the IMF in October 2011. Although job creation tops governments' agendas in this region, there may be as many as 2 to 3 million additional unemployed GCC citizens by 2015.[20] The GCC countries are also experiencing a period of rapid growth in their youth population at the same time overall education levels are increasing. Yet these higher educational achievements have not made pursuing a private-sector career any more desirable.[21] The key reason for this is that the salaries associated with the public sector continue to be considerably higher than those of the private sector, which naturally lures nationals to such jobs. If the current government policies are not updated to properly reflect contemporary demographic and labor-market realities, increasing numbers of unemployed nationals will be likely to express their dissatisfaction with such policies.[22]

These countries also face additional challenges addressing the employment balance between their nationals and non-nationals. The growing level of national unemployment in the GCC countries poses one of the region's core domestic policy challenges. A third of all public-sector and two-thirds of all private-sector positions are staffed by expatriate workers.[23] In addition to unemployment problems for nationals, rising food prices and food security issues could have serious ramifications for the region. Despite the ongoing threats of violent extremism, terrorism, war, and social upheaval in the Arabian Peninsula, coming to grips with the challenge of food security has never been more essential in the incredibly water-stressed Middle East.

The peninsula's constituent countries are highly dependent on essential food imports (wheat, rice, maize, soybeans, sugar, and barley are among the major items) and thus seriously exposed to global food inflation and crisis. With declining agriculture, a growing population, and scarce water resources, the vulnerability of GCC member states will surge markedly in the future. Given that the majority of the population in these countries consists of expatriates, food price increases or any future food crisis will seriously undermine the legitimacy of these governments, triggering social unrest and protests by migrant workers.

The GCC countries, including Saudi Arabia, Qatar, and the United Arab Emirates, have made impressive aid pledges totaling nearly $18 billion to Egypt while avoiding specific commitments to Tunisia.[24] Although there are questions about whether such pledges would be eventually fulfilled, their aid might well come with numerous political strings attached. This is because although these GCC states have a good reason for wanting to uphold stability in Egypt and Tunisia, they may see democratic transitions in any Arab country as a tacit challenge to their own legitimacy. As a result, they may not share Western enthusiasm for creating strong democracies in the region.[25]

Contending Views on Technology

Whereas some view the role of technology in social change as overly exaggerated, others regard social tools as capable of bringing about an epochal change by "dramatically improving our ability to share, cooperate, and act together."[26] Increasingly, activists, nongovernmental organizations (NGOs), and even policymakers have turned their attention to the ways new information technologies and social networking can mobilize and organize credible opposition to the status quo. A combination of ICTs and social media, such as Facebook and Twitter, has increased the informational capacity of protesters and voters in the MENA region, providing tech-savvy and disaffected youth a new tool for political communication that is now critical to democratic transitions. Furthermore, as one scholar notes, the Internet as a source of information has helped open up a freer space for public debate, making it extremely difficult for governments to censor information. In fact, Internet censorship has become a "ridiculously ineffective strategy."[27]

The so-called information revolution and the spread of modern technology, experts point out, have helped level the playing field between citizens and their governments, as well as the battlefield between dissidents and dictators, while opening up these realms to the rest of the world—to the disadvantage of rulers who appear to be obsessed with the issues of national boundaries and state sovereignty.[28] Yet the questions of how to use social media and how to avoid technological determinism—namely, giving the tools more credit than the activists—remain critical.

Regarding the democratizing effects of the Internet and its surrounding technologies, a key question remains: are these technological tools inherently democratizing or contingent upon the intentions and attitudes of agents using them? In terms of the context and contingency of the public spheres, another critical question arises: under what conditions and how might the Internet and social media foster democratizing efforts? Events in China, Syria, Vietnam, the Maldives, Cuba, Moldova, Iran, and Zimbabwe, experts remind us, demonstrate that repressive governments can still coexist alongside an information revolution.[29] There is no question that modern technologies have dramatically increased the contagion effects and information cascade. However, while social media lower the organization and transaction costs among citizen activists, they equally lower the cost of government monitoring and authoritarian policies.[30] The dictators are rapidly becoming able to use ICTs to arrest key opposition leaders, disrupt efforts to organize smart mobs, and spread dissension online. The new authoritarianism in the next decade, so goes the argument, will likely see the advent of Arab Dictatorship 2.0.[31]

Insofar as technology diffusion and social change are concerned, it is worth noting that the Internet and social media are, at best, the intervening variables—and not causal ones. It is the collective action that makes protests possible. Grievances—economic or otherwise—alone do not make protests and revolutions happen. Many revolutions (France in 1789, Russia in 1917, Iran in 1979, and Eastern Europe in the 1990s) have taken place without social media and the Internet. Social media are basically new forms of expression, in which the source of the message (the person or activism behind the movement) is more important than the medium (the technological tools). Their use is, therefore, simultaneously independent of the protests and dependent on the individuals who use them. Individuals use social media in order to influence the outcome of protests. In fact, all revolutions have involved the media of their times. Use of such technologies, however, will tell us more about the protesters' motivation, intention, intelligence, and expectation than about what has actually caused the protests in the first place. Moreover, the many variations between and among the cases and conditions under study here render determining causality impossible.

Some experts have argued that social media have made protests possible and have resulted in net improvement for democracy throughout the world, even as a state's forceful reaction has increased in both vigor and sophistication.[32] Vint Cerf, a vice president of Google, has stated that the transparency enabled by Internet connectivity is a powerful, universal solvent that ultimately erodes deceit and misrepresentation. Today, Cerf claims, "there is much more openness and tolerance of criticism in China than most in the West believe."[33]

Others, by contrast, have argued that it was not Twitter and Facebook but television that was absolutely fundamental to the unfolding of events, playing a critical role in expanding protests of thousands into protests of millions. Al Jazeera and many of the other television stations helped to frame and give meaning to events in Tahrir Square and elsewhere in Egypt, legitimizing public participation and galvanizing massive support for these protests.[34] Al Jazeera is often wrongly thought of as a regional station. According to one study, upward of 70 percent of Egyptians have access to satellite television in their homes (95 percent have televisions), thus rendering Al Jazeera's content widely available.[35] This expansion of global television, experts note, has stripped government's ability to control the political narrative. It has also reduced the local, government-controlled media's credibility. During the 2008–2009 Israeli war with Hamas, for example, more Egyptians turned to Al Jazeera not only because it provided more extensive coverage of the war but largely because the public identified with its narrative.[36] It should also be noted that social media have not been helpful in facilitating political bargaining in constitution-writing processes, nor have they played a pivotal role in helping form new political parties.[37]

Still others point out that Internet communication has helped awaken online youth activism. On a much broader level, ICTs not only spread the power of ideas and information but also confer new meaning and legitimacy upon notions of power, participation, transparency, and accountability.[38] In the last analysis, it is the case that new media technologies and the Internet are most effective in those countries where there is already a modicum of freedom and individual autonomy to organize freely.[39] Under the most repressive conditions and regimes, such opportunities have been either brutally suppressed or nonexistent in the first place.

Finally, it is important to note that technology is not a remedy; it is a tool that connects the people and disseminates information to the masses, but it cannot create social change on its own. Social media, one commentator notes, cannot meet the tenets of social change: activism, strategy, discipline, organization, and personal connection. Traditional activism is high-risk activism that leads to "strong-tie" social bonds, while activism associated with social media is built around weak ties that seldom lead to high-risk activism.[40] Even though this critique is credible, one can no longer assert that online activism is not high-risk, especially in the context of authoritarian regimes. An example of this is Egypt under Hosni Mubarak, where Wael Ghonim, known for his online, anti-regime activism, was kidnapped and jailed for twelve days (January 27–February 7, 2011), during which time a massive uprising forced Mubarak to step down.

This is not to deny the importance of traditional activism and personal commitment and connection to those uprisings; rather, the point here is to underline the significance of both human agency and the role that new technologies play in the formation of social movements. It was the youth of Tunisia and Egypt who, through their courageous actions and incredible sacrifices, made history. In the words of Ghonim, head of marketing for

Google's Middle East and North Africa division, "history is made on the street, not on the Internet."[41] This view is in sync with the observation that the Internet—"the ultimate technological fix"—can help mobilize people around certain causes, but conceptualizing all problems in terms of mobilization is fundamentally misguided. Technology visionaries have yet to explain the practical details of how technology really transforms the world and how the Internet can nudge authoritarian societies toward democratization. We simply have no definitive answer to the question of whether the Internet undermines or strengthens democracy. Some commentators argue that the old and new media strengthen democracy.[42] Others note that many social and political problems, such as corruption, nepotism, and authoritarianism, are not technological in nature. Confronting these problems requires thoughtful policies, planning, and management.[43]

Some observers even call our attention to the antisocial effects of social media, arguing that increasingly social media have come to replace face-to-face communications. Emotions drive behavior and are central to self-reflection and what is going on between individuals and groups and within them.[44] Connecting emotionally is the key to all relationships as well as to personality growth and development.[45] It is through person-to-person and/or peer-to-peer communication that one can build trust and coalitions of like-minded people necessary for winning political campaigns, causes, and elections.

Sustainability and Setbacks

Significantly absent from the flurry of media coverage of the Arab Spring has been a more considered assessment of whether spontaneous social movements are sustainable over time. The conditions that render successful popular revolt and those required for successful democratization bear some resemblance, but they are far from identical. Experiences with democratization elsewhere have shown that these processes entail complicated and lengthy transitions that require proper institutions, the right leadership, adequate amounts of public pressure, and cultural and perceptual changes.[46]

Another missing aspect of analysis in this context is that although technology and social media tell us how and when the Arab Spring happened, such technology does not point to why it emerged. Although this book focuses on the role of technology, youth, and human rights, the basic question being asked is, how big of a role did social media and the Internet play in the 2011 Arab awakening? Insurgencies, as experts remind us, have depended and continue to rely on ICTs for the timing and logistics of protests. Having an active online civil society today has become a critical factor enabling democratization, but nearly everyone agrees that the Internet and mobile phones have yet to cause a single democratic revolution.[47]

The fact remains that governments today can no longer fully control popular perceptions, nor can they shape all public narratives owing to these new channels of popular communication. Yet no one can deny the crucial role that internal political dynamics and leaders' strategic choices play in the success or failure of such protests. The integration of moderate or mainstream Islamic elements into the political process within the context of post-revolt Tunisia and Egypt has raised some concerns about democratic governance. It is too early to say that the victory of Islamists in parliamentary elections portends any major attitudinal shift toward the 1979 Egyptian-Israeli peace treaty. Thus far, calls for its annulment have been rare—not even the Muslim Brotherhood, despite its occasional outcries against Israel, has gone so far.[48]

More recently, Muslim Brotherhood leaders have said that as members of the governing party they will honor Egypt's peace accord with Israel. Some of its leaders, such as Reda Fahmy, who oversees its Palestinian relations and is currently chair of the Arab Affairs committee in Egypt's upper house of Parliament, have pointed out that such coexistence can become a model for Hamas as well, provided that Israel moves toward embracing a fully independent Palestinian state.[49] As it moves into a position of authority in Egypt, the Muslim Brotherhood has begun overhauling its relations with the two main rival Palestinian factions—Fatah and Hamas—in an effort to put new pressure on Israel for an independent Palestinian state. The shift in the Brotherhood's stance toward neutrality between Hamas and Fatah may relieve US policymakers who have long worried about the Brotherhood's relationship with the more radical Hamas. This diplomatic posturing is the indication that, having assumed power in Egypt, the Muslim Brotherhood, the main victorious party in the country's parliamentary elections, intends to both moderate its positions on foreign policy and reconfigure Egypt's domestic politics to accept a new reality.[50]

It is possible to argue, as do many experts, that a more democratic Egyptian leadership is likely to behave more assertively than the previous administrations of Anwar Sadat or Hosni Mubarak toward Washington, a foreign policy that may bear greater resemblance to the government of Turkish prime minister Recep Tayyip Erdoğan, which has maintained a relatively independent posture from the US foreign policy toward the region without undermining it.[51] The exclusion of liberal or secular groups or parties from any future decision-making processes, however, would be alarming. The challenge for liberal or secular parties in the coming years, then, will be to forge an alliance with Islamists and nationalists. Accomplishing this goal will be no easy task, but it is much better than going back to the status quo.

While liberal or secular parties are at a great disadvantage compared to Islamists and nationalist pragmatists, especially in terms of organizational capabilities and resources, they must seek a new way to participate in governance processes. Ironically, both Islamists and secularists are more likely to look to the army (the Supreme Council of Armed Forces—SCAF) as the neutral arbiter or referee in their struggle for power.[52] In the case of Libya, by contrast, the absence of institutions may or may not be entirely negative. Yet another irony is that in building the infrastructure of a new system virtually from scratch, Libyans might be less burdened by the institutional remnants of such authoritarian bureaucracies as Egypt's SCAF.[53]

The transformation from authoritarianism to democracy has never been smooth and mistake-free. The success of the next phase of the Arab Spring will depend to some extent on the degree of international support. That support must be based on the recognition that there will be numerous setbacks along the way, but once overcome, they will fortify the development of democratic institutions in the region. "For the first time in their history," writes Hussain Abdul-Hussain, the Washington bureau chief for the Kuwaiti newspaper *Al Rai*, "the Arab people are experimenting with democracy. They cannot succeed if the world is too scared that they will make mistakes."[54]

Implications for Foreign Policy in the West

Both European and US experts have acknowledged their lack of influence over the 2011 revolutionary uprisings. The European Union and the United States, a German analyst notes, "may assist or obstruct, but they cannot determine the course of events."[55] Europe's interest in the success of these transformations, Volker Perthes stresses, is no smaller than it was twenty years ago in Eastern Europe.[56] Echoing a similar sentiment, a former member of the US intelligence community points out that despite its limits, the Arab Spring is a boon for US strategic interests in the MENA region.

These revolts embrace American values and, at least in Tunisia and Egypt, have achieved some political change through nonviolent methods, dealing a fatal blow to the appeal of radical Islamists.[57] Yet the fact remains that the new Middle East and North Africa will be more open and democratic, more Islamist, and ostensibly more volatile than in the past.

Since the 1978 Camp David Accords, Egypt has managed to remain the stable linchpin of US foreign policy in the Middle East. A staunch ally of the United States and Israel, Egypt's sudden collapse has left the country in the hands of a military that delivered a coup de grâce to its civilian ruler. Arguably, the United States' influence in both Egypt and Tunisia has had a positive influence on ensuring stable democratic transition in the postrevolutionary period, although the sustainability of those transitions remains a significant concern. In Iran, the US role was minimal and ineffective, with almost no impact on or leverage against the Islamic Republic. Acknowledging the limits of information technology in rentier states—states that largely live off of oil revenues—many analysts take the view that Iran's Green Movement, which emerged in reaction to disputed 2009 presidential elections, failed because the existing regime was strong. It has remained powerful and stable in large part because its oil revenues were used to defuse that challenge.[58]

In Libya, the NATO-led intervention ended the security-dominated state—a government tightly controlled by an omnipresent security apparatus. Unlike other Arab countries of the Persian Gulf, Bahrain faced an internal revolt, as its Sunni minority ruled and continues to rule over a majority Shia population. The US interests and values conflict in this small island state ruled by the Al Khalifa royal family. Similarly, the US blocked the Palestinian bid for statehood at around the same time it pushed for imposing sanctions on Syria in the UN Security Council. Syria presents a much tougher challenge, and the US role is constrained and uncertain as the Assad regime appears committed and poised to crush the opposition. Many keen observers of US foreign policy have warned that "the Arab Spring is seen more widely in the Muslim world as reflecting America's declining influence in the region, and that this perception will increase as the US prepares to withdraw from Afghanistan."[59]

The search in the West for a new foreign policy toward the MENA region has just begun. The traditional policy of containing chaos and Islamists is untenable given that Islamists are likely to win at the ballot box. The call for a new paradigm in foreign policy has never been more urgent. The question is no longer whether US foreign policy should address unrest and pressure for change in the MENA region; the question is how? Given that the United States is limited in its ability to force adequate reform and change, some experts note that "providing [for] the transfer of advice, planning, and training will often be far more important than money."[60] Cutting off US foreign aid and involvement overseas, however, is not necessarily the solution.[61] US foreign policy must orient itself toward the right side of history as soon as possible. Much is to be made up for if the United States is to regain any semblance of moral authority or democratic/liberal legitimacy in the region.

From an ethical point of view, the Arab Spring has refocused our attention on the call for responsibility to protect (RtoP), particularly in situations where mass slaughter has become or continues to be a realistic possibility. The RtoP is the international community's response to some of the most extreme violations of human rights of the past two decades. Emanating from the 2006 UN Security Council Resolution 1674 on the protection of civilians in armed conflicts (POC), RtoP is built around the notion that intervention must be motivated and authorized by a concern for rights, not for political reasons, and that it is only justified in such extreme cases as genocide, massacres, ethnic cleansing, and crimes against humanity.[62] A new debate, however, has raged over the gains, capacities, and consequences of the military intervention. While RtoP has heightened awareness of duties to prevent mass atrocities, it has simultaneously exposed the riskiness of employing forceful means under certain circumstances. Consider, for example, NATO intervention in Libya, which, as noted above, has raised the question of whether this intervention has done more harm than good. The current uncertainties in Libya and subsequent violent disorder in the aftermath of the sordid killing of Muammar Qaddafi threaten to eclipse the hope for democratic integration of the country's eastern and western parts. This violence has delayed substantial progress toward achieving state-building and economic development.

It appears that a great deal of patience, peacemaking, and proactive diplomacy might be more prudent than precipitous attempts to intervene in indigenous conflicts. Some experts have poignantly underlined the notion that RtoP's primary tools are persuasion and support, involving calls for persistent negotiations, proactive diplomacy, and the use of noncoercive force.[63] The difficulty will be to know when, in exceptional cases, intervention is morally imperative at virtually any cost. In the case of Syria, it is a conundrum that presents no easy solution, in large part because of a disparate rebel movement and crisscrossing ethno-religious fault lines.

Additionally, the absence of consensus in the international community—especially among the UN Security Council's five permanent members (China, the United Kingdom, France, Russia, and the United States)—has led to a stalemate in Syria. At regional level, the crisis has created a tension between several countries, namely, Iran, Turkey, Qatar, and Saudi Arabia. Despite seeking conflicting interests in Syria, these regional powers have shown, to varying degrees, an overlapping prudential objection to armed intervention. The problem of post-combat difficulties in Syria reinforces the emphasis on a diplomacy that would leave some kind of government in place—a kind of post-Assad regime as a transitional regime. In socially and politically fractured nations such as Syria, what will happen after a long-standing autocracy has collapsed or been overthrown is never very clear. For now, media identity in Syria has assumed a special significance. As the Syrian government has prevented foreign reporters from entering Syria, the role of social media users has proven crucial to the outside world. Mainstream television channels in the region, such as Al Jazeera, CNN, and the BBC, have become increasingly dependent on sites such as YouTube to get inside footage of Syria's upheavals.

For mediation to work when so much is at stake for various communal groups of Syria, potent economic and political incentives need to be placed on the negotiating table. Given the possibility of regional mediation and the complex political mosaic of Syria, military intervention is certain to be the most costly alternative and likely to have discouraging results. Arguably, selective and inconsistent application of the norm of RtoP is inevitable given the changing nature of geopolitical considerations of major international and regional powers involved in such decisions. If there had been tools and levers to coax and coerce such leaders as Qaddafi and Assad, rather than arm their opponents, within a generation, perhaps without so much bloodshed, there could have been transitions to broader human rights regimes. RtoP may under certain conditions be better fulfilled by mediation than intervention.

From an economic standpoint, some experts have encouraged the region's Arab countries to seek a competitive private sector and strong trade relations with the West. Given that the Arab uprisings were driven at least in part by economic grievances, they note, helping the region to move from civil strife to political transition requires getting it on a path to sound economic growth. The best tools available to do so are enhanced trade agreements. The region's core challenge is to rectify the absence of a vibrant private sector—one that can compete internationally, that can create sustainable jobs for the 4 million young people entering the labor force each year in the MENA region, and that no longer depends on regulatory rents and political connections.[64] For Egypt and Tunisia, joining the European Union (EU) Customs Union over a period of ten years, as was the case with Turkey, will mean benefiting from free trade in goods and services. The United States should also work on a parallel track to negotiate free trade agreements with these countries. These policies will push newly elected governments in Egypt and Tunisia to embrace increased transparency in government procurement and regulation as well as better investor protection.[65]

Conclusion

The 2011 Arab uprisings proved that the notion of human dignity was at the heart of these peaceful democratic protests. If nothing else, the Arab Spring illustrated how human rights–inspired movements could open up space for the ordinary and marginalized people to claim a public role in politics. Apart from different political contexts in which these uprisings broke out, they all culminated in a heightened sense of pan-Arabism, drawing together people of every ideological and political stripe and social class. More importantly, a cohort of youth throughout the Middle East and North Africa, wired up and equipped with the new methods of communication, spearheaded a momentous event of unprecedented significance. Jobless but educated, frustrated but tech-savvy, weary but fearless, this young generation turned to online activism, toppling patriarchal and dysfunctional regimes as never before.

It is worth noting that modern technologies of communication and social media entail both opportunities and constraints. They are crucial to organizing, instigating, and upholding nonviolent movements aimed at seeking representation, democracy, and human dignity. On the flip side, online activism is likely to turn into a visionary platform unless it can generate momentum in the street. This was evident during the 2011 uprisings in Egypt when shutting down access to the Internet failed to hinder political activities that the Mubarak government wished to extinguish.

Online activism alone lacks the necessary venom to put an end to authoritarianism if it is not buttressed by building trust and coalitions on the ground. The power of social media to transform political systems is blown widely out of proportion. What social media and other modern technologies alone cannot do is bring about democratic governance and change. What these mediums can do is hold ruling elites and governments accountable to the general public only if there is a degree of freedom that allows social activism. Social media without human action is bereft of what it takes to prompt a truly revolutionary change. Messages posted to social networking sites alone cannot lead to formidable and sustainable change, unless they are followed up by action on the ground.

Chapter 2
THE DIGITAL AGE, DEMOGRAPHICS, AND AN ETHOS OF PROTEST

The development of new digital technologies, especially online social networking, has enhanced the level of youth participation in cyberspace in a variety of ways, including accessing information and participating in informal and formal groups. Marked by the elements of anonymity, speed, wider reach, and connectivity, these new technologies have become the most effective tools of organizing and instigating uprisings, making the search or the need for a populist leader unnecessary and making mass mobilization and protest possible.[1] These elements have enhanced young people's capacity to effectively engage and participate in mobilizing civic movements as well as to advocate for human rights and social change. For the region's many young people, especially those who are female, ICTs and social networking technology are enabling tools. Evidence suggests that women are especially active users of social networking, blogging, and other online activities, in part because the keyboard doesn't require them to cover their heads or be accompanied by a man.[2]

By prompting interactivity and participation, where one becomes not only consumer but also creator of online content and where sharing ideas and exchanging feedback become the norm, these new digital technologies enable youth to redefine patterns of participation, civil involvement, and self-expression.[3] Access to new media has transformed communications throughout the MENA region and, together with the emergence of a wide variety of new satellite television channels (e.g., Al Jazeera and Al Arabiya), is likely to help its citizens to form public discourse around notions of accountability, justice, and freedom.[4] This has led to the emergence of a new political culture informed by modern ideas, ideals, and values, often known as "technological citizenship." This form of citizenship emphasizes inclusive rights of an individual as "citizen" and of "social justice" as opposed to those of exclusive prerogatives such as sectarian and ethnic identities. Technology must therefore be seen not just as a set of neutral tools, but as a *practice*—that is, a way that things are done.[5]

Following the Arab Spring, the public's mood in the Muslim world has turned against militants and autocrats. Tunisia's "Jasmine Revolution" demonstrated new ways of expressing dissent and expanding political space for protest. Such new methods of communication appeared crucial not only for mobilizing collective action in the form of civil disobedience but also for serving as a tool for gauging efficiency, transparency, and accountability. To be sure, even the most authoritarian states now appear dependent on such tools, in part because their economies, service infrastructure, and communication systems include integration of such modern ICTs.

Although the revolts in the MENA region have many roots, there is a broad consensus that economic stagnation and lack of income growth have been fundamental motives. Given the rapid population growth and soaring import prices for basic food items, some protests were not totally unexpected.[6] The concept of emotional identification has recently regained prominence among international relations experts. *Emotional identification* refers to fear, sympathy, anger, resentment, and similar emotions that link domestic groups and even all human beings regardless of national borders in the face of common—if not identical—economic deprivation, misery, calamity, and threat. It has evolved from the study of human rights in the post–Cold War era, when genocide and ethnic cleansing in the 1990s evoked the justifications for humanitarian and military interventions. Today, there are pragmatic and analytical reasons for taking seriously the role that moral ideas and emotions play in the formation of new identities and solidarities—on both the local and global scales. Given the influence that economic deprivation, social injustice, genocide, and ethnic cleansing have had on the protesters' behavior and mind-set, understanding their role is central to the study of modern uprisings. This chapter examines the relationship between demographic trends and revolt and the spread of technology and democratization with a view toward demonstrating the difficulties of democratic transition.

Demographic Trends

There were more than twice as many people (7 billion) on the planet in 2011 as there were in 1960 (3 billion).[7] World population has never doubled this rapidly before, but it is unlikely to double again. The overwhelming young populations of developing countries will generate virtually all the future population increase. The developing world will account for more than 95 percent of future population growth. Even with declining fertility, the world's population is still growing by about 80 million people a year.[8] Similarly, the world's gross domestic product (GDP) more than doubled from 1980 to 2009.[9] A combination of the enhanced prosperity and sheer numbers of people will dramatically increase demands on the Earth's finite resources. As a result, the consumption of resources currently enjoyed in wealthy nations of the developed world will be difficult to sustain world-wide.[10] This is arguably the reason world population is unlikely to double again—because we will kill ourselves off by our unsustainable practices.

According to a study conducted by the Pew Forum on Religion and Public Life in January 2011, the Muslim population in the MENA region is expected to grow by more than a third (37 percent) in the next twenty years. It is projected to grow from 321.9 million in 2010 to 439.5 million in 2030, which is more than double the number of Muslims in the region in 1990 (205.9 million).[11] The annual growth of the Muslim population in the region is projected to be 1.4 percent between 2020 and 2030, down from 1.8 percent between 2010 and 2020 and 2.1 percent between 2000 and 2010.[12] Trends show that average life expectancy at birth has been rising in this region in recent decades, from approximately sixty-five years in 1990–1995 to about seventy-one years in 2010–2015.[13]

With fertility rates in the MENA region dropping and life expectancies rising, the Muslim population in the region is aging. Nevertheless, the population in this region is expected to remain relatively youthful. In the Middle East, about 54 percent of the population in Muslim-majority countries is expected to be under age thirty in 2030; in North Africa, about 49 percent of the population in Muslim-majority countries is expected to be in this age bracket in twenty years. In Israel, by comparison, the UN estimates that about 43 percent of the general population, which includes a growing share of Muslims, is expected to be younger than thirty in 2030.[14]

According to the *2009 Arab Human Development Report*, the region continues to be characterized by water shortages, the lack of arable land, soaring food prices, and population growth at rates that are bound to put enormous pressures on the carrying capacity of lands and further threaten environmental sustainability. The urban sprawl adds more to the existing problems, as the growth of Arab cities and towns poses formidable challenges to the ruling regimes. "Accelerating urban drift in the region," the report notes, "is straining already-overstretched infrastructure and creating overcrowded, unhealthy and insecure living conditions in many cities. In 1970, 38 percent of the Arab population was urban. By 2005 this had grown to 55 percent, and it is likely to surpass 60 percent by 2020."[15]

Although demography alone is not necessarily the main source of conflict and tension in these countries, it surely contributes to the problem if correct economic policies and political actions are not pursued. In this section, we turn our attention to the population age structure in the MENA region. Of the numerous problems facing the region, unemployment is the most urgent one. The unemployed in North Africa are known as the *hittistes*, Arab slang for those who lean up against the wall. The Arabic word for "wall" is hit, and the term was used in the Islamist struggles against the state in Algeria and Egypt. The young urban dispossessed male in Algeria became known as a *hittiste*. In October 1988, the *hittistes* ran out of patience and became engaged in riots. In Gilles Kepel's words, the riots of 1988 "marked the emergence of the young urban poor as a force to be reckoned with." The *hittistes* alone, however, could not mount a coherent political challenge to the leadership of the dominant ruling regime under the National Liberation Front (Front de liberalization nationale—FLN). This task was left to militant Islamists, many of whom were teachers and students already active in preaching and ministering to the working class. Naturally, they tapped into this reservoir of discontent and disenchanted young people, recruiting many of the *hittistes*.[16]

Fearing these prospects and the globalized impacts of Western culture and what are perceived to be its immoral values, including HIV/AIDS, premarital sex, drugs, and suicide, states in the MENA region have explicitly viewed themselves as surrogate parents for the country's youth. According to one expert, this explains the establishment of Ministries of Youth and Sports throughout the region during the 1990s. The purpose of such ministries has been to develop national youth policy and programs. States have also attempted to guide youth through ideological work of institutions devoted to education and health, conscription into the military, and numerous state-run youth and student unions. These projects have been aimed at "ensuring that young people do not deviate from the transcendent goal of maintaining the integrity of the nation."[17]

Population Growth and Urbanization

Swift population growth in the MENA region entails significant implications for employment, access to services, and the cost of subsidies. The increase in subsidies means trouble for many governments that are under pressure to properly manage budget cuts and restrictions in the face of conditions imposed on them by international financial institutions such as the International Monetary Fund and the World Bank. This can be immensely unsettling given that the subsidies are inevitably targeted at basic goods and services. In many rentier states of the MENA region (i.e., states that live off of the petroleum rents), the drop in oil prices will leave governments with the dilemma of trying to balance the budget versus the political consequences of attempting to reduce subsidies on basic goods and services.[18] This collection of factors could spell numerous political consequences, including unemployment, fast-paced urbanization, water and food insecurity, and ultimately political instability.

An overview of demographic trends points to the steeper population growth in the region and the expected rural-to-urban migration projections. The region's lesser urbanized nations all have recently experienced sharp urban population increases—a trend that is likely to continue in the coming years.[19] By 2010, with the exception of Egypt and Iraq, all MENA countries saw an increase in urban population. The future projections of population in the MENA region all point to decline in the annual average growth rates (see Table 2.1). The population of MENA's largest cities, especially the Cairo metropolitan area, has increased from 2.4 million in 1965 to nearly 10 million in 2010 and is expected to reach 11.5 million by 2015.[20] That said, the whole region has experienced a decline in total fertility rate (TFR), manifested in a transition from high mortality and fertility to low mortality and fertility, even though this has transpired at very different rates in different countries. By 2005, all MENA countries had a TFR of less than 4.0, except for Iraq, Saudi Arabia, the Palestinian Territories, and Yemen.[21] It is projected that during 2010–2015, all MENA countries will have a TFR of less than 3.7—except for Yemen at 4.7.[22]

Several factors accounted for the decline in fertility: a sharp decline in infant mortality, a tendency toward later marriage, better and faster access to family planning services, and improved educational opportunities for girls. Despite continuing fertility declines, MENA's population is expected to reach 690 million by 2050.[23] The youth cohort (typically defined as young people below the age of twenty-four) continues to be numerous in size compared to all other age groups. The number of youth in the MENA region is projected to reach its upper limit at 100 million by 2035 and decline slowly thereafter.[24] In 2010, the median age in the region ranged from 17.6 in Occupied Palestinian Territories and 17.8 in Yemen to 31.7 in the United Arab Emirates and 31.1 in Qatar.[25]

Table 2.1 Demographic Trends

	Population						
	Total (millions)			Average Annual Growth (%)		Urban (% of total)	
	1990	2010	2030	1990–1995	2010–2015	1990	2010
UAE	1.9	4.7	6.6	5.3	2.0	79.1	84.1
Qatar	0.5	1.5	2.0	2.4	1.6	92.2	95.8
Bahrain	0.5	0.8	1.1	3.2	1.8	88.1	88.6
Kuwait	2.1	3.1	4.3	−4.3	2.2	98.0	98.4
Libya	4.4	6.5	8.5	2.0	1.8	75.7	77.9
Saudi Arabia	16.3	26.2	36.5	2.3	1.9	76.6	82.1
Iran	56.7	75.1	89.9	1.8	1.1	56.3	70.8
Tunisia	8.2	10.4	12.1	1.7	1.0	58.0	67.3
Jordan	3.3	6.5	8.6	5.6	1.4	72.2	78.5
Turkey	56.1	75.7	90.4	1.7	1.1	59.2	69.7
Algeria	25.3	35.4	44.7	2.2	1.5	52.1	66.5
Egypt	57.8	84.5	110.9	2.0	1.7	43.5	43.4
Syria	12.7	22.5	30.6	2.8	1.7	48.9	55.7
Morocco	24.8	32.4	39.3	1.7	1.2	48.4	58.2
Yemen	12.3	24.3	39.4	4.6	2.7	20.9	31.8
Djibouti	0.6	0.9	1.2	2.1	1.6	75.7	76.2
Sudan	27.1	43.2	61.0	2.6	2.0	26.6	40.1
Iraq	18.1	31.5	48.9	3.0	2.6	69.7	66.2
Lebanon	3.0	4.3	4.9	3.2	0.8	83.1	87.2
Palestine	2.2	4.4	7.3	3.9	2.9	67.9	74.1
Oman	1.8	2.9	4.0	3.3	1.9	66.1	73.0

Note: Countries listed based on Human Development Index Rank (from high to low to other countries).

Source: United Nations Development Program, *Human Development Report 2010* (New York: UNDP, 2010), 184–187.

Demography and Security Implications

Demographic concerns and factors have attracted more interest in the dynamics of change by both scholars and policymakers since the end of the Cold War. Increasing levels of globalization, as evident in the expansion of new social media tools—such as the Internet, Facebook, Twitter, and satellite TV—have made it more difficult for US policymakers to ignore demographic-induced instability across the globe.[26] The three most pervasive demographic trends have the potential to generate significant security effects: (1) the bifurcation of high-fertility developing countries into those that are beginning to curb fertility rates and those that are not; (2) the emergence of chronic low fertility in developed countries of Europe and East Asia; and (3) increasing urbanization in the developing world.[27]

Turning now to the third trend—that is, the increasing urbanization in the MENA region—it is evident that relatively more conflict will occur against an urban backdrop.[28] Contributing to the urbanization problem is the degree to which younger citizens in developing countries put pressure on the educational, health care, sanitation, and economic infrastructure.[29] Urban areas and their surrounding cities, including poor shantytowns, are likely fertile recruiting grounds for radicals and revolutionary groups fighting existing regimes.

Contrary to the widely held view—that in high-fertility developing countries, the emergence of high structural unemployment at a time when the national age distribution is highly skewed in favor of those ages eighteen to twenty-four years old is likely to result in many of the youthful unemployed throwing their support behind the radical political alternatives[30]—what happened in Egypt was that these educated but unemployed youth sought new goals via peaceful democratic change.

Thus the relationships among demography, security, conflict, and democracy require a fresh look. A country's political demography is indicative of its vulnerability to revolt as well as its potential for democratic change. Countries with youthful age structures are highly likely to have nondemocratic regimes, but once age distribution becomes more balanced, countries are more likely to achieve and sustain democracy. This is because the youth bulge—a high proportion of young adults, resulting from a large share of the population composed today of children who will become tomorrow's young adults—and the threat of volatility may typically be used by autocratic regimes to justify their emergency rule, fraudulent elections, and use of systematic coercive capacity to suppress dissent. Egypt under Mubarak is a case in point, as Mubarak repeatedly reminded the Egyptians that they face a stark choice between "chaos or stability."[31]

According to a 2003 report from Population Action International (PAI), countries with a high number of young adults (at least 40 percent of the adult population between the ages of fifteen and twenty-nine) were 2.3 times more likely to suffer a civil conflict through the 1990s.[32] Richard Cincotta and Robert Engelman of PAI note that most countries tend to progress through a demographic transition—the shift of all populations from high death and high birth rates to low death and low birth rates— that most industrialized countries have experienced. Although this phase initially boosts the population, it eventually stabilizes it. Countries that undergo such transition are less likely to experience political instability. In most cases, they note, the "youth bulge" was strongly associated with the likelihood of a new outbreak of civil conflict.[33]

Tunisia's age structure is changing in response to a rapid decline in the country's fertility rate, from an average of five children per woman in the early 1980s to fewer than two children per woman today. Young adults comprise 41 percent of the country's working-age population, but this "youth bulge" is already shrinking.[34] In Yemen, by contrast, where women have an average of six children each, nearly three-quarters of the population are younger than thirty. This is no surprise because half of all married women in Yemen want to avoid pregnancy but are not using family planning. As age structures grow more mature, societies become less willing to accept the regime's proposed trade-off, and the attempt to put in place democratic reforms has a greater likelihood of success. Based solely on demographics, Tunisia has a better chance at attaining a representative government than Yemen or Egypt.[35]

The Youth Unemployment Predicament

Many developing countries have limited means and ways of providing employment to their young, fast-growing populations (see Table 2.2). Many would-be laborers are likely to be attracted to the labor markets of the aging developed countries of Europe, North America, and Northeast Asia.[36] Youthful immigrants will become crucial to sustaining advanced economies of the developed world. These demographic dynamics and their implications will be palpably visible in the Muslim world, where many economically fragile and poor countries will continue to experience dramatic population growth in the decades ahead. The attendant surge in the immigration of Muslim workers, especially to Europe from the MENA, will be the trend in coming years and decades. "Worldwide," experts note, "of the 48 fastest-growing countries today—those with annual population growth of two percent or more—28 are majority Muslim or have Muslim minorities of 33 percent or more."[37]

Nearly one in five people living in the MENA region, according to a 2007 study conducted by the Population Reference Bureau, is between the ages of fifteen and twenty-four—the age group defined as "youth"—resulting in the youth bulge, as mentioned above.[38] Despite the fact that mortality in the MENA region began to decrease in the late nineteenth and early twentieth centuries, the decline in fertility (births per woman) did not take place until the mid-1960s and early to mid-1970s. Consequently, the second half of the twentieth century saw explosive population growth throughout the region as births far outnumbered deaths.[39]

The combination of a noticeable decline in child mortality and the relatively slow advent of fertility decline resulted first in an increase in the proportion of children under age fifteen and then in a rise in the proportion of young people ages fifteen to twenty-four, as the proportion of children fell after fertility began to decline. This youth bulge, when combined with the rapid growth in the overall population, has resulted in the most rapid growth in the number of young people in the region's history.[40]

In the MENA region, another study demonstrates, two-thirds of the population are under eighteen. They face one of the highest unemployment rates in the world, as the MENA region ranks among the worst in the world for youth unemployment—approaching 30 percent—high population growth, and poor education. Many graduates from high school or college are poorly prepared for employment.[41] In some countries of the MENA, such as Egypt, nearly 40 percent of the population is ten to twenty-nine years old.[42] Those under the age of thirty account for 90 percent of Egypt's total unemployment.[43] For many of the young unemployed, getting a job takes *wasta* (connection) to a country's ruling party, tribal leader, or a powerful businessman.[44] Moreover, many university graduates have the highest unemployment rates. Two reasons account for this: (1) university students are the fastest-growing group among new entrants to the job market; and (2) students are the group most dependent on public sector employment, which is not growing as fast or might even be shrinking.[45] Young people make up 80 percent of the total unemployed, and 95 percent

Table 2.2 Unemployment Rate

Total unemployment is expressed as a percentage of total labor force, whereas youth unemployment is expressed as a percentage of labor force aged 15–24 years.

Country	Year	Total	Female-Male	Youth
Qatar	2007	0.5	2.4	1.6
Kuwait	2005	2.0	−0.2	11.3
UAE	2008	4.0	10.0	12.1
Saudi Arabia	2008	5.0	9.5	28.2
Bahrain	2001	5.5	6.4	20.1
Israel	2008	6.1	0.8	12.6
Syria	2007	8.4	20.5	19.1
Egypt	2007	8.9	12.8	24.8
Lebanon	2007	9.0	1.5	22.1
Morocco	2009	10.0	0.7	21.9
Iran	2008	10.5	7.7	23.0
Algeria	2006	12.3	2.6	24.3
Jordan	2009	12.9	13.8	27.0
Tunisia	2005	14.2	4.2	30.7
Yemen	2008	15.0	29.4	—
Iraq	2006	17.5	6.3	—
West Bank and Gaza	2008	26.0	−2.7	—
Djibouti	2002	59.9	14.0	—
G6Average	2009	7.8	−0.52	17.4

Source: Credit Suisse, ILO, "Middle East and North Africa: Demographic Highlights," *Economics Research*, February 25, 2011, 7, www.credit-suisse.com /researchandanalytics.

of the unemployed youth have at least a secondary degree.[46] Similarly, in Lebanon, according to a study carried out in 2003, there were not enough jobs for young graduates of universities and high schools. Those who were employed suffered from low pay as well as a disparity between their education and employment.[47] The upshot has been politically explosive, with a generation of young people that is far more educated than their parents yet is economically worse off.

Furthermore, according to the *2009 Arab Human Development Report*, unemployment in Arab countries affects youth disproportionately. Not surprisingly, however, unemployment rates for young Arab women are higher than those for young Arab men, and are among the highest in the world. In 2005, the youth unemployment rate for men was 25 percent of the male labor force compared with 31.2 percent for women. The female youth unemployment rate varied from a high of about 59 percent in

Jordan (compared with 35 percent for males) to a low of 5.7 percent in the UAE (compared to a male unemployment rate of 6.4 percent).[48] Figures demonstrating the combined effects of high unemployment and the youth bulge may be seen on the website for this book: www.paradigmpublishers .com/Books/BookDetail.aspx?productID=321173.

The rapid rise in the number of job seekers in the job market, combined with the declining role of the government in hiring and lingering barriers for young women to enter the private sector, has led to very high female unemployment rates. There are several reasons for the failure of private firms in the MENA to replace the public sector in employing young women, "including highly segregated labor markets along gender lines; employers unwilling to assume the added cost of maternity leave and child care; women's limited geographic mobility; and the limited growth of labor intensive, export-oriented industries that might otherwise employ women."[49] On balance, to face the challenge of youth unemployment, some leaders in the region, such as Jordan's King Abdullah II, have said that the Middle East must develop 200 million jobs by 2020.[50] To do this, countries in the MENA region need 6 to 7 percent sustained annual economic growth. Oil revenues aside, the current rate of growth is 3.6 percent.[51]

Demographics of Revolt

Those factors that contributed to the Tunisian uprisings—such as high unemployment rates, high prices of food, and falling real wages—are widespread in the region, from oil-rich Libya to impoverished Yemen. The problem of youth bulge and unemployment has mounted enormous pressures to the region's education and health care systems, natural resources, and labor markets. Ultimately, however, the greatest strain is in the labor market: in some cases such as Egypt, it takes five years before 75 percent of all graduates obtain work.[52] On balance, however, Tunisians are better educated and more urbanized than their neighbors. With 7.2 percent of their GDP spent on education, Tunisians are steadily ranked among the most modernized countries in the Middle East and North Africa. In contrast, Algeria spends 4.3 percent of its GDP on education, Egypt 3.8 percent, Libya 2.7 percent, Jordan 4.9 percent, and Yemen 5.2 percent.[53]

Ironically, but understandably, the question persists: why did the revolt occur in Tunisia? Those who have traveled throughout the region, one expert reminds us, could see that Tunisia enjoyed a relatively high standard of living and quality of life. The country's per capita income is almost double that of Morocco and Egypt. It is higher than Algeria's, even though Algeria is an oil-rich nation and Tunisia lacks such national resources. Similarly, Tunisia scores high in poverty-reduction programs, literacy, education, population control, and women's status. It is far from a rentier state in that it has built a middle-class society based on its human resources and investment rather than pumping oil from the ground. Tunisians export clothing, olive oil, and produce and are host to hundreds of thousands of European tourists each year.[54]

The fact remains that, like Iran, Tunisia has become a middle-class society imbued with rising expectations and demands for political freedoms. The façade of stability in these countries is misleading, and the preservation of the status quo is no longer sustainable as long as their citizens cannot freely express their economic and political grievances. A quick glance at the demographics behind the resurgence of Iran's Green Movement in 2009 explains why educated young women were at the forefront of it. In the 1970s, toward the end of the Pahlavi monarchy, nearly 5 percent of college-aged youth went to college. By 2009, the figure had reached 31 percent.[55] The girls outnumbered the boys in secondary schools (1996), primary schools (1999), and higher education (2001).[56]

Roots of Youth Unemployment

The root causes of youth unemployment can be attributed to a number of demographic, socioeconomic, and political factors, including the absence of proper development strategies, weaknesses in the business environment, poor governance, absence of transparency and accountability, and widespread corruption.

- **Demographic factors:** As a significant part of the population in every MENA country is below the age of thirty-five, the youth represent a prominent share of the labor force. This large section of the population, particularly those between the ages of fifteen and twenty-nine, puts immense pressure on the labor market.
- **Low economic growth and weak economic diversification:** Economic growth in the region cannot absorb the flow of job seekers entering the labor market. Additionally, private investments are

flowing primarily to informal sectors that create few or poor-quality jobs, particularly the small retail industries.

- **Inept education system:** College graduates are struggling to find a job, let alone one that matches their qualifications and expectations. Ultimately, the educational system is ill-suited to the labor market, providing graduates with a type of training that fails to serve the needs of potential employers.
- **Institutional factors:** Public institutions and policies are neither efficient enough to deal with labor-market reforms nor able to implement the macroeconomic strategies necessary to deliver long-term growth. This weakness in governance hinders job creation by discouraging potential investors and fostering the growth of the informal sector.[57]

Expanding Educational Opportunities

The link between access to formal education and the attempt to curb population growth is beyond dispute. Free and state-provided education has been one of the central pillars of the social contract in virtually every country in the MENA region since these countries gained their independence from British and French colonial regimes. Postindependence governments significantly extended their education systems, driven by the rapidly growing youth bulge, the need to build nationhood, and the desire to establish state sovereignty predicated on political legitimacy and popular support for new regimes through rendering access to basic education a fundamental right of citizenship.[58] The adult literacy rate, as shown by the percentage of people age fifteen and older, has received considerable priority (see Table 2.3).

Many studies have shown that education is a major underlying factor influencing age at first marriage and access to reproductive health care, including the use of contraceptives and the determination of family size. It is evident that universal access to primary education and reproductive health care make a huge difference. Likewise, good health and education are the very foundation for reducing poverty and constructing a decent, dignified life. In most MENA areas, including Oman, Iran, Egypt, Bangladesh, Sri Lanka, and Kerala in India, women with primary education have fewer children than women with no education.[59] Other studies have shown that universal completion of compulsory education would create higher levels

Table 2.3 Educational Achievements

Human Development Index Rank (high to low to other countries)		Adult Literacy Rate (% age 15 and older) 2005–2008	Population with at least secondary education (% age 25 and older) 2010
32	UAE	90.0	—
38	Qatar	93.1	54.1
39	Bahrain	90.8	48.1
47	Kuwait	94.5	56.9
53	Libya	88.4	—
55	Saudi Arabia	85.5	48.8
70	Iran	82.3	29.5
81	Tunisia	78.0	23.1
82	Jordan	92.2	54.2
83	Turkey	88.7	22.3
84	Algeria	72.6	25.9
101	Egypt	66.4	36.1
111	Syria	83.6	33.5
114	Morocco	56.4	—
133	Yemen	60.9	—
154	Sudan	69.3	11.5
	Iraq	77.6	26.3
	Lebanon	89.6	—
	Palestine	94.1	47.3
	Oman	86.7	—

Source: United Nations Development Program, *Human Development Report 2010* (New York: UNDP, 2010), 192–196.

of literacy and mathematical skills in society and wider dissemination of individual social skills necessary for a country's national development.[60]

Paradoxically, but understandably, these uprisings started in Tunisia, where there was a high level of education, a sizeable middle class, and a greater degree of gender equality. The 1956 Tunisian Code of Personal Status (CPS), which profoundly altered family law and the legal status of women, represented one of the initial reformist policies known in the Arab world. This was, in one expert's view, a manifestation of the different vision of society held by Habib Bourguiba's victory over other factions immediately following the proclamation of the nation's independence.[61] The CPS changed, among other things, regulations on marriage, divorce, alimony, custody, and to a lesser extent inheritance. The code decreased the prerogatives of extended kin in family matters, giving women greater rights by broadening the range of options available to them in their private lives. The code abolished polygamy, terminated the husband's right to repudiate his wife, allowed women to file for divorce, and increased women's custody rights. Absent any feminist movement or women's mass protest movement in Tunisia in the 1950s demanding such reforms, the move can rightly be labeled as a reform from above.[62] Table 2.4 illustrates the value of investing in education relative to GDP throughout the region.

Social Media and Hunger for Freedom

Resistance to ineffective and failing policies of governments in the MENA region made the Internet, social networking, and satellite television useful tools for the revolutionary youth on Arab streets. All over the world, from Tunisia and Egypt to Athens, from Occupy Wall Street to Moscow, the protesters shared a conviction that their countries' political systems and economies had grown impaired and corrupt. The Web and social media became key tactical tools in these nonviolent struggles.[63] Nowhere were

Table 2.4 Education Expenditures in Selected Countries of the MENA Region

Rank	Country	% of GDP	Date of Information
15	Tunisia	7.2	2007
30	Israel	5.9	2007
40	Saudi Arabia	5.6	2008
41	Morocco	5.6	2008
54	Yemen	5.2	2008
60	Syria	4.9	2007
72	Iran	4.7	2009
90	Algeria	4.3	2008
109	Oman	3.9	2006
110	Egypt	3.8	2008
112	Kuwait	3.8	2006
121	Qatar	3.3	2005
136	Bahrain	2.9	2008
137	Turkey	2.9	2006
159	Lebanon	1.8	2009
162	United Arab Emirates	1.2	2009

Note: Rank is based on the percent of GDP a country has spent on education.
Source: CIA, *The World Factbook*, www.cia.gov/library/publications/the-world-factbook/rankorder/2206rank.html?countryName=Tunisia&countryCode=ts&regionCode=afr&rank=15#ts.

these protests more dramatic and ground-shaking than in the Middle East and North Africa, where Mohamed Bouazizi's self-immolation galvanized an uprising in Tunisia that swept across the region and unleashed democratic forces previously unseen in the Arab world.

A demographic bulge of young people unable to find employment has found in social media a way to address its grievances and a tool by which to organize opposition against the government. Accessibility to ICTs and social media has rendered any form of totalitarian control over information and political expression both implausible and obsolete. Although technology diffusion and democratization processes are significantly linked, the connection between the two is not necessarily causal. The successful transition to democracy in the MENA region rests on wide-ranging socioeconomic and political parameters, vibrant social movements, effective communication means, and ruling elites willing to accommodate popular demands for democratic change.

Experts have noted that countries with some form of censorship and content filtering have experienced little regime change.[64] It is equally important to bear in mind that "in many Muslim countries, censorship is not simply about protecting political elites, it is about managing cultural production and consumption."[65] The rules of censorship of newspapers and broadcast media hardly, if ever, apply to digital content and tools. That ruling elites and autocratic states relentlessly seek to manage gender politics and identity formation suggests that digital media pose a serious challenge to the traditional practices of cultural production, consumption, and management.[66]

Supporting and promoting ICTs for civil Islam, experts remind us, is likely to undermine the appeal of fundamentalist discourse. In Turkey and Indonesia, democratic governance and accessible information infrastructure can surely provide a counter-narrative to fundamentalist Islamic groups in ways that secular authoritarianism cannot. One comparative study demonstrates that having an active online civil society is both a necessary and sufficient cause of transition out of authoritarianism.[67] Many young people in the MENA region today are keen on formulating their own definition of who they are and what their cultural inheritance entails. In Iran, the rise of the Green Movement demonstrated that the Iranian youth have abandoned political apathy and embraced the political space.

Despite their failure to change the regime in Iran, they have become the trendsetter in the MENA. The dramatic changes sweeping the Arab world since late 2010 and early 2011 have shown that the Western world's traditional bargain with autocrats has crumbled. It was not a revolution led by Islamist groups or organized opposition political parties, nor an external military intervention, but rather a popular uprising spearheaded by youth that overthrew Zine El Abidine Ben Ali's twenty-three years of despotic rule in Tunisia. This leaderless uprising, with young men and women yearning for democracy and political participation, has set in motion a wave of unrest throughout the MENA region ever since.

Although the trigger appeared to be the widely reported self-immolation of twenty-six-year-old Tunisian fruit vendor Bouazizi, whose cart and scale were confiscated by the police, the underlying circumstances of economic insecurity, police brutality, political repression, and social injustice all combined to pave the way for the massive internal implosion. The pressure cooker exploded as a result of the presence, activism, and willingness to sacrifice personal security embodied by so many Tunisian youth. Images of repression, torture, and cruelty were broadcast to the rest of the world through social media and the Internet. It is important, however, not to lose sight of the fact that what connected Tunisian youth with the rest of their counterparts across the Arab world was indeed a dignity-based narrative, found in a larger regional identity.

In Egypt, economically and politically alienated young professionals from middle-class backgrounds led the revolt against Hosni Mubarak's regime while he was consumed by his own succession of power. Known as the Facebook generation, Egyptian young men and women went online, opting to remain anonymous and faceless for security reasons. Over the past thirty years, these young people have sought a confluence between the appeal of liberal ideals and the positive and dynamic energy that they can bring to the country's political, economic, and cultural scenes.[68] Caught between the military and Islamic movements, this generation of Egyptians, Tarek Osman writes, "is animated by a passion to escape the failure it feels it has inherited."[69] And now, they face new challenges of the postrevolutionary era.

Turning Elections into Democracy

The all-too-familiar question that has dogged the region for centuries is this: Can democracy work in the Middle East and North Africa? The momentous events of 2011 undermined the argument often made for the durability of authoritarian regimes, demonstrating the persistent vulnerability of these regimes to mass protest and resistance. In the West, the works of experts such as Bernard Lewis and Samuel Huntington have represented an essentialist thinking: that there is something inherently hostile to modern and Western notions of secularism, democracy, civil society, and human rights in the Muslim world. Denying that democracy was a universal creed, Huntington points to the spread of "third-wave" democracy, which began in 1974, to all other regions of the world except the Arab Middle East.[70]

In Egypt and Tunisia, as well as across the Arab world, the old bargain between authoritarian regimes and people—who were promised economic well-being and public services in return for submissive behavior, reduced freedom, and the muting of political voices—crumbled.[71] The legitimacy of these regimes, generally perceived in terms of economic performance, came under question—a reality marked by the collapse of regimes in Tunisia, Egypt, and Libya.

In the rest of the region, uncertainty reigns as the popular demands for political opening and reform have stalled. After Muammar Qaddafi's death, Libya's rebel militias have turned on each other. Confidence in transitional leaders is eroding. Saudi Arabia's monarchy has preserved its tight grip on society and is determined to stem the tide of democracy in the neighboring country of Bahrain. The latter's repressive state apparatus has effectively curbed mass protests, even as public anger is growing. The uprising against Syria's Bashar al-Assad has turned into an open war, with the opposition increasingly resorting to violence. In Yemen, many factions are jockeying for power in the post–Ali Abdullah Saleh period as the country's economy is suffering a sudden decline.[72]

Subsequently, debate rages over the new challenges and difficulties facing democratic transition in these postrevolutionary societies. Much of this debate continues to revolve around the timing, procedures, and efficacy of elections. Elections, known as one of the most important symbolic and substantive elements of democracy, may not necessarily lead to democratic transformation, but they are still the best hope for conveying authority to an elected body that can take up the mantle of popular will. Turning elections into a sustainable democracy involves creating rights-sustaining institutions, favorable economic conditions, and a viable civil society. Regarding Egypt's nascent democratic system, Dan Tschirgi of the American University at Cairo notes that the process is a learning experience that is slow, pain-ful, and fraught with uncertainties and tensions.[73] Mohammad Nassar, of Al-Alsun University, Cairo, echoes a similar sentiment, pointing out that democracy is an accumulation process that takes time and experimentation in the face of mounting constraints.[74]

Egypt's young protesters may have brought a new politics—that is, bottom-up, grassroots opposition with no ideological platform or political leaders—to the streets since January 25, 2011, but organization on the ground trumps the enthusiasm of Facebook and Twitter when it comes to influencing a country's political future. Even though many observers seem hopeful about elections, others fear chaos and disorder. Still others fear the rise of Islamist political movements, calling into question their commitment to democratic principles. Those who view such fears as exaggerated argue that the issue is not whether the Muslim Brotherhood in Egypt believes in liberal democracy or Lockean liberalism. Most of the major political players in Egypt do not. The fact remains that the Muslim Brotherhood has not supported, pursued, or instigated violence since the 1970s for the simple reason that it has not been in its best interests to do so.[75]

In both Tunisia and Egypt, Islamists have demonstrated their power at organizing action and mobilizing votes in the parliamentary elections. In Egypt, the Freedom and Justice Party (FJP), affiliated with the country's Muslim Brotherhood, won 47 percent of the votes in the newly elected parliament. In Tunisia, the Islamist Al-Nahda (Renaissance) Party won 41 percent of the votes. But as the power of the Islamic parties expands, they have yet to convince their domestic and foreign critics of their commitment to democratic values.[76] The decades-old state of emergency was partially lifted to mark the anniversary of the revolt, an act directed at mollifying those who are discontent with the brutal police tactics of the Supreme Council of Armed Forces (SCAF).

In addition to the military and Islamists, there are also remnants of the old regime. With Mubarak removed from power, a parliament dominated by Islamists, and the military still in the background, Egypt's revolutionary narrative has become a deeply divisive issue, raising tough questions as to who owns and who speaks for the revolution.[77] It may be the case, as some analysts argue, that the younger generation will have no choice but to form pragmatic alliances with Islamists, secular nationalists, and residual regime actors in order to become viable participants.[78] This may in turn broaden the interests of the reformers and force liberals to reassess their ground game in an attempt to win votes, something that was notably absent from the most recent elections. It is too early to determine if the young people who launched these revolts are prepared to deal with the hard bargaining they will inexorably be involved in in the postelection period. This bargaining entails negotiations with groups whose economic interests persist, as well as with Islamist parties who are poised to win large numbers of votes and defend their cultural and political agenda.[79] Without adopting pragmatic positions, secular liberals could risk becoming marginalized, especially as Islamists may be prepared to deal with the military in a power-sharing arrangement of sorts.

More critically, however, the December 29, 2011, Egyptian security forces' crackdown on the pro-democracy nongovernmental organizations (NGOs) on charges that they received millions of dollars annually in US government funding and that these NGOs sought to destabilize the country, ratcheted up the pressure on Egyptian liberal and human rights groups who have often relied on external support and training. The Egyptian court's inquiry into foreign funding of NGOs strained US-Egyptian relations and jeopardized—at least temporarily—US aid to the Egyptian military. Among forty-three employees of four democracy promotion organizations who were charged with illegally accepting foreign funds and operating without a license, nineteen Americans faced trial; most recognizable among them were Sam LaHood—head of the International Republican Institute and the son of President Obama's transportation secretary Ray LaHood—and Julie Hughes, who was the country director for the National Democratic Institute.[80]

Egypt's ruling generals defused the crisis by lifting the travel ban on some NGO workers and dropping the prosecution. Subsequently, the US government authorized $1.3 billion in annual military aid to Egypt. Yet, Nancy Okail, the Cairo director of the US-based Freedom House, and a dozen of her Egyptian colleagues still face trial as of this writing. Critics have noted that support for these civil society groups, such as Freedom House, should not be sacrificed for the sake of strategic stability in the relations between Egypt and the United States.[81]

Moreover, Egyptian liberal and secular groups encounter another serious problem: they are divided and beset by infighting.[82] It is also important to envision the possibility of a massive brain drain among young members such as human rights activists and NGO workers in the face of the political exclusion of these groups. Contrary to the earlier optimism that the Arab Spring would help encourage the return of Arab scholars and experts, as well as the arrival of professional and highly skilled migrants able to build knowledge-based institutions, if the Arab youth avoid negotiating and forging alliances with other groups that are poised to join the country's power structure, they are likely to become politically disenfranchised, resulting in massive youth migration to Western countries and/or East Asia. Contemplating the future possibilities, Negad El Borai, a human rights lawyer and advocate in the Cairo law firm United Group, describes this scenario as disastrous for Egyptians. This reminds him of the flawed and shaky Sudanese model, where military regimes have allied with Islamic-oriented governments since the country's independence. The result, El Borai notes, has been a political fiasco for Sudan.[83]

Difficulties of Democratic Transition

The concerns following the collapse of dictatorial regimes highlight the inherent difficulties of democratic transition that include, among other things, the emergence of powerful splinter groups or parties that will exert a great deal of influence on the range of possible outcomes between semi-democracy and full democracy—not to mention the possibility of backsliding into traditional authoritarianism. The trajectory of democratic transition in the late twentieth century confirms the view that there is a need to decouple the process of authoritarian breakdown from the process of transitioning out authoritarianism and supplanting it with democracy. Only a few countries that successfully went through that process between 1974 and 1999 had evolved into stable democracies by the turn of the century. More than two decades after the fall of the Berlin Wall, the vast majority of Central and Eastern European countries that had replaced communism in 1989 are still not democracies; they are hybrid regimes at best.[84]

In the Muslim world, some political regimes undergoing democratic transition have either reverted back to some form of authoritarianism or have been described as having just as much of a hybrid nature. Algeria's brief experiment with democratization (1989–1991) came to an abrupt halt when the army canceled the second round of parliamentary elections on January 11, 1992. Fearing that the Islamic Salvation Front (Front Islamique du salut—FIS) majority in the National Assembly would lead to the emergence of an Islamic state, the army stepped in to prevent such an eventuality—a takeover tacitly supported by some secular groups who similarly feared Islamization and Arabization. Since the January 1992 coup, the army has reclaimed its dominant role in the country's politics and power structure.

Turkey, Indonesia, and Pakistan, by contrast, have blended some aspects of authoritarianism and semi-democracy for a long period of time in the presence of an intrusive military. Since the Republic of Turkey was established in 1923, the armed forces have directly intervened in the country's politics several times. Historically, Turks are cognizant of four regime changes when the military crushed elected politicians. A 1960 army coup led to the execution of Prime Minister Adnan Menderes and two of his senior ministers, as well as the imprisonment of many Menderes followers. Through several coups, the military removed the ensuing administrations that pursued an Islamist agenda bent on negating Kemalist influences and traces in society and politics. And in 1997, the army ousted Prime Minister Necmettin Erbakan, an Islamist-minded technocrat.

In Indonesia, since the country's independence in 1945, its armed forces have been frequently involved in local politics and regional conflicts. In the post–Suharto period (1998–present), the military continues to see itself as "the guardian of the state," and its political influence remains extensive. Pakistan has been more or less dominated by the military/security establishment since 1958. In the postindependence era, the military has four times administered martial-law governments in Pakistan to gain legitimacy en route to democratization. In short, military rulers have been arbiters of the nation's destiny.

Having acknowledged the continuing importance of the military establishment in the political order of these countries, some experts have pointed to the crucial role that an external actor can play in catalyzing democratic change in the MENA region. The EU's approach to Turkey, for instance, has been decisive in altering the interests of and constraints on important political actors—such as the armed forces—in Turkey. The overwhelming desire to join the European Union has in fact made the Turkish democratic transition possible. The United States and France can arguably play a similar role in Egypt and Algeria, respectively.[85] Others have argued that democracy may spread slowly in transitional countries such as Egypt and that this may be a more favorable long-term outcome for democracy advocates in the Arab world largely because too rapid a diffusion of democratic governance may carry the seeds of its own destruction.[86]

It is worth noting that elections do not equal democracy as long as the previous power structure remains intact and the ensuing justice system remains reluctant to condemn the crimes of the past, punish the perpetrators, and put in place legal mechanisms that deter human rights abuses in the future. "Democracy," as one observer asserts, "is a long road, with many perilous intersections, and Egypt has barely started on its way."[87] Egypt's SCAF remains the most potent political force in the country by far, simultaneously presenting conflicting messages: a desire to cede power to a new civilian government on the one hand and a similar determination to preserve their own grip on power on the other.[88]

Just as important, the army in authoritarian Arab states has thus far been able to balance the need to respond to regime requests to reestablish order whenever internal security forces have lost control with that of the preservation of its corporate interests.[89] It should come as no surprise that a fair amount of US military aid winds up in firms controlled by Egypt's senior military officers. In Egypt's specific case, the army runs factories, farms, telecommunications and service sectors, and high-tech corporations—what Robert Springborg describes as a parallel "officer economy," which is linked to a system of supplemental patronage for the officer corps. This explains why SCAF has drawn a red line to protect its businesses from closer scrutiny and accountability, effectively eliminating any possibility of meaningful civilian oversight.[90]

Though it is premature to say with certainty that we are witnessing the dawn of a new democratic era in the MENA region, it is evident that the digital protesters have shaken the foundation of the old order, enhancing the prospects for change toward democracy. It may be the case that ICTs and social media have increased the number of hybrid systems that are not entirely democratic or authoritarian but a combination of the two. Some Egyptians criticize the army, arguing that the biggest confrontation is not among Islamist parties (the FJP and al-Nour), the nationalist party (Wafd), and the Egyptian Bloc (a union of secular liberal groups), but rather between the SCAF and the newly empowered groups in Egypt.

It is not yet clear what authority the Egyptian parliament will have, given that the military generals running the country appear unlikely to cede control easily.[91] Many questions remain as Egypt undergoes a difficult and tumultuous transition: Do parliaments really matter? Are they important only on a symbolic level? And if they are mainly symbolic, how can one gauge the significance of elections? Do elections also have only symbolic and not legitimizing and output functions, such as participation, efficiency, and transparency?[92]

It should be noted that there are many Egyptians who regard the army in the post-Mubarak era as the only institution that holds the country together. The old political power structure and institutional arrangements associated with the Mubarak regime have either collapsed or been fragmented.[93] What happens in Egypt will have ramifications for the broader region. Success in Egypt may determine the political future of the Arab Spring—and deliver a model for democratic change in the region. Failure could have devastating consequences, dashing the hopes of millions of Muslims who have come to believe in peaceful ways of challenging the status quo.

Although civil disobedience and other forms of nonviolent insubordination have produced peaceful democratic change in some countries, the track record of success is uneven. Some groups successfully challenged the legitimacy of authoritarian rule (Tunisia and Egypt), others were able to prompt governmental reform (Morocco), but in other cases these movements have either failed to generate necessary change without outside intervention (Libya) or were unable to produce lasting results through peaceful democratic opposition (Syria and Bahrain). In the case of Libya, hopes for holding future elections coexist with fears of an emerging civil war. Concerns about Iraq fuel such fears, where elections after the US invasion deepened divisions so perilously that they helped unleash a civil war.[94] In Jordan, several factors unique to the country contribute to its stability. Both East Bankers and Jordanian Palestinians, for example, fear that if Jordan disintegrates, outsiders may try to convert it into a Palestinian state. This fear, along with the bloodshed in Syria, where many Jordanian families share tribal bonds, tends to weaken the prospects of large-scale protest against King Abdullah II. Yet discontent often bubbles just beneath the surface—whether among ethnic minorities or among the youth—about the country's economy and lack of reform.[95]

In most cases, as one expert notes, repression only backfired when the opposition movements remained nonviolent in spite of regime provocations. On balance, however, in almost all cases repression is costly. Maintaining an active security force entails a hefty cost. Politically, repression is likely to undermine the legitimacy of the government, creating even more grievances against the government and thereby fueling more destabilizing unrest and protests.[96] The Syrian regime's slaughter of unarmed civilians and its continued repressive measures have stripped the Syrian government of its legitimacy. Yet the major-power politics at the UN Security Council protects the Syrian regime from accountability for its brutal repression against its own citizens. The Russian and Chinese vetoes shield Syria from the ratcheting up of international pressure, as the veto-wielding powers continue to place their narrow geopolitical agenda ahead of international humanitarian law.[97]

The uprisings in the MENA region have also set off a debate over the relationship between economic development and democracy. Though it is clear that economic development and human security—defined in terms of "income" and "education"—are the keys to maintaining sustainable democracy in the long term, many argue that the causality runs instead from democratic institutions to development. Those who argue against the existence of any significant and direct links between democratic institutions and economic development assert that there is little evidence to suggest that democratization leads to higher educational attainment or faster long-term growth. Thus, they conclude, one should not expect Middle Eastern countries to achieve high and sustained levels of democratization until they more fully embrace economic modernity and development.[98]

Conclusion

The rise of social movements and demands for freedom in the MENA region—as empowered by digital networks and the ethos of protests—reflect the emergence of a real sense of hope and possibility among the younger generation. These protests have provided a counter-narrative to terrorism and Islamic extremism, while challenging the local inept and corrupt regimes in power. Today's youth in the Muslim world seem to be more interested in employment and freedoms than in radical Islamic ideology and an agenda to topple autocratic regimes and wreak havoc on Western imperialism. Young Egyptians' most important contribution today is in constructing a new identity.

Demographic trends, low economic growth, an inept educational system, weak governance, and the unemployment predicament have combined to create the youth revolts throughout the MENA region. While these protests have brought new politics to the streets of the Arab world, it is organization that trumps the enthusiasm of protests in the post-revolt period when a country's future will be determined by elections. How to turn elections into democracy continues to be the key question, given the difficulties of democratic transition, especially in countries where the army has had a long-standing history of involvement in politics.

In sum, the emergence of nonviolent and democratic outcomes in the MENA region turns on a number of factors, including economic development, the degree of ethnic homogeneity, the existence of a functioning civil society, a sense of national identity and pride, the level of demographic urbanization, and the existence of a modernized industrial infrastructure. Equally critical is the occurrence of democratic transition in neighboring countries. Internet technology broadens awareness of other countries in which democratic transition is taking place. Social movement leaders are aware of other successful examples, consciously emulating prior successes in neighboring countries, learning from them, and attempting to apply them.[99] All of this collectively contributes to the likelihood that gains made in the pursuit of peaceful democratic change can in the future be sustained via the ballot box.

Chapter 3
YOUTHFUL MOMENTUM, SOCIAL MEDIA, HUMAN RIGHTS, AND POLITICAL ECONOMY

The uprisings in the MENA region, which were the culmination of a century of Arab popular struggle for freedom, dignity, and social justice, have awakened the Arab soul. These struggles are, according to one observer, "the single most significant movement of Arab citizens and citizenries since the modern Arab world was created in the early 20th century."[1] These revolts revealed versatile political mobilizations that transcended the categories of ideology, formal organization, and charismatic leadership long associated with revolutionary transformations—democratic or otherwise.[2] The active role and participation of many young people in opposition movements to challenge and—in some cases—topple the incumbent rule has made these uprisings starkly different from those of the past. What caught the world's attention was the region's young demographic, overwhelming unemployment, and gravitation toward urban centers. The demographic profile and the levels of dissatisfaction among youth make for an explosive situation to sweep the MENA region in the coming years.

These young men and women seek a confluence of growing demands for peaceful democratic change and shifting identities in a globalizing world. Young Arabs' most important identity construction lies in formulating their own definition of who they are as citizens of their own country as well as of the twenty-first century.[3] The drive to become part of the twenty-first century—manifested in growing demands for democracy and empowerment, as well as the rejection of extremism and autocracy—not only defines today's Islamic world but also consumes its young members' energy. In a fundamental sense, the 2011 Arab revolts, counter-jihadist movements, and rebellion against extremist Islamic ideologies such as Salafism, Shiite theocracy, and Wahhabism demonstrate a new reality: that commonality of civilizations has replaced the so-called "clash of civilizations" so simplistically portrayed and advocated by the late Samuel Huntington.[4]

This situation, though somewhat unique to the region, is not entirely uncommon in the rest of the developing world. Throughout the world, the demands of the younger generation have often put it at odds with those of the older ones, as the changes in cultural traditions and global resurgence of cyberspace and communication technologies have provided the youth with unique opportunities for experiencing a higher degree of personal choice and freedom. When the evolving youth culture and state instinct for survival, which is predicated on the maintenance of the traditional cultural patterns and established societal norms and values, have come to a head, clashes between the two over who defines and determines the course of cultural politics have become inevitable.[5] If and when combined with economic decay, political suffocation, and social restrictions, these clashes tend to assume revolutionary character by posing major challenges to the political authority of the state. But what authoritarian states find more ominous is the way social media has helped turn internal cultural and political clashes into uprisings and unrests of great magnitude, spearheaded largely by youth.

In Iran, such clashes have given rise to frequent student protests and a broad-based social movement as well as political opposition—dubbed the Green Movement because green is the color of the descendants of the Prophet Muhammad, among whom Mir Hossein Mousavi, the movement's leader, is counted—which led to widespread unrest in Iran in the summer of 2009. In the cases of Tunisia and Egypt in 2011, the result was the retreat of the state and lingering unrest that shook the foundations of both regimes. And what began as peaceful youth protests in Yemen turned violent when key players—such as tribesmen, the Joint Meeting Parties (JMP) (an umbrella group of opposition parties, including the powerful Islah party), and President Ali Abdullah Saleh's loyalists—began jockeying for influence and a place in a new government. Since he came to power in 1978, Saleh did not spare any opportunity to spend blood and treasure to placate his rivals. Saleh was ultimately removed from office by his opposition, who coalesced around the young protesters to cause the regime's downfall.[6]

Similarly, protests in Libya sparked riots in eastern parts of the country, deepened division between eastern and western parts of the country, and provoked further unrest and violence. Various opposition groups in rebel-held areas in eastern Libya, as well as abroad, launched their own affiliated newspapers, websites, radio, and satellite TV stations to counter the so-called "propaganda" of the state-controlled broadcaster.[7] Voice of Free Libya radio stations went on air in Benghazi and Al Bayda, as well as the besieged rebel-held port of Misrata in the western part of the country. Many new opposition satellite TV channels, including Libya TV, were launched to counter Libyan state TV and undermine Qaddafi's regime. Libya TV was based for a time in Qatar, the first Arab country to recognize the Transitional National Council, the opposition shadow government.[8] In the aftermath of an assault on the US Consulate in Benghazi on September 11, 2012, when US ambassador J. Christopher Stevens and three other Americans were murdered by a group of militiamen, many Libyans took to the online tools such as the Internet and Twitter to register their grief, resentment, anger, and disapproval of such terrorist acts.

While Syria has weathered more antigovernment protests in Deir Ez-Zor, Hama, Hasakeh, Ar-Raqqa, and Idlib since early 2011, the regime has blamed the militia for the violence and has reported the deaths of security personnel. Protesters have blamed the killings on the government, while alleging massive human rights abuses. In the cases of both Libya and Syria, it became evident that controlling the economy, building patronage networks, managing tribal affairs, and providing basic social services was not enough to sustain political stability over time.

Views differ on the role that electronic and social media play in fostering uprisings. Of particular relevance is the extent to which social media tell the narrative of street protests as well as shape the protesters' agenda. Some experts minimize such a role, arguing that the popular uprising in Egypt should not be attributed to Twitter, Facebook, or any other Internet-related development. People protested and brought down governments before the advent of social media. They did it before the Internet came along. Barely anyone in East Germany in the 1980s had a phone—and yet they showed up with hundreds of thousands of people in central Leipzig and brought down a regime that was stable by any stretch of imagination. "In the French Revolution," as one expert notes, "the crowd in the streets spoke to one another with that strange, today largely unknown instrument known as the human voice. People with a grievance will always find ways to communicate with each other. How they choose to do it is less interesting, in the end, than why they were driven to do it in the first place."[9]

Following a similar line of logic, another observer has argued that there is a great deal more to the recent uprisings than just the incidental effects of social media. The media must focus on the economic brutality of governments as the root cause of popular unrest. Although information technology has been a shaping force in these uprisings, things have erupted for one reason and one reason alone: "There is a global crisis of capital."[10] Other analysts have likewise warned that one should not confuse tools with root causes, or means with ends. The protests in the MENA region are against dictators who have held sway and suppressed their own people for a long time. The struggle against repression and injustice is "the fuel for the engine of dissent."[11] Although local conditions in these countries vary greatly, similarities abound. These popular uprisings are rooted in backlash against autocratic regimes, lack of representative institutions, glaring income inequalities, corruption, nepotism, and private and wasteful management of public resources.[12]

Some journalists, however, insist that social media have been absolutely crucial to recent revolts in the Arab world. Though no one can deny the power of images that find their way onto the Internet via social media sites, they argue, recent uprisings demonstrate that the "barricades today do not bristle with bayonets and rifles, but with phones."[13] It was through Facebook that support groups followed what happened in Sidi Bouzid, the town where Mohamed Bouazizi self-immolated—an event that triggered subsequent uprisings in both Tunisia and Egypt. Social media proved to be critical at a time when everything else was censored.[14] A journalist's encounter with a group of young Tunisians during a demonstration in Tunis best summed up this notion in their response, when the reporter asked them what they were photographing with their phones: "Ourselves. Our revolution. We put it on Facebook. It is how we tell the world what's happening."[15]

This chapter first examines the reasons why many scholars have failed to predict these uprisings. It will next turn to analyzing the prevailing socio-economic and political grievances behind such revolts, with a view toward explaining the nature of popular movements that are bent on permanently altering the terms of governance in the region. The ensuing parts of this chapter explore the role of youth in cyberspace, the Internet penetration in the MENA region, and how ICTs have made regional borders porous. The chapter concludes by demonstrating how the widespread use of such technologies has given human rights struggles a major boost.

Failure to Predict Uprisings

A debate is under way over the issue of why Middle East specialists, including scholars, experts, and policymakers, have all failed to forecast political uprisings in the Arab world. Some analysts argue that "revolutions are inherently unpredictable" and that structural analyses regarding the timing and content of the revolutions are generally post hoc studies that are always playing catch-up.[16] Others attribute the failure to forecast such instabilities to the prevailing view that economic liberalization and reform could establish new and wider bases of support for authoritarian governments in the Arab world, while fostering the economic growth necessary to meet the challenges of growing populations. The example typically cited to warrant this approach is the way economic reforms in Turkey have led to greater support for the ruling Justice and Development Party (Adalet ve Kalkinma Partisi, or AKP). This rationale lay behind Western governments' policies that embraced the notion "economic reform represented a step toward political reform."[17]

For many Tunisians and Egyptians in similar economic circumstances, however, fundamental rights and freedoms outweighed economic considerations, proving wrong those experts who underestimated the Arab public's aversion to the corruption and crony privatization that accompanied the reforms.[18] "In every single country where Arab citizens have revolted against their regime," Rami G. Khouri writes, "the main demand is for constitutional changes that protect the rights of individuals."[19] In keeping with these explanations, this chapter's central argument is that change and transformation in the MENA region have resulted from bottom-up concrete social struggles, as well as popular movements that will not only permanently alter the terms of governance in the region but will also most likely challenge the conventional US policies toward the region in the coming years. Several other questions come to mind: Will these popular uprisings resemble the 1989 Berlin Wall opening in Eastern Europe? Or are these changes transient, cosmetic, and susceptible to backsliding? What do these uprisings portend for the region's future?

Given the internal dynamics and diversity of countries in the MENA region, no satisfactory answers to these questions exist. What is clear, however, is that the underlying causes of what is happening across the MENA region (unemployment, housing issues, rising food prices, inflation, social restrictions, and lack of democratic governance) are both socioeconomic and political in nature. In the current unrests in Bahrain and Syria, following the uprisings in Tunisia, Egypt, Libya, and Yemen, religious language has been remarkably absent.[20] Whether young people in the region will view the rising influence of the Muslim Brotherhood in the political process as a threat or a problem in the immediate or near future remains to be seen.

While the increasingly educated, globalized, and young segments of these societies have provided the impetus behind these revolts, and while they were particularly motivated by the indignity of their political and economic context, it is too early to determine whether the forces of religion will play a divisive or uniting role in public life in these societies.[21] To gain a better understanding of what caused these revolutions and what are the ramifications of these democratic changes, it is important to contextualize the role of emotion, identity, and solidarity in a context heavily influenced by demographic factors and mobilizing impacts of information explosion and technology. Several basic research questions motivate this chapter: (1) What has prompted these peaceful democratic protests in the MENA region? (2) Are we witnessing the Arab version of the opening of the Berlin Wall? If yes, can democracy work in the Middle East and North Africa? And finally, (3) why should the Western world support these uprisings given that the democratization of politics in the region is likely to make Western countries' relations with these Middle Eastern countries more difficult to manage?

The Revolts in the Arab World

Since the global resurgence of democracy in the late 1980s, most observers have sought to provide a wide range of explanations for why the Arab world has bucked a global trend of democratization. A broad consensus holds that most Arab regimes, ruling over artificial states and with dubious legitimacy, maintain power only through coercive means and apparatuses. Except for oil and natural gas, some argue, the Arab world today exports little or no economic value. Its public sectors are inept, bloated, and rife with corruption. The region has seen little growth during the past several decades. In real terms, per capita GDP grew just 0.5 percent per year in Arab countries from 1980 to 2004, according to World Bank statistics.[22]

Others have asserted that the search for democratic governance is not new in the Middle East. Contrary to widely held views, Eugene Rogan, the director of the Middle East Center at Oxford University, argues that the events of 2011 have deep historical roots that can be traced back to the early nineteenth century. Arab reformers have pondered and deliberated over the merits of constitutional government since the 1830s and have sought to constrain absolutism with elected assemblies and popular sovereignty since the 1860s. Moreover, even in the nineteenth century, it was Egypt and Tunisia that led the reform agenda in the Arab world. Liberal political-reform movements subsequently emerged in the broader Middle

East with constitutional revolutions in Iran (1906) and in the Ottoman Empire (1908). The past half century of political despotism in the region might well be remembered as but a setback and hiatus in two centuries of domestic and popular pressure for constitutional rule and democratic rights.[23]

In many countries of the region, the tradition of a democratic past remains, debunking "the myth that the Arabs as people, or Muslims more generally, are somehow incompatible with democratic values."[24] On December 17, 2010, fruit vendor Bouazizi's desperate act of protest sparked an uprising in Tunisia—the Jasmine Revolution, as the Tunisians called their movement—that ended with the forced resignation of the country's longtime leader, President Zine El Abidine Ben Ali. This act of burning oneself to death became the symbol of a widespread popular uprising that initially deposed an authoritarian regime in Tunisia and subsequently those in Egypt and Libya.

A look at Tunisia before the case of Bouazizi shows that Tunisians were well educated in Internet campaigns and activism. One of the crucial moments of contentious politics prior to the 2011 uprisings in Tunisia came when a protest was organized by six young activists via Facebook and Twitter called Tunisie en Blanc (Tunisia in White) on May 22, 2010. Promoting peaceful demonstration against Internet censorship, these activists encouraged people to take part in a protest in front of the Ministry of Technology in downtown Tunis as well as dress in white and have a coffee in one of the many cafés on Avenue Habib Bourguiba.[25] Although "Tunisia in White" never became a successful social movement, the event laid the groundwork for future Internet campaigns and a public forum for political debate.[26]

A combination of several factors, but most notably the poor government's development strategy to reduce regional disparities, prevented the generation of enough jobs in the interior for a rapidly growing population. More specifically, scarce natural resources, climate constraints, and the need to lower transport costs made it difficult to attract large numbers of tourists or export-oriented producers to the hinterland. As a result, 80 percent of current national production in Tunisia remains concentrated in coastal areas. Only 20 percent of national production is generated in the southwest and center-west regions, home to 40 percent of the population.[27]

Bouazizi died on January 4, 2011, but a momentous chain of events sparked by his act of despair led to the successful revolution that inspired popular uprisings across the region, toppling the government of Egypt and leading to armed conflicts that culminated in the violent murder of Libya's leader Muammar Qaddafi and the departure of President Ali Abdullah Saleh in Yemen. On February 20, 2011, a forty-nine-year-old man, an employee of an oil company, drove a car rigged with four propane tanks and filled with makeshift explosives into the gates of the al-Katiba military base in Benghazi, Libya, and blasted its gate open. A few hours later, the base was overrun and the city was in the hands of pro-democracy forces.

Fueled by high youth unemployment, soaring food prices, and autocratic rule, these spontaneous and leaderless protests have resulted in the rising Arab identity and a newfound sense of empowerment and potential, especially among the younger generation who are driven by secular impulses and demands, such as employment, economic prosperity, and political rights. A combination of population growth, rural-to-urban migration, and socioeconomic changes has had a radical impact on MENA societies. As a result, many leaders in Morocco, Saudi Arabia, and the United Arab Emirates (UAE) have put a massive emphasis on both employment and housing so that young men and women can afford to get married and buy a house.[28]

Coverage of civil resistance by the press, the Internet, and television played an increasingly important part in its success. Al Jazeera correspondent Ayman Mohyeldin notes that this was a revolution of awareness, based on access to fast-traveling information. The participants in these uprisings, also known as the "January 25 Movement," included farmers and the peasants who were completely aware of their rights.[29] Although the uprisings at Egypt's Tahrir Square did not deliver a complete revolution, they did arouse an exhilarating sense of possibility and empowerment that had been conspicuously absent for far too long. The revolt's impact "has been felt in Cairo's political and intellectual scene, where conversations are no longer colored by hopeless cynicism about the future."[30]

Even though the conventional political processes and power relations within the region failed to produce any democratic change, a combination of youth and technology facilitated massive social unrest capable of transforming society-state relations in coming years. Optimists argue that new social media are likely to empower individuals to coordinate, communicate, form a new public sphere, mobilize collective contentious action against authoritarian states or hierarchies of any kind, and fundamentally challenge existing sociopolitical order by privileging horizontal networks over hierarchical organizations such as the modern nation-state.[31] Skeptics, by contrast, warn that the effects of social media will not be directly translated from changing individual attitudes, competencies, and identities into political change. They will create new resources available to authoritarian states, as their effects will be mediated through massive state control mechanisms and capacities for surveillance, repression, and infiltration. Although it is true that a new public sphere will fundamentally alter the conditions of political possibility, the direction of that change as well as its long-term consequences are still to be seen.[32]

Questioning the sustainability of such revolts, another critic argues that street-based movements lack the organization and leadership—and thus continuity over time—to project, let alone foist, a new political or social order. Their power is confined to their ability to pressure existing elites and institutions, not to supplant the state and economy.[33] Although the uprisings have commenced a new epoch in the MENA region, in some cases, eventual outcomes are still uncertain. It remains to be seen whether the old order has completely crumbled. Half of Egypt's voters, for example, live outside major cities, in places where the power structure has hardly been fundamentally altered. The old order likely will retain a significant base of support in towns and in the countryside.[34] Great battles lie ahead. People have no idea who and what comes next. Just as a revolutionary mood can be infectious, so can be disillusionment. The key to endurance of positive change is good governance, but the role of external players and pressures should not be underestimated. Will the key external actors support the democratic trajectory in these countries? It is too early to answer this question.

The Political Economy of Uprisings

To better grasp the political economy of the Arab revolts, experts point to the gradual collapse in the postindependence era of the populist social contract that combined authoritarian rule with a redistributive welfare state maintained by a large bureaucracy. The state-owned enterprises employed a large urban workforce, provided agricultural support to the peasantry, and supplied extensive subsidies for basic consumer goods. This corporatist or developmental state consolidated its power by trading development for the political loyalty of key groups, such as workers, peasants, professionals, and many others in the educated middle class.[35] In many middle-income Arab countries, such as Egypt, Jordan, Lebanon, Morocco, Syria, and Tunisia, this model was subsequently followed by economic liberalization, deregulation, and privatization programs, leading to impressive developmental accomplishments in terms of increasing life expectancy and rates of education.[36]

Unlike their counterparts elsewhere, these countries neither democratized nor were endowed with the petroleum resources of other rich Arab states to defray the expenses of economic liberalization and sustain political stability. Over the years, the authoritarian populist social contract began to collapse. GDP growth rates that averaged 6 percent per year in the 1960s dropped to less than 1 percent in the 1980s.[37] By 2009, one study found that about 40 percent of Arabs lived in extreme poverty.[38] By the late 1990s, much of the MENA region had gone through two decades of structural adjustment, resulting in states largely abandoning their legacy of support for workers and peasants. In Egypt, some 1.7 million workers participated in more than 1,900 strikes between 2004 and 2008.[39]

Many experts view the 2011 unrest in the MENA region as revolts against neoliberal economic policies imposed on these countries by the international financial institutions, such as the IMF and the World Bank, arguing that these policies have led to contradictory and negative impacts on poverty reduction, unemployment increase in the labor market, privatization of the access to basic services such as education and health care, and high food prices. According to neoliberal economic policies, governments should deregulate economy by reducing deficit spending, limiting subsidies, removing fixed exchange rates, promoting free trade by containing protectionism, privatizing state-run businesses, and allowing private property. Under pressure by the international financial institutions to liberalize their economies, many of the Arab countries have undertaken neoliberal reforms. As a result of such economic reforms, welfare programs such as public subsidies (for food, unemployment, cooking oil, gas, transport, health, and education) for the poor have been lessened or eliminated and state employment has been drastically curtailed, closing off one of the few opportunities for educated youth.[40] These neoliberal policies, some experts note, have shattered the paternalistic ties through which the rulers curbed the discontent of the young and the poor, as well as clerical elites and tribal chiefs. The neoliberal policies reinforced the concentration of wealth in the hands of a few while attenuating state controls over the street masses.

A combination of a "modern" rentier economy and the implementation of neoliberal policies has relegated the newly educated young into the poorly paid, unprotected, "informal economy" of the streets working as venders, transport and contract workers, and in personal services.[41] The modern, urban, industrial working class that has small, independent trade unions is banned. Civil society is underdeveloped, as evidenced by the fact that middle-class civic associations are either under state control or limited to petitioning the absolutist state.[42] Under such circumstances, it comes as no surprise that the central place for protest action was the street, led not by workers in industry—a meager sector of the economy—but rather by unemployed and underemployed part-time youth engaged in the informal sector, who were typically found in the plazas, at kiosks, cafés, street-corner society, and markets. These groups were joined by oppressed professionals, public-sector employees, small-business people, and the self-employed, who feared no loss of jobs or possible reprisals from their place of employment.[43]

In 1987, in a bloodless coup in Tunisia, on the grounds of incompetence, the left-leaning and nationalist government of Habib Bourguiba was replaced by a new regime, which was firmly committed to "free-market" reforms. Since the late 1980s, efforts to liberalize the economy were vigorously pursued by this new regime. During the past twenty-three years, the country's economic and social policy was dictated by the "Washington Consensus"—an IMF economic formula that recommended that government pursue macroeconomic stability by reducing fiscal deficits and privatizing domestic economy—a policy that President Ben Ali vigorously enforced. These policies in the end destabilized the national economy and impoverished the Tunisian population. Moreover, the IMF's insistence on fiscal austerity and the removal of subsidies coincided with a renewed upsurge in staple food prices. The latter, which was in large part the result of speculative trade by major financial and corporate agribusiness interests, served to impoverish people throughout the world.[44]

From 2006 to 2008, there was a dramatic surge in the prices of all major food staples including rice, wheat, and corn. The price of rice tripled during a five-year period, from approximately $600 a ton in 2003 to more than $1,800 a ton in May 2008.[45] Ironically, against this backdrop, the IMF recommended the removal of the subsidies with an eye toward reaching the goal of fiscal austerity. The uprisings that unfolded in late 2010 and early 2011 in Tunisia were part of a nationwide reaction to an economic process that destroyed people's lives through the deliberate manipulation of market forces. Critics of neoliberal policies argue that the harsh economic and social realities underlying IMF intervention led to soaring food prices, local-level famines, massive layoffs of urban workers and civil servants, and the destruction of social programs. Internal purchasing power collapsed, health clinics and schools closed down, and hundreds of millions of children were denied the right to primary education.[46]

Under programs in Tunisia, more than 150 state enterprises were privatized. The socioeconomic costs of the privatization measures proved to be prohibitively high, as these measures led to rising unemployment and poverty levels unprecedented in the country's history. Despite the promising diverse economy relying on agriculture, mining, tourism, and manufacturing sectors, poverty in Tunisia downgraded the living conditions of millions of the people, while gains accrued for long-term investors and a handful of elites. These deregulation measures were largely imposed by an alliance of army, business, and civilian politicians. The poor classes, including farmers and workers, were excluded from benefiting from such gains. A significant portion of the youth turned their attention to Europe in their attempt to seek economic survival and opportunity. The percentage of unemployed graduates doubled those employed. An estimated 55 percent of the population is under the age of twenty-five.[47] Unemployment soared to 18 percent, reaching an exceptionally high 32 percent in Sidi Bouzid, the town where the initial protests erupted. Uneven investment in tourism and other global-market-oriented industries along the narrow coastal strip captured more than 80 percent of total investment.[48] With access to the Internet and social media such as Twitter and Facebook, Tunisia's younger generation found new ways of expressing their disenchantment with the country's economic woes: burgeoning unemployment, privatization, and food insecurity.

By the same token, although social media helped organize the movement that eventually toppled Mubarak's regime in Egypt, what really brought people to the streets was economic grievances that were intrinsic to neoliberalism. Mubarak's economic policies degraded schools and hospitals and exacerbated existing wage inadequacies and inequalities, particularly in the private sector.[49] Three decades of neoliberal "reform" made the country much more vulnerable to the 2011 crisis—a crisis caused by massive widening of the levels of inequality and debilitating mechanisms of social support. At the same time, a small group of elite benefited enormously from these economic measures. Neoliberalism produced rapid growth rates but simultaneously led to lessening living standards for the majority of the population and the increased concentration of wealth in the hands of a tiny minority.[50] Poverty increased from 20 percent in 2008 to 23.4 percent in 2009. By 2009, poverty afflicted more than one-fifth—or 18 million—of the Egyptian population.[51] Today, some 40 percent of Egyptians live on less than $2 per day.[52] By 2008, inflation had risen to 18 percent and stood at 12 percent in 2009.[53] Unemployment and low wages pushed the basic necessities out of the reach of millions of Egyptians and rendered many people insecure in the face of the 2008 food crisis.[54]

These neoliberal policies can be traced back to a series of policy measures known as *infitah* (opening) that were launched in the 1970s under President Anwar Sadat. After Mubarak came to power in 1981, his government continued the same policy. With the encouragement of the IMF, World Bank, and USAID, structural adjustment programs were enacted to transform social relations in the rural areas. Egyptian agriculture shifted toward export-oriented production. Many Egyptians lost their livelihood on the land and streamed into the informal sector of urban centers, such as Cairo. A key feature of the 1990–1991 IMF structural adjustment programs was the transfer of wealth to the private sector. As a result, a few massive conglomerates—such as the Osman, Bahgat, and Orascom groups—whose activities stretched across construction, import/export, tourism, real estate, and finance, gained access to cheap labor, government contracts, and other kinds of largesse distributed by the state.

In the meantime, state employment began to decline sharply with the privatization. The number of workers in public-sector companies was halved between 1994 and 2001. At the same time, nearly 20 percent of the banking system was transferred from public control to the private sector.[55] Although Egypt achieved significant economic growth during 1990–2009, averaging a decent 4.5 percent annually, only a small minority enjoyed most of the gains. A balanced, all-inclusive development was not achieved, however.[56] The result was a massive degradation of working conditions and the further pauperization of large segments of the Egyptian population. These economic insecurities contributed greatly to the expansion of the large numbers of informal workers that came to characterize the unrest in Egyptian cities and played a critical role in the ensuing uprisings. In response to these neoliberal policies, a wave of strikes engulfed Egypt between 2006 and 2008. During 2006, there were 220 major strikes involving tens of thousands of workers in the largest strike wave that Egypt had seen in decades.[57]

In both Tunisia and Egypt, a combination of similar factors paved the way for the uprisings: a sharp rise in food prices, high unemployment rates (especially among the youth), and widespread resentment directed at corrupt and repressive governments. Many of these economic difficulties were attributed to neoliberal IMF and World Bank interventions in the region, implicated in privatization, falling real wages, and the accumulation of wealth in the hands of ruling families and their cronies. These revolts were a clear expression of people's rejection of neoliberal policies imposed by the IMF and World Bank.[58] Some observers foresee a pessimistic outlook for Egyptian workers, arguing that the current trends suggest that what awaits them in the post-Mubarak era is not a happy ending but rather new challenges and greater uncertainty. Egyptian workers are likely to remain marginalized by the continuation of the same economic liberalization programs undertaken under the previous regime. Workers' protests and demonstrations, while pervasive in the past, will most likely be disallowed in the name of turning the country's economic wheel forward, maintaining national security, and providing for the public welfare.[59]

The Youth in Cyberspace

The year 2011 began with the social media–driven uprisings and protests in the MENA, toppling the regimes of Tunisia's Zine El Abidine Ben Ali and Egypt's Hosni Mubarak, both of which had seemed firmly entrenched. This peaceful democratic change has posed the most formidable challenge to the rule of autocrats and monarchs throughout the region. By way of comparison, Fareed Zakaria writes, these peaceful revolutions were reminiscent of popular uprisings 162 years earlier that began in Sicily and France. The revolutions of 1848 keenly resemble, in mood, recent developments in the MENA region. The backdrop then, as now, was a recession and rising food prices. The monarchies—archaic and resistant to change—were challenged by the young. Mass newspapers at the time connected the crowds. The difference between those movements and today's is that while the old regimes reconstituted themselves subsequently, these new waves of change in the MENA region seem irreversible.[60] Especially in authoritarian regimes, where freedom of expression and assembly are nonexistent, a combination of the demographic youth bulge and new technological resources, also known as digital social networks on the Internet—Twitter, YouTube, Facebook, and other tools of communications—has created new dynamics of change in the region, making it possible for the virtual and actual participation of people in the affairs of their communities.

The digital world has drastically altered the face of the Middle East and North Africa. Social networks have practically replaced the old public sphere, occupied by the traditional meeting places such as the *suq* (bazaar or marketplace) and mosques, where the general public used to gather for exchange of ideas and social intermingling, as well as for many other types of interactions. As modernizing and globalizing forces challenge traditional identities, experts note, new technologies and opportunities provide newer forms of identities based on individual choice and accountability. Increasingly, young people view their own decisions as a choice rather than an unmitigated force imposed by cultural traditions and social norms.[61]

With few exceptions, teen life in the MENA region is generally characterized as straddling tradition and modernity. Turkish teens hold onto old beliefs, values, and cultural traditions while also being vividly exposed to new technology, Western ideas, and changing social norms.[62] Increasingly throughout the region, especially in the case of Iran, young people have become more pragmatic, more autonomous, less conformist, and more conscious of the outside world.[63]

More and more young people in the MENA region have come to express their opposition to the repressive regimes under which they have lived through the larger strategies of nonviolence, noncooperation, and civil disobedience. Contrary to the widely held view that Arab youths are often raised in an environment of religious radicalism and anti-Americanism and that these values thus have "become the formative elements of a new and dispossessed generation," in reality, these protests have illustrated that young people "were a big part of the silent, moderate majority."[64]

Internet Penetration in the MENA

The most influential medium of globalization—that is, the worldwide spread of global music, film culture, and information—has arguably been the Internet. Along with other means of globalization, the Internet provides new opportunities by exposing young people to many new experiences beyond national and cultural boundaries. Today throughout the MENA region, cybercafés are occupied mainly by young people who, by using the Internet, feel liberated from social restrictions and norms of their own societies (see Table 3.1 and website for additional data). The young generation in Morocco, for example, spends considerable time in cybercafés, where they meet others and have experiences in real or virtual life. In cyberspace, as Ines Baune notes, "young people are free from social pressure and the many demands they are faced with in the real world. Undergoing experiences without being controlled by parents or others constitutes a critical change."[65]

Arguing that "connective technologies" such as the Internet have proven to be a double-edged sword, US assistant secretary for democracy, human rights, and labor Michael Posner warns that the same technology can also give governments "greater energy in curtailing freedom of expression."[66] This has clearly been the case in China and Iran, where governments have used filtering and other devices to control the flow of information on the Internet.

This information revolution has in many respects contributed to the fragmentation of authority and opening up of new spaces. Many new sources of authoritative information have emerged, creating tremendous potential for spontaneous organizational activities by dissidents and government critics. By providing the endless and boundless flow of information, ideas, and values, multimedia and new technologies have created new opportunities for the general public to address economic and political grievances. Some human rights lawyers and activists have argued that one of the most powerful tools at the disposal of the legally powerless is the media. Used properly and effectively, media can serve as the court of public opinion, raising people's awareness of their rights, an awareness from which no oppressive authorities can escape.[67]

The emerging information revolution has coincided with a dramatic and massive demographic youth bulge in the MENA region. More than half the total population of these countries is under the age of thirty; many of these youth are unemployed. Although youth unemployment is a global problem, young people in the MENA region have the highest unemployment rate in the world. What makes this segment of the population explosive and rebellious is the fact that youth unemployment often is highest in these countries among those with the most education.[68]

Why Human Rights Matter

There can be no doubt that the prevailing use of modern communication technologies has given human rights struggles an unprecedented jolt and momentum. As noted above, the free flow of information has created a new generation that is plugged in and proactive, less conformist, and more cognizant of the outside world. This combination has made the young generation far more receptive to modern ideas of internationally recognized human rights. At the same time, international borders have become more porous in this era of globalization than at any time in the past—thanks in large part to cyberspace. The debate over how one can have a clear grasp of the place of human rights in global politics has, in the past, invited

Table 3.1 Access to Information and Communication Technology

Human Development Index Rank (high to low to other countries)		Telephones % of population covered by mobile phone network 2008	Internet Users (% of population) 2008	Personal Computers (% of population) 2006–2008
32	UAE	100	65.2	33.1
38	Qatar	100	34.0	15.7
39	Bahrain	100	51.9	74.6
47	Kuwait	100	36.7	—
53	Libya	71	5.1	—
55	Saudi Arabia	98	31.5	68.3
70	Iran	95	32.0	10.4
81	Tunisia	100	27.1	9.8
82	Jordan	99	27.0	7.2
83	Turkey	100	34.4	—
84	Algeria	82	11.9	—
101	Egypt	95	16.6	3.9
111	Syria	96	17.3	8.8
114	Morocco	98	33.0	5.7
133	Yemen	68	1.6	2.8
154	Sudan	66	10.2	10.7
	Iraq	72	1.0	—
	Lebanon	100	22.5	10.2
	Palestine	95	9.0	—
	Oman	96	20.0	16.9

Source: United Nations Development Program, *Human Development Report 2010* (New York: UNDP, 2010), 211–214.

different views and many controversies, but today it has received a great deal of attention in the face of the uprisings in the MENA. A discussion of human rights in this context is particularly relevant.

Let us turn to revisit the perennial question of what place human rights occupy in world politics in general and foreign policy in particular. History has shown that whenever the issue of human rights has gained prominence in US foreign policy, it has thrust the debate upon world politics, making the destiny of each human being a matter of global concern. But at the same time, given that foreign policy is full of trade-offs, many questions still remain about the degree to which human rights concerns can be taken into account when making foreign policy decisions and whether human rights policies actually improve domestic conditions.

Some scholars, while accepting the premise that human rights, like other goals of foreign policy, must at times be compromised, have noted that human rights should be treated as a genuine national interest and that "we must *integrate* human rights into foreign policy rather than occasionally tack them on."[69] Others, who describe the practice of human rights as part of the emerging global normative order, have reminded us that "today, if the public discourse of peacetime global society can be said to have a common moral language, it is that of human rights."[70] While cautioning about the overreaching human rights doctrine in certain respects, they argue that there is a growing—though hardly unanimous—agreement in the discourse of human rights practice that a plausible strategy of action by outsiders can be grounded in the case of antipoverty rights, rights of political participation, and the rights of women and other marginalized groups as matters of international concern.[71]

Still others, seeking a middle ground and pragmatic approach, argue that the inclusion of a wide range of human rights in foreign policy is not practical. This is especially true, they assert, of the implementation of the full liberal agenda on human rights. Foreign policymakers—especially presidents—must respond to strong domestic pressure for economic advantage and national security—not to mention strong pressure on behalf of particular special interests. Pursuit of economic gain, however, can be accompanied by such policies as reduction of labor rights violations, and the pursuit of national security need not have to entail torture and other abuses of suspected terrorists or enemies—even of Islamic militants committing atrocities.[72]

Finally, a growing number of studies indicate that human rights have gained increasing salience in foreign policy and aid bureaucracies in many countries of the Northern Hemisphere. Although human rights considerations have been neither the only factor nor the primary one in determining foreign aid, several studies have shown how human rights as part of "good governance" has increased in saliency. Some states have demonstrated a principled commitment to build global governance by reshaping the meaning of sovereignty and instilling a slowly emerging legitimacy norm in their foreign policy. Such states—referred to by Alison Brysk as "global citizen states" and including Sweden, Canada, the Netherlands, Costa Rica, Japan, and South Africa—face the changing and rapidly evolving challenges of globalization and hegemonic forces, while leading the world in promoting global governance and humanitarian intervention, as well as providing resources for development, relief, and the rule of law. For these so-called "global citizen states," given their history, evolving domestic structure, and relationship to others, such notions have converged in a specific package of human rights identity and promotion.[73]

Equally noteworthy is the fact that the application of human rights standards has been uneven. Geostrategic considerations, for example, have consistently overridden such concerns in much of the oil-rich or strategically significant Arab world and for many key Asian countries. That said, transnational advocacy networks and international media attention given to deteriorating human rights conditions around the world have pressured states and international organizations to take human rights concerns seriously.[74] As to whether current foreign policy instruments—such as foreign aid, sanctions, and military interventions—are effective means to improve human rights conditions abroad, there is no consensus. It is fair to say, however, that the combination of norm diffusion, spread, and development as a result of promoting and protecting internationally recognized human rights; nongovernmental mobilization; and state foreign policies and multilateral action have made considerable progress in reducing human rights abuses worldwide.[75]

Although views differ about the effectiveness of human rights norms and institutions, human rights issues today merit particular attention as they have become a dominant framework for many political struggles within and across national boundaries. It is in this context that we should turn our attention to the uprisings in the MENA region. The aspirations of the people in this region for basic human rights, articulated in universal terms, are emblematic of a yearning for the same basic civil and political liberties that Westerners have sought—both conceptually and institutionally. As the entire region experiences an Arab awakening, the political parlance is changing. The notion of *sha'b* ("the people") has become the decisive marker of identity in Tunisia, establishing itself as the pertinent signifier of consensus.[76] The social movement that has transpired since 2011 has had a profound impact on the country's political consciousness, turning individuals from people into citizens.

These uprisings were "about dignity and justice, not collective self-pity. It is very unlikely that a za'im [leader] claiming to have miraculous healing powers will be able to seduce Tunisians, who are advocating a politics of justice, not compassion."[77] To merely translate the people's economic woes into unrest misses a larger point. Ordinary Arabs themselves depict the heart of this movement as a revolution for dignity. Eating bread is no longer enough; liberty and dignity equally drive their revolts.[78] Through their uprisings, as one expert notes, Egyptians have created a more favorable terrain in which their power relative to the state has increased.[79]

Modern-day dictators in the MENA region have used food subsidies to ensure obedience and dependence on the state and to maintain power: from Egypt's Gamal Abdel Nasser, who used subsidies as a means of managing and controlling society, to Saddam Hussein's self-serving and corrupt use of the UN's oil-for-food program, to the food subsidies that for many years helped shore up Egypt's Hosni Mubarak. But in 2008, when grain prices went up, a wave of bread riots spread throughout the region, forcing governments to respond by increasing subsidies, raising wages, or simply lavishing cash grants on their people. By 2010, Egypt had become the world's largest wheat importer by far, spending nearly $3 billion a year on food subsidies. When prices soared even higher in 2010, Mubarak and other rulers in the region responded by announcing a new round of handouts. This strategy, however, could no longer subdue the unrest, as rioters demanded something more than just bread: they asked for freedom, justice, and security.[80] Human rights have entered the discourse on the Arab street with a vengeance. As one commentator has aptly put it, "Human progress comes in moral stages, usually each higher than the last one."[81] Increasingly, youth in the MENA region tend to articulate their demands largely in internationally recognized human rights terms. The younger members of Egypt's Muslim Brotherhood are attempting to articulate a new vision sensitive to the new reality of the region by rejecting the group's old and conservative platform that bars women and Coptic Christians from becoming the head of the state.[82]

The fact remains that US foreign policy toward the MENA region has in the past been handicapped by conflicting agendas and paradoxes. It is imperative to reconsider several aspects of US foreign policy given these changing and challenging times. The policy of quiet diplomacy has not borne fruit in some cases, but neither has supporting the status quo in the name of long-term geostrategic considerations. In the face of the social unrest and protests now spreading across the Arab world, the need for a US foreign policy toward the MENA region that represents a new strain of thinking is aptly captured by Tom Malinowski, Washington Director of Human Rights Watch: "If we bet on the stability of authoritarian states, we will be right most of the time, but wrong at the crucial time."[83] Both Bush's crusading moralism and Obama's policy of engagement failed to convince

Hosni Mubarak to lift Egypt's state of emergency and to permit international observers to monitor both the 2005 and 2010 parliamentary elections. In both cases, Mubarak turned the other way, using the bogeyman of the Muslim Brotherhood and Islamic militants' takeover.[84] There is a need for different policies to help us navigate a new path to this critical region.

Arguably, the outcomes of these uprisings may dovetail nicely with long-term strategic interests of the West more generally and the United States more particularly. These youth revolutions are driven more by secular demands of human dignity, jobs, rule of law, economic prosperity, and participation in national affairs than by grand ideological statements.[85] What the recent popular movements in the MENA region, such as Iran's Green Movement and Arab revolts, have in common is an unprecedented desire to achieve social justice, human rights, and democratic governance. "We may be witnessing," Asef Bayat observes, "the coming of a post-Islamist Middle East, in which the prevailing popular movements assume a post-national, post-ideological, civil, and democratic character."[86] The youth and their political organizations (within the "Facebook Generation") have created a new "center" in Egypt—a balance aligned with neither the Mubarak regime nor the Muslim Brotherhood—where the US foreign policy focus should be. Aligning interests with values should become the task of US foreign policymakers, recognizing that the US national interest is no longer reducible to geopolitics and power alone.

Democratic Values and Economic Reform

It is now widely believed that support for democracy and economic development are the most effective policy tools to fight terrorism. Because of the democratic deficit in the Middle East, one expert notes, the streets became the political and emotional outlets for the masses. Bin Laden spoke in the vivid language of popular Islamic preachers, built on a deep and widespread resentment against the West, and local ruling elites identified with it. The lack of formal outlets to express opinion on public concerns created the democracy deficit in much of the Arab world, and this made it easier for terrorists, such as bin Laden, to act in the name of religion, to hijack the Arab street.[87]

A growing consensus is emerging that helping the region's countries, such as Pakistan, educate their youth will not just eradicate the culture of violence by mitigating poverty and ignorance, but it will also advance the cause of long-run economic development.[88] As an antidote to Islamic militancy, the recent Arab revolutions in Egypt, Tunisia, Libya, and Yemen, and the significant upheaval in Syria, Jordan, and Bahrain, serve as a potent counter-commentary to Islamic radicalism. While bin Laden preached hate and violence under Islam, it was the street youth that called for peaceful protest and universal democratic ideals. In this vein, it seems that a pan-Arab identity, which accounts for a broad swath of religious, ethnic, and political thought within the Middle East, better drives the protest movements in the Arab street.

Some scholars have warned against the reductionism of focusing primarily on religion as the main cause of conflicts between Muslim and Christian communities. "There are many perspectives in the Muslim community," J. Dudley Woodberry points out, "and even these are changing, and conflicts between Muslim and Christian communities in places like Indonesia and Sudan have ethnic, economic, and political, as well as religious, roots."[89] The Muslim world has, in recent years, seen rising and encouraging voices of moderation, religious tolerance, democratic social movements, and human rights. Arguing that the United States could benefit from supporting the call for open society and the rule of law in the Muslim world, one observer cautions that "it will be highly imprudent, even reckless, to treat the Middle East and neighboring Muslim societies, with a population of half a billion, merely in terms of their available energy resources and strategic values."[90]

In the post–Cold War era, the Muslim world has seen an internal struggle regarding the role of Islam in public life, where forces of change and continuity have clashed with those of the status quo. This struggle has taken the form of a self-critical approach in the aftermath of the September 11 tragedy, becoming in the process a struggle for the soul of the Muslims. At the heart of this political and cultural struggle lie two key questions: Whose Islam? And what Islam? The first question has to do with who should lead or decide in Islamic societies: elected or unelected officials? The second question concerns the issue of whether or not to restore past doctrines and laws or to reinterpret and reformulate laws in light of the new realities of contemporary society.[91] The real issue is if and when this trend will lay the groundwork for a Muslim reformation, a development whose encouragement should be an important objective of US policy.[92]

The Obama administration was wise to allow the Arab protesters to wrest authority from their autocracies, although his support and that of his regime could have come much sooner and with greater force. However, the deficit of dignity in the Middle East has become palpable. The Arab street feels monopolized and abused by foreign interests. This did indeed need to become a revolution for Arabs, by Arabs, whatever the outcome. The region now faces a war of ideas that must be waged from within. Al Jazeera (Arabic for "the peninsula"), the independent, all-Arab television news network based in Qatar, has popularized investigative reporting and freedom of information around the Muslim/Arab world in the events following the September 11 attacks and the subsequent war waged in Afghanistan. The official motto of Al Jazeera, *al-rai wa rai al-akar* (the opinion and the opposite opinion) has virtually become a political slogan for many Arabs, who favor anchoring wide-ranging ideas and discussing them peacefully.[93] Its impact on the struggle for free press and public opinion in the Arab world has been drastically visible. For the first time, the Arab public is getting a taste of free press and free journalism.[94]

The September 11 tragedy also vividly illustrated that the growth of Islamic radicalism poses a huge threat to the existing Middle Eastern regimes and leaders, hence the Saudis' peace initiative amid the intensification of the second Intifada (uprising), and hence the argument that US public diplomacy should foster genuine avenues for political participation that would create space for moderate and reform-minded Muslim leaders, scholars, lawyers, and journalists and other beleaguered liberals to freely express their views.[95] The policy of supporting democratic movements and regimes offers not only better prospects for stability but also long-run credibility to US foreign policy in the region.

Conclusion

The demographic youth bulge, particularly when accompanied by high unemployment rates and poor governance, is among the leading causes of the brewing tensions and revolts throughout the MENA region. While it is too early to gauge the long-term outcome of the uprisings in the MENA region, it is even more difficult to foretell whether the current ferment could fundamentally reshape the region by bringing real democratic change, as revolutionary changes are not only slow to emerge but usually take many years to become fully operative. The political drama is in its initial act and far from its final scene. The real question is whether authoritarian states in the region can adapt to new challenges and absorb the shocks of change in the coming years.

The traditional bargain with the region's autocrats has collapsed, and US strategic interests are better served in working with governments that genuinely respect the will of their people. The Arab awakening has upended assumptions about orientalist views of Arab societies—views that have characterized common aspects of Arabs and their societies as being regressive, fanatics, backward, and resigned to national politics. This orientalist construction has typically overlooked complexities, specificity, and inner dynamics of the Arab people and their societies. The Arab world is now much more politically mobilized, and the habit of deference to authoritarian rule has been broken.[96]

Furthermore, these uprisings, in addition to the subsequent regional and global response to them, are likely to greatly impact a wide range of issues, including oil prices, democratic transition, neoliberal economic policies, US strategic interests, and human rights conditions in the region. There is a unique opportunity to use this occasion to promote the counter-narrative of peaceful democratic change—a narrative that views the spread of democratic values and norms as a strategy to undermine the influence of terrorist groups such as al-Qaeda. There are risks associated with promoting reforms, but those risks are far more manageable than the continuing support for autocrats. These young people and their leaderless movements are driven by secular impulses, and in the long term, US strategic interests will be better served by working with them than with the old, corrupt regimes that have lost legitimacy in the eyes of their own people.

Some observers have warned that the era of Western meddling in the region is coming to an end. The ongoing Arab uprisings have demonstrated that the people of the Middle East have "an organic capacity to engineer change themselves" and that they need no outside oversight, guidance, or protection.[97] The bottom line is "the century-long battle for the control of the Middle East and North Africa is over. We lost. They won. No amount of high-tech ordnance can alter the outcome."[98] New media, also known as citizen media, have come to play an important role in fostering peaceful democratic change in the MENA region—in both instigating anti-regime protests and content consumption. Moving toward greater democratic measures and more economic opportunities is the only way to defuse current tensions. The younger generation in the region feels empowered to move forward on its own.

Chapter 4
EMERGING IDENTITIES

Emotions, Protests, and New Media

The Arab revolts demonstrated not only rage and rebellion against autocratic regimes but also a deep and protracted struggle over identity. The latter came down to the very essence of what it meant to be a modern, revolutionary Muslim. In some countries (e.g., Tunisia and Egypt), these struggles showed a move away from basic and exclusive notions of identity, such as sect and ethnicity, toward universal and inclusive notions of identity, such as citizenship. In others (e.g., Syria and Bahrain), the reverse proved to be the case. On balance, however, these events elucidated the emergence of a new and powerful form of identity—Arabism—unprecedented in recent decades. What gave birth to the renewal of this identity were not only the sustaining bonds of common language and historical experience, but also an ideational and inspirational energy unleashed by each other's methods and goals.[1]

The expression of new, multiple, and shifting identities among the MENA youth was facilitated by social media. Social media have shaped and played a key role in contributing to the reconstruction of societal identities as well as to rising new demands on governments. By facilitating much easier information-sharing, the Internet has dramatically increased the speed with which people can communicate and exchange information around the world, circumscribing government censorship. Though it is not a perfect tool, it is the fastest and the most effective instrument to mobilize a group for a particular cause.

Since the 1980s, young Muslims have struggled to come to grips with the massive changes in world politics—changes associated with globalization and the so-called third wave of democratization across Europe, Asia, and Latin America. Witnessing these movements, Muslim youth have tried to a find a way to reconcile their interests and values with modern moral orders and legal principles that are based on accountability, transparency, and participatory politics. Similarly, Islamic feminists and secular feminists have also reasserted their identities and interests, as they have become further concerned with being in control of their own lifestyles and politics. More importantly, youth organizations have insisted on a human rights framework that is legally and morally acceptable. The Muslim world's social realities have pointed to a rising and vibrant forum for positive change.

Unlike in Iran, where modern technology was used to mobilize the opposition against disputed election results, an effort led by the Green Movement's political leaders, known for their previous positions within the Islamic Republic in Egypt, people used new social media tools for a different cause—toppling a thirty-year regime. With the increased usage of ICTs, the Internet, and new social media tools in Egypt, the quest for authenticity, recognition, self-assertion, and new meanings in life has become inseparable from social change and power politics. Egyptians' struggles for identity construction have led to intense debate over the digital self versus the on-the-ground self. Egyptians used Facebook primarily for organizing at Tahrir Square. The events unfolded rather organically with no apparent leader.[2] Advocates of Facebook argue that if a message is potent enough, it can spread to a vast sea of connected individuals, irrespective of where it originated.[3] Facebook has leveled the playing field by giving everyone the same power to transmit a message that traditional media have often monopolized.[4] Emphasizing qualities of universal connectivity, Mark Zuckerberg, the creator of Facebook, asserts that this social networking site serves as an effective tool to build bridges and share information between people.[5]

On balance, experts note, Twitter "isn't the maker of political revolutions, but the vanguard of a media one."[6] Twitter has indeed become a crucial tool for understanding the momentous changes sweeping the Arab world. Likening it to a broadcast platform, analysts assert that "If there is indeed such a thing as a Twitter revolution in the Middle East, it's the way the tool is transforming how the outside world looks at the region."[7] Whereas hunting through Facebook pages, which are often in the local/national language, is time-consuming and requires a keen sense and responsibility of judgment about the veracity of attached information, Twitter is the most effective tool to get protesters' messages out to the world, especially given that these messages are more often in English.[8]

In many respects, one expert argues, the Green Movement that arose after Iran's contested presidential elections in 2009 was not so much a catalyst but a harbinger of the momentous transformation to come.[9] Although the Green Movement came to a standstill after it was brutally suppressed, in the period since the 2011 uprisings in the MENA region, when the Green Movement's leaders called for street demonstrations in solidarity with the uprisings in the MENA, it assumed a more radical stand. The movement, as Hamid Dabashi rightly asserts, entered a new stage: "the phase of organized opposition to the state apparatus."[10]

In this chapter, we turn our focus to different but interrelated developments in the MENA region that proved to be crucial for the peaceful democratic change: the 2009 Green Movement in Iran, the April 6 Youth Movement in Egypt followed by the 2011 uprisings in Tunisia and Egypt, women's role in the Arab Spring, and the power of moral emotions in influencing Arab hip-hop culture as well as identity formation and social protest. The Green Movement again made its presence felt in Iran's streets on February 14, 2011, as tens of thousands of Iranians rallied and clashed with police in solidarity with the uprisings in Tunisia and Egypt.[11] Two questions persist: (1) what does the reappearance of this movement mean for the future of the Islamic Republic? and (2) how does it relate to the uprisings sweeping across the region? The rise of Islamic identity and feminism in the post-conflict societies of Tunisia, Egypt, and Libya needs careful scrutiny, as does the role that the Arab hip-hop culture has played and continues to play in forging new identities throughout the Muslim world—identities that reject violence, militancy, and autocratic rule.

The Rise of the Green Movement in Iran

In the lead-up to the June 2009 Iranian presidential elections, all political campaigns—from labor leaders and journalists to students and women— were accused of jeopardizing the Islamic Republic's national security and inciting the so-called Velvet Revolution. Led by Mir Hossein Mousavi—a reformist politician, artist, and architect whose impressive credentials as the last prime minister of Iran during 1981–1989 remained indisputable—the Green Movement provided a solid opposition against the incumbent Mahmoud Ahmadinejad, who was running for his second term (2009–2013). Mousavi's supporters were typically tech-savvy, disaffected youth—men as well as women—educated, urbanized, and largely from the middle and upper classes. The older supporters of Mousavi were drawn largely from the same group that supported President Mohammad Khatami in his two consecutive landslide victories (1997 and 2001).

The official results of the June 12, 2009, presidential elections remain highly disputed. The results from 39.2 million handwritten ballots gave Ahmadinejad 24.5 million votes, compared to Mousavi's 13.2 million, a ratio that Mousavi called a "dangerous charade."[12] Given that the Ministry of Interior had put the number of eligible voters at 46 million,[13] the voter turnout was noticeably high at 85 percent, making the results utterly implausible given the huge support among the youth for the Green Movement. One journalist astutely captures the tense political climate: "Power, wealth, and ideology were all at stake as the new leadership troika—the Revolutionary Guard, the Supreme Leader, and Ahmadinejad and his neoconservative cabal—tried, once and for all, to attain political invincibility."[14]

Mousavi's reaction to the disputed elections was best captured in a remark that pointed to the possibility of a second Islamic Revolution:

> If the large volume of cheating and vote rigging, which has set fire to the hays of people's anger, is expressed as the evidence of fairness, the republican nature of the state will be killed and in practice, the ideology that Islam and Republicanism are incompatible will be proven. This outcome will make two groups happy: One, those who since the beginning of revolution stood against Imam and called the Islamic state a dictatorship of the elite who want to take people to heaven by force; and the other, those who in defending the human rights, consider religion and Islam against republicanism.[15]

Even before the popular wave from the rise of the Green Movement reached Iran, many experts pointed to mounting pressures for change and demands for democratic participation emanating from the spread of transnational satellite television, the Internet, and social networking tools such as Facebook and Twitter. Satellite television networks—Persian or foreign-language—exposed Iran's urban, young, and educated population to a new sociocultural and political world. Many of these young people felt increasingly frustrated when they saw citizens in democratic societies outside Iran enjoying basic freedoms that they were denied.[16] Some analysts noted that these protests reflected a remarkable phenomenon: the rise of a new middle class whose demands to participate in the discourse of democracy and create its own indigenous secularism stood in contrast to the core conservative values of the clerical establishment.[17] Others argued that this movement was neither a class struggle against a pro-rural government nor a secularist war against theocracy. Rather, it embraced a post-Islamist democracy struggle to reclaim citizenship within a religio-political order. It typified the long-standing aspirations for a dignified life free from fear, moral surveillance, corruption, and arbitrary rule. Homegrown and nonviolent in its approach, this movement represented "a green wave for life and liberty."[18]

Access to the Internet gave rise to new forms of political expression and political mobilization, substituting traditional print media with the preferred medium that helped give a voice to the many dissidents and disenfranchised.[19] This medium was particularly attractive in light of the fact that print media made for easier targets of attacks by Islamic conservatives who have often used the threat of the "external enemy" to silence internal dissents. These experts predicted that in the not too distant future, the progress toward achieving a more democratic future, and perhaps a transformation of the Islamic state in Iran, would be facilitated by high-tech communication technologies.[20] Likewise, opposition campaign managers discovered that Internet applications allowed them to get messages out and organize unprecedented campaign rallies. Without access to broadcast media, Philip N. Howard notes, "opposition campaigners turned social media applications like Facebook from minor pop culture fads into a major tool of political communication."[21]

Many young people used both Facebook and Twitter for street-level communications during the protests. More than 90 percent of Iranian Twitter users live in Tehran; a quarter of the current Iranian user base created accounts during the last three months of political campaigning.[22] Twitter was also used to help street protesters find safe hospitals, where injured people could be treated without drawing the attention of Basij militias. Any incident of attacks on people's residence by security agents was shared with family and friends. Protest leaders also used Twitter to recruit more international cyberactivists.[23] Significantly, online social networking services have become influential as communications media. But they are also a fundamental infrastructure for social movements.[24]

The emergence of the Green Movement and postelection insurgency was a testament to the emergence of a digital revolution, facilitating expanded capacities and possibilities for democratic change. This peaceful, massive democratic uprising—called by some experts an "electoral fraud revolt"[25]—was primarily a civil rights movement, the first of its kind in contemporary Iran. It is difficult to measure the effectiveness of such movements, in large part because their effects and success must be gauged over time. Despite all efforts by the authorities to depict it as a perilous counterrevolution, one expert notes, the Green Movement continues to draw supporters and sympathizers from clergy and conservative Iranians.[26] The movement morphed from a political campaign—during the 2009 presidential elections—to one that aimed to restore civil and political rights. The majority of supporters still want peaceful reform of the Islamic Republic and not necessarily a wholesale revolution—bloody or otherwise. Radical ideas and actions are still confined to a minority of protesters.[27] The movement is real, cannot be completely suppressed, and will undoubtedly have long-term effects on the nation's politics. It will put pressure on the regime to implement reforms—a pressure that it can only ignore at the risk of its own demise.[28]

Aptly capturing the essence of this movement, Hooman Majd notes that "the Green Movement may have started as a symbol of opposition to a government, but in reality it is more symbolic of a desire for something better than what Iran now has, a desire to move forward and not backward, and the hope of reform politicians and clergy is that *all* Iranians, not just angry protesters, might one day be able to call themselves Green."[29] Defiant protesters—young and old—took to the street to express their anger and frustration with the much disputed election results. The widely used and seen protest mantra became "Where is my vote?" This mantra spoke volumes about how a peaceful democratic movement soon turned into a violent backlash to a regime bent on retaining power at any cost.

The ensuing death of Neda Agha Soltan, a twenty-six-year-old girl who was shot in the chest by security forces, caught on a cell phone video, captured the unfolding drama of a peaceful resistance withstanding the heavy-handed and brutal tactics of a regime bent on wantonly punishing dissidents. Given that Iran lacked a free press and that the government restricted the access of foreign and Iranian media to the protesters, most of the information, films, and photos of the demonstrations came from protesters themselves, who captured images on their cell phones and posted them on the Internet and on social networking websites, such as Twitter, Facebook, and YouTube. Aware of this reality, Iranian leaders announced that they would create a special court focusing on "media crimes," a move that will certainly deter journalists and citizens alike from using the Internet to disseminate information about the protests. Even the regime's moderate conservatives, such as Majlis speaker Ali Larijani, have demanded that opposition leaders face trial for the February 14, 2011 protests. Some Majlis deputies have even called for their execution.[30]

The Guardian Council rejected the charges of fraudulent election results, agreeing only to recount 10 percent of the ballots—a too-little, too-late practice that further exposed the flawed election process altogether. When Iran's Supreme Leader, Ayatollah Ali Khamenei, declared the election of Ahmadinejad a "divine assessment," he clearly chose to come down on the side of the state, arguing that the rationale behind sustaining the state lay in its Islamic authenticity and anti-imperialism mandate. The idea of *velayate-e faqih*, rule by the Supreme Jurist, has now assumed a different meaning, but it cannot escape the reality that the struggle between secular and religious faiths and ideologies is far from over.

Reformist presidential candidates Mehdi Karroubi and Mir Hossein Mousavi, both former senior officials, came under fierce attack and were placed under house arrest by regime hard-liners for renouncing the brutal means used against protesters and pressing for charges against rape assailants in prisons. The increasing violence at both street level and in prisons eventually received global attention. President Obama finally reacted by saying that he was "appalled and outraged" by these developments. Those events intensified the Obama administration's foreign policy dilemma that sought to avoid any entanglements in the country's internal politics in its new diplomatic gesture to Tehran, hoping to convince Iranian leaders to forgo their nuclear program.[31]

The post–2009 presidential election protests in Iran shook the foundation of the Islamic Republic more than the three decades of sanctions and containment imposed by the United States and the United Nations.[32] What made this possible was the use of communication technologies and digital social networks, which served as vital and new communication tools during and after the 2009 presidential elections and the ensuing protests in Iran. Following the contested 2009 presidential election, disillusionment has begun to set in, with a growing realization among many Iranians that the Islamic Republic has inflicted an inept and archaic political and ideological system on them.

As in many other regimes, the Islamic Republic owes its political survival to constructing and imagining an omnipresent external threat. Indeed, suspicion of meddling by outside powers—Great Britain, Russia, and the United States, in particular—is deeply ingrained in the minds of many Iranians. The country's revolutionary power structure, however, felt threatened this time by a homegrown and popular movement. On the street, the use of brute force to quell unrest rendered the Ahmadinejad administration "fragile, contested, fissured, and militaristic" in the coming months and years.[33] Leaving aside the issue of elite fragmentation, the clerical regime or superstructure has ruled a society that has in many respects grown even more secular and globalized.[34]

A new generation of activists works behind the scenes to sustain the movement's momentum. Students and youth are still the driving force behind the movement, but it is swiftly spreading to the older generation, parents actively supporting their children.[35] Unlike the 1999 student protests, however, the Green Movement has expanded far beyond university campuses to encompass heterogeneous and overlapping groups, including human rights advocates, women, disgruntled clerics, unemployed and underemployed workers, and many young people who are angry at the current order.[36] Although the Islamic Republic has declared the demise of the Green Movement, it has gone to extraordinary lengths to criminalize it and conduct a campaign of repression against its leaders and followers. The logical question is that if the Green Movement is extinct, why does the government continue to violently suppress it?[37] There can be no doubt, one expert approvingly argues, the Green Movement and associated peaceful civil disobedience have posed the regime with its most significant challenge to date. For the Muslim world more generally, Iran has again become a trendsetter.[38]

A pessimistic view holds that an analysis of the degree to which the Islamic Revolutionary Guard Corps (IRGC)—Iran's most potent military entity—has come to call the shots in the Islamic Republic reveals an Iran that has become a bona fide militarized state, one in which guards are gaining enormous might if not full control. The successful clampdown against the Green Movement has further solidified the position of the guard in a theocratic regime only in name. The Green Movement, according to this view, is currently not powerful enough to transform the Islamic Republic.[39] That said, it is worth noting that the background for the rise of the Green Movement was set well before the 2009 presidential election. Since Khatami's presidency, a group of reformists worked on the expansion of civil society and amending laws. Although the struggle for women's rights and encountering feminist problems predated the Green Movement, for many female activists, these protests provided a unique opportunity to broach the subject tactfully.

Iran's Gender Discourse

In keeping with modern notions of rights and the rule of law, the civil society discourse fostered the idea of adjusting to the prevailing standards of international legality and legitimacy. There have emerged sharp disagreements among the ruling elite as to how to respond to civil society's growing demands on the political regime, with the conservatives favoring the all-too-familiar mode of social control and reformists calling for an open society. Supporters of President Khatami's reformist agenda advocated—largely on pragmatic grounds—a regional détente and improved ties with the West, especially with the United States. Public opinion grew increasingly supportive of such foreign policy initiatives, challenging the conservative camp and their allied Islamic radicals to put forth a credible foreign policy agenda.

Conservatives blocked any reformist measure, as the power struggle between the two camps reached a new deadlock during the second term of the Khatami presidency. At the same time, conservatives could reach a consensus among themselves as to the pace and direction of change. They clearly failed to run a modern country and economy with all its attendant complications and, most importantly, the people's rising expectations. As a result, they alienated large segments of society, especially the younger generation. These internal divisions further revealed the Islamic Republic's political contradictions, stemming largely from the lack of clarity about who actually heads the state and who controls the levers of power. Although conducted within certain limits, elections are held regularly in

Iran. The public elects the president, the Majlis (an Iranian term for the parliament), and the Assembly of Experts (Majles-e-Khobregan). But the *velayat-e faqih* and the clerically dominated Council of Guardians determine who can compete in these elections. The power of the Council of Guardians to vet parliamentary candidates remains a huge barrier to the enactment of a reform agenda.

Undoubtedly, the absolute powers of the *velayat-e faqih* posed and continue to present a major hindrance to the effective operation of democracy and civil society. Objections to such absolutism greatly mounted as the globalizing dynamics struck a chord in Iranian society, raising the level of public awareness of democratic rights and individual freedoms. The interaction of external influences—such as global trends of democratization and human rights—and internal dynamics—such as calls for open society and economic development—reinforced an enormous need for change, intensifying the internal cultural clash between conservatives and reformists. It was in this context that Iran's gender crisis resurfaced. A new strand of feminism—in both Islamic and secular forms—embraced the idea that the independent understanding of women's rights, based on *ijtihad* (autonomous reasoning), was compatible with the provisions of the UN Convention on the Elimination of All Forms of Discrimination Against Women (CEDAW, passed on December 18, 1979), to which Iran has yet to commit itself. The most obvious discrepancies between Islamic laws and CEDAW relate to adulthood age, blood money (*diyah*), and witnessing rule, which equates two female witnesses with one male witness in the courts.

Likewise, according to Iranian civil law, men reach puberty at age fifteen and women at age nine. Thus there is a considerable age difference between males and females in determining legal eligibility for marriage. This runs counter to the universal standards of human rights, which specify equality in all matters relating to marriage and family relations.[40] This definition of puberty entailed different criminal responsibilities for the same criminal act. If a fourteen-year-old boy committed a crime, he would be exonerated from any criminal responsibility. But if the same crime was committed by a ten-year-old girl, she would be held accountable.[41] Marriage before reaching the age of puberty was possible through legal means. According to Iranian civil law, the father or his side of the family had the right to enter into a marriage contract regarding an adolescent daughter or son. Only the father and his side of the family would be in a legal position to cancel such a marriage if they decided that such a marriage compromised the boy's or the girl's welfare. The girl or the boy would have no say in confirming or denying the choice of her husband or his wife in the future.

Shirin Ebadi, an Iranian lawyer and prominent feminist, likened this practice to a form of slavery.[42] Since the Iranian government, she noted, has joined the Treaties to Abolish Slavery (1904, 1926, and 1956), it was obligated, both formally and legally, to determine a minimum age for marriage and to require, before either a state official or a religious authority, both the husband's and the wife's consent prior to marriage. The current practice was also incompatible with Article 11(a) of the Cairo Declaration on Human Rights in Islam: "Human beings are born free, and no one has the right to enslave, humiliate, oppress or exploit them, and there can be no subjugation but to God the Most-High."[43]

In 2003, the granting of the Nobel Peace Prize to Ebadi opened a new chapter in Iran's upcoming political drama. Iran's hard-line conservatives felt threatened and undermined by this global notoriety. Their immediate backlash to this prize as interference in Iran's internal affairs was emblematic of the fear of losing ground as the 2005 presidential election approached. In the long run, however, conservatives were concerned about losing their grip on power. Ebadi, who has since 2009 chosen to live in exile, appears to be unoptimistic about remarkable change in Iran. She insists, however, that during the last three decades Iranians have experienced a revolution and an eight-year war with Iraq and that they are tired of violence and bloodshed. They want peaceful democratic change and reform. That is why we should expect change to be a lengthy process.[44] At the moment, Ebadi asserts, Iranian government is weak; it has lost a great deal of its popular base and the economic situation is fast deteriorating. Ruling elites are divided and the country faces enormous international pressures.[45]

It should be noted, however, that the awarding of the Nobel Peace Prize was the harbinger of future gender politics in Iran. With many uncertain and paradoxical features, the shifting Iranian society is fast approaching a gender conundrum. The dramatic growth of educational and professional capacities of Iranian women has become a social issue in a country in which females constitute 64 percent of university graduates and the female literacy rate exceeds 80 percent.[46] Despite these achievements, no woman held any key position in President Khatami's or President Ahmadinejad's first cabinets, women's testimony is half that of men, women cannot travel abroad on their own without the permission of their husbands, a woman's life is worth half that of a man under Iran's blood money law, and men continue to have a unilateral right to divorce.

Worse yet, the official unemployment rate among youth ages fifteen to twenty-nine is 20 percent.[47] Iran continues to suffer from double-digit unemployment and inflation. The latter climbed to a 28 percent annual rate in 2008.[48] Underemployment among Iran's educated youth has convinced many to seek jobs overseas, resulting in a significant "brain drain."[49] The figures released by Iran's Central Bank for November 2008 showed prices of basic commodities and services were rising at a 19 percent while overall inflation was running at 16.8 percent annually—double the pace it was when Ahmadinejad took office in 2005. But independent economists and experts put the inflation rate well above 30 percent.[50] The overall unemployment rate is estimated to exceed 16 percent this year, as more than 4 million young Iranians remain unemployed.

A report by Tehran University's Center for Women's Studies noted that women's unemployment rate in 2004 was 17.80 percent, compared with that of men at 11.30 percent.[51] Even though women outnumber men in the entering classes of universities by two to one, when they graduate, women are a third less likely to have equal employment opportunities. This is because a large number of women are enrolled in humanities and social sciences programs, which are not marketable. In contrast, men prefer, for example, engineering: in 2006, 40 percent of men were engineering students, compared with 13 percent of women.[52] The unemployment rate among female university graduates has risen in the past five years. According to a UK-based feminist organization, the reason for nine out of every ten women who are drawn into prostitution in Iran is poverty.[53] The second most cited reason is unemployment.

As a female lawyer who for the past quarter century has fought the Islamic penal code and other archaic laws while defending the rights of women and children, Ebadi epitomizes the next generation of Muslim feminists. The awarding of the Nobel Peace Prize to her has already exposed the inherent contradictions in Iran's conservative ideology. It has also fostered more convergence between certain elements of Muslim feminists and secular feminists.[54] What is perhaps most noteworthy is the increasing range of Iranian women who have embraced human rights as a source of empowerment. Many Iranian women feel vindicated and emboldened, even as the risks to them for asserting their claims have not been drastically curtailed. This unique opportunity revitalized Iranian civil society, posing new challenges to the control of the theological state—a dysfunctional state held together by coercive means and sheer intimidation. Many Iranian women, regardless of their ideological bent, saw a rare opportunity in the 2009 elections to advance their struggles.

Women and the Arab Spring

Since the protests in the Arab world began in early 2011, women—both Muslims and Christians—have emerged as a political force challenging repressive regimes throughout the region. This trend captured even further attention when Yemeni activist Tawakkol Karman won the 2011 Nobel Peace Prize. At the same time, a new wave of Islamic feminists determined to inject feminine perspectives into Islam's teaching and practices, as well as to distance themselves from state policies, has embraced the notion that Islam can liberate rather than restrict them. This new generation of Islamic feminists is determined to win equality through Islam, not despite it.[55] Many Muslims and Christians have begun to challenge the social authority of al-Azhar and the Coptic Church in the aftermath of Mubarak's departure, viewing these institutions as insensitive or indifferent to their interests over personal status law.[56]

More specifically, two incidents fueled feminists' struggle in the post-Mubarak era. First, the practice of subjecting women to the so-called "virginity tests" came under attack when a large group of women in Tahrir Square on March 9, 2011, were subjected to this practice. These tests were used by the riot police to raise the charge that these women protesters were prostitutes and thus not entitled to any rights. In an interview, Nawla Darwish, a prominent Egyptian feminist of the New Woman Foundation, pointed to the difficult and dangerous times ahead in Egypt's transition to democracy. She specifically criticized the practice of "virginity tests" as a demeaning practice that is an egregious violation of women's rights.[57] The real war on women in the Arab societies, Mona Eltahawy notes, is rooted in misogyny. It is because of this hatred that women throughout the Middle East lack freedoms. Critical of the current situation in Egypt, Eltahawy writes that during parliamentarian elections of 2011, when fielding female candidates, Egypt's Salafi Nour Party ran a flower in place of each woman's face. The Muslim Brotherhood, with almost half the total seats in the newly elected parliament, does not believe women—or Christians, for that matter—can be president.[58]

The second event happened on December 19, 2011, when security forces beat and stripped a female protester half-naked in Tahrir Square. This act of brutality that went viral over the Internet and social networks, not to mention in the international media, called into question the systematic way that the police have degraded women protesters. A member of the military council sought to discredit the protesters, questioning their motives and morals and speaking of a conspiracy to "topple the state." Maj. Gen. Adel Emara defended the use of force by troops, while refusing to offer an apology for the brutality shown by troops toward female protesters.[59] Nearly 10,000 women marched on December 21, 2011, through downtown Cairo, demanding Egypt's ruling military step down in an extraordinary expression of anger over images of soldiers beating, stripping, and kicking demonstrators in Tahrir Square. This demonstrated the outrage over soldiers' treatment of protesters in the street during a fierce crackdown on activists.

The *New York Times* described this event in a dramatic fashion: "Historians called the event the biggest women's demonstration in modern Egyptian history, the most significant since a 1919 march against British colonialism inaugurated women's activism here, and a rarity in the Arab world. It also added a new and unexpected wave of protesters opposing the ruling military council's efforts to retain power and its tactics for suppressing public discontent."[60] This backlash pushed women to the center of the Egyptian political landscape after they had been left out almost completely. Although women stood at the forefront of the initial revolt that ousted President Hosni Mubarak in early 2011, few had prominent roles in the various revolutionary coalitions formed in the uprising's aftermath.[61]

Unlike Tunisian feminists and activists, who have been the major beneficiary of the oldest progressive family laws, Egyptian women have shown a clear interest in distancing themselves from the institutional and political legacies of state feminism.[62] That said, it is worth noting that Egyptian women face a familiar dilemma: many of their contemporary gains are associated with authoritarian states. This is also true in the case of Tunisia, where the 1956 Tunisian Code of Personal Status (CPS), which profoundly altered family law and the legal status of women, represented one of the initial reformist policies publicly known in the Arab world. This was, in one expert's view, a manifestation of the different vision of society held by Habib Bourguiba's victory over other factions immediately following the proclamation of the nation's independence.[63]

In May 2011, Tunisia passed a progressive parity law, which required all political parties to make women at least half of their candidates. Ennahda, which strongly supported the parity law, enjoyed more credibility than other groups by having a greater number of female candidates run than any other party. Many Tunisian women have formed a political consciousness as a backlash to President Ben Ali's severe oppression of Al-Nahda in the 1990s. As a major winner in 2011 elections, Al-Nahda will send the largest single bloc of female lawmakers to the 217-member constituent assembly. These female representatives are well educated, and their brand of Islamism, like Tunisian society as a whole, is moderate and progressive. Tunisians are seeking to reconcile their legacy of French-inspired civil rights policies with their religious aspirations. Their challenge lies in striking the proper balance.[64]

To explain the role of women in the Arab Spring more fully, it is important to address the question, why did women choose to take part in the Egyptian revolts? In an extensive and riveting interview with Professor Mayy ElHayawi, a scholar of postcolonial and gender studies at Al Alsun University and the Arab Academy, in Cairo, Egypt, I became convinced that "what drew women to the streets on January 25th was precisely what drove men—that is, three decades of political corruption, social injustice, and economic decay."[65] Since assuming presidency one week after the controversial assassination of President Anwar El-Sadat in 1981, Mubarak enacted an emergency law that extended police powers and intensified brutality against all opposing voices—Islamists as well as secularists—while maintaining one-party rule by means of fraud and political manipulation, which in part paved the way for his son to succeed him in presidency. In doing so, Mubarak ruthlessly devastated all Egyptians' dreams for a better future.[66] Women during Mubarak's regime, ElHayawi pointed out, served as window dressings, giving the world the impression that Mubarak was ruling over a democratic state. The laws passed that granted women the right to divorce, travel without the consent of her husband, pass Egyptian nationality to their children, and issue birth certificates for their children—even if the father declines paternity—were all crucial in promoting women's status.

Many Egyptian women, ElHayawi continued, were directly and traumatically affected by the tragic loss of life when one thousand Egyptians were intentionally left to die after the seriously defected Salem Express Ferry sank into the Red Sea. On December 15, 1991, the Salem Express departed Jeddah bound for Safaga, carrying passengers who were pilgrims returning from Mecca. It was estimated that 464 people drowned in total, many of them trapped inside the ship.[67] One of the most controversial aspects of this tragedy was that under Mubarak's regime, the owner of the ferry was allowed to leave the country without trial.

The same can be said about what happened to the Duwayqa Slum inhabitants on September 6, 2008, when 107 people died and 58 lay injured when huge boulders and rocks crashed down Al-Muqattam Hill in Al-Duwayqa onto Ezbet Bekhit in the Manshiyet Nasser neighborhood of east Cairo, home to approximately a million of the city's poor residents. In addition to neglect, corruption, and mismanagement, the Mubarak era was replete with numerous examples of police brutality. Recent examples include Khaled Said (a man who exposed police brutality by capturing it on a video) and Sayed Belal (a member of a Salafi group arrested in connection with the attack on Al-Qeddesine—The Church of Two Saints—in Alexandria), along with many others who have been tortured to death by state security officials, while their killers were simply acquitted or mercifully punished after Al-Qeddesine was bombed in order to agitate antagonism between Muslims and Christians.

Turning to the question of the role of women prior to and during the revolution, ElHayawi asserted that in spite of the systemic exclusion of women from politics—largely through sexual assaults during protests and elections—women have played a major role in fighting corruption and dictatorship especially during the last decade of Mubarak's rule. Ten days before the start of the protests on January 25, 2011, a video posted online by Asmaa Mahfouz, the twenty-seven-year-old political activist, went viral on the Internet, urging Egyptians to rise and defend their rights. During the eighteen-day uprising that culminated in the ousting of Mubarak's regime, ElHayawi noted, women's role proved vitally significant to the success of the Egyptian revolution. In many important ways, ElHayawi continued, "Egyptian women have daringly led marches, compassionately treated injuries, emotionally identified and sympathized with protesters' cause, defiantly challenged the brutality of security forces, and above all patiently endured the tragic loss of family and friends. There can be no doubt that Egyptian women have not only tried to renegotiate their agency in a patriarchal regime but also to reserve their leading role in the new national dream."[68]

As to the question of what is the status of women under military rule, ElHayawi pointed out that adopting Mubarak's authoritarian style, the SCAF immediately resorted to sexual assault as the most effective means of intimidating women and driving them out of Tahrir Square. However, women demonstrated resiliency when it was publically announced that they had been sexually assaulted; they were unwilling to abandon their feminist rights or their pro-democracy fights for fear of public scorn. "I could see," ElHayawi opined, "such incredible insistence and perseverance in the rallies protesting against the brutal treatment of women in Tahrir Square." Thousands of women and men were chanting "Oh Tantawi! Wait, wait, Egyptian women will dig your grave!" ElHayawi then went on to astutely capture the main thrust of her message in this engaging interview: "With a dream to share, a nation to love, an anthem to sing, a goal to attain and a future to plan, Egyptian women and men will surely resolve negotiating agency to focus on navigating a nation."[69]

The Satellite Dish and New Media Tools

Just as the Arab satellite network helped bring about a popular uprising in the MENA, Iranians' access to satellite television has made it possible for many to witness the democratic changes that transpired across the European continent. Iranian youth watched profound economic and political transformations sweeping the globe and suddenly felt that change seemed possible and within grasp in their own country. The Obama presidency heartened Iran's younger generation, and his administration's decision concerning the abandonment of the Green Movement in return for Iran's cooperation in Iraq, Afghanistan, and on nuclear issues left a bitter taste in some people's mouths.

Regardless of Western support or lack thereof, the revolution in online campaigning played an instrumental role in shaping presidential candidate Mir Hossein Mousavi's Green Movement. Captured best in Mousavi's slogan, "Every person is a campaign office," the so-called "green wave" of the pre– and post–June 12 election days made it very difficult for the Islamic Republic to stuff the genie back into the bottle. More importantly, the homegrown, popular movement in Iran revealed the Islamic Republic's hand and made it extremely difficult, if not impossible, for the regime to hide behind the mask of enemy construction.

What separated the 2009 Green Movement from the previous protests in Iran was that a significant portion of the populace rejected the state's sanctioned narrative of enemy construction and replaced it with its own unique version. The fact that the Islamic Republic, with its hardened monopoly over the means of mass communication—including all six nationally televised channels, dozens of radio networks, and all but a few newspapers and magazines—was unable to sell its narrative to the public is a testament to the reach and penetration of digital communication networks in Iran. According to the Central Intelligence Agency, Iran ranked fourteenth globally in the number of Internet users in 2008, as the number topped 23 percent of the population.[70] Iran boasts even more impressive statistics when it comes to mobile phone penetration. By the first quarter of 2009, nearly 50 million Iranians owned mobile phones, leaving the penetration rate at more than 70 percent.[71] Not surprisingly, the Iranian government shut down the short message service (SMS) communication networks for several weeks beginning on June 12, the election day. In fact, immediately after the election, the Iranian government stepped up its cyber censorship efforts, unleashing a massive campaign to prevent online access by filtering opposition websites, reducing Internet bandwidth to lowest possible levels, and setting up fake opposition websites.

Nevertheless, the Green Movement in Iran will be remembered around the world by the varied images transmitted amidst the protests. These images documented not only the oppression and violence the Iranian protesters faced but also the Iranian people's yearning for democracy and human rights.[72] Further, as Robin Wright rightfully notes, these uprisings are not a passing phenomenon like the student protests of 1999, which were quickly and forcibly squashed. This time, Iranians' resolve is firm and reminiscent of civil disobedience in colonial India before its independence in 1947 or in the American South in the 1960s. Although the current uprising is not as widespread as that of 1979, which ushered in the Islamic Republic, the activism has created a new political space in Iran. What is unique about this movement is that opposition figures, such as Ayatollah Rafsanjani and Mousavi, are in fact responding to sentiment on the street rather than directing it.[73]

The Green Movement (or "green wave") highlighted the political and social energies of resistance and suggested a new movement that will not settle for anything short of a just and democratic order. The continuing images of the show of resistance that now emerge on a daily basis in Iran are in fact powerful symbols for the strength of the green wave. Facilitated by constant digital interaction via instant messaging and social network services, the green wave drew immediate attention to human rights violations and political violence in Iran. In the meantime, the Islamic Republic has failed to terrorize the public into submission. Many Western states are adopting legislation that requires penalizing the companies that provide the Islamic Republic with the technology of surveillance and suppression.

Iranian Revolution Gone Astray

Iran reasserted its culture, people, civilization, and ideals on the world stage in 1979 with a revolution that captured the imagination of many in the world. Today, however, that revolution has gone awry, as it is challenged by a popular democracy movement and young Iranians whose aspirations for progress, prosperity, and democratization remain mostly unfulfilled. The 2009 presidential election marked a new era in the country's political history. Nearly thirty years after the 1979 Islamic Revolution, protests and demonstrations came back to Iran's streets with a vengeance. Why have the Iranian people, who were chanting "death to America" three decades ago, turned inward, shouting vociferously "death to dictator"? By adopting the same policies that it once defied as justification for its rise to power, the Islamic Republic has shot itself in the foot. Both the state and society in Iran suffer from deep divisions and a cultural divide that have propelled society further away from the state and its ruling elite.

All the indications point to the fact that lingering tensions in Iran may not subside anytime soon. The difficulties facing the Islamic Republic are mounting as the regime faces multiple crises. To begin with, many Iranian youth are grappling with a crisis of belonging-ness, as they have for a long time felt alienated from the Islamic Republic. For the Iranian youth, the bitter irony was (and still is) that the Islamic Republic supports such regional causes as the Palestinian Intifada (uprising), while at the same time it brutally suppresses its own domestic uprisings. Likewise, the Islamic Republic of Iran supported 2011 popular uprisings in North Africa and the Middle East, but kept suppressing the legitimate aspiration of the Iranian people for human dignity and fundamental human rights. How could the Islamic Republic advocate democracy for the Tunisians, the Egyptians, the Bahrainis, the Libyans, the Iraqis, the Syrians, the Afghans, and the Palestinians, yet deny it to its own people? The Islamic Republic has built a vast Internet police system based on an extensive system of censorship and surveillance of cyberspace.[74]

It is worth acknowledging the limits of social media in a rentier state such as Iran. Although social media strengthened the Green Movement in Iran, the country's petroleum economy insulated the regime from protest activity. The movement failed, experts remind us, because the Islamic Republic relies on oil—not taxes—to sustain itself economically. Political protests in 2009, unlike the 1979 revolution, did not jeopardize oil production.[75] Regardless, Facebook continues to be a way for Mousavi's supporters to spread information and organize action in response to arrests in the postelection period. With each passing day, there has been an increasing link between activity on Mousavi's Facebook page and the size and intensity of support for peaceful, democratic change.[76]

Kefaya: A Prelude to Change

The Egyptian Movement for Change (EMC), also known as Kefaya—an Arabic term for "enough"—was founded by 300 Egyptian intellectuals from various ideological backgrounds in November 2004 at a meeting at the home of al-Wassat party leader Abu 'l-Ala Madi. This group, also known as New Islamists, represented a moderate centrist and reformist Islamic mainstream vision, as embodied by the New Wassat Party that emerged in the mid-1990s.[77] The New Islamist trend emerged out of the Muslim Brotherhood, shaped as much by reaction to its failures as by its successes.[78] This group includes renowned Islamic scholars, jurists, historians, lawyers, and journalists: Yusuf al Qaradawy and the late Muhammad al-Ghazzaly, Islamic scholars; Fahmy Huwaidy, Egypt's most prominent Islamist journalist; Kamal Abul Magd and Selim al Awa, highly regarded lawyers and public figures in Egypt and the Arab world; and Tareq al Bishry, a distinguished member of the judiciary and renowned historian. Together they represent a major intellectual force in Egypt and beyond.

Kefaya called for political reforms and excoriated the extension of Mubarak's presidential term, the succession of Gamal Mubarak (his son), government inefficiency corruption, and Egypt's state of emergency in place since 1981. By 2005, the movement organized anti-regime demonstrations throughout Egypt. Kefaya soon became the first political initiative in Egypt to explore as well as exploit new social media and digital technology for the purposes of advancing its political cause. Most notably, this movement popularized such trends as political blogging in Egypt—currently in vogue and widely employed in youth activism and opposition campaigns. In particular, bloggers mobilized support by spreading the movement's ideas of political reform and broadening its efforts to document human rights abuses by posting uncensored audiovisual and photographic images. The use of social media, as well as e-mail and text messages, online advertisements, and an official website, was in fact the primary means of communication.[79] Kefaya's significance lay in its cross-ideological framework that potentially created a new mainstream and a movement in Egyptian politics. With so many restrictive laws imposed on political parties, and with the Muslim Brotherhood banned from elections, the Kefaya movement played a significant role in shaping Egyptian political life.[80]

The April 6 Youth Movement

As noted above, the roots of social media–driven uprisings can be traced back to the Kefaya movement (2004–2005) that was in solidarity with textile workers who were planning a strike on April 6, 2008, hence the origin of the name, "April 6 Youth Movement," which referred to a loose coalition of many several groups of activists, opposition parties, lawyers, professors, and student protesters.

Ahmed Maher, thirty, gained prominence in 2008 as one of the co-founders of this movement—a solidarity group launched to support protests. Organizing mostly online, especially on Facebook, it was a decentralized network of activists who used the tools of social media to broadcast economic and political grievances against the Mubarak regime, mobilize support, evade the government's ubiquitous security forces, and later help bring down the Mubarak regime. Ahmed Maher and Ahmed Salah, young members of the Kefaya opposition group, branched off and helped launch a Facebook group to promote a protest planned for April 6, 2008.[81] The movement attracted 70,000 members on Facebook, making it the largest youth movement in Egypt at the time.[82] In 2008, workers at Al-Mahalla Textiles called a strike on April 6. Although no major protests ensued, two activist workers were killed and the city became, albeit briefly, a site of violent confrontation between workers and security forces.[83]

Given the limits of social networking as a tool of democratic revolution, leaders of the April 6 Youth Movement sought to study and learn from both post-communist democratic change in Eastern Europe and NGOs in the West. In the summer of 2009, Mohamed Adel, a twenty-year-old blogger and April 6 activist, went to Belgrade, Serbia, where he received training at the Center for Applied Non-Violent Action and Strategies (CANVAS)—an organization that was vociferously involved in the mass mobilization against Slobodan Milošević in the late 1990s. CANVAS helped Adel figure out how to turn a cynical, passive, and fearful public into activists.[84] By attending several workshops, Adel learned how to use new media and technology to galvanize and mobilize a large-scale, nonviolent revolutionary effort by stressing unity, setting clear goals, and keeping members engaged.[85]

In early 2010, Bassem Samir, the twenty-eight-year-old director of the Egyptian Democratic Academy, led a small delegation to the United States for media training. This US-based NGO with funding from the State Department oversaw training sessions led by digital journalists from *Time* magazine and documentary filmmakers affiliated with human rights organization Witness, in which the Egyptian activists were taught camera operation and ways of using effective online videos.[86] During the 2011 uprisings, Samir used his office for the purposes of feeding images taken by the activists on the ground to the international media. The way these young activists used new-media tools and methods proved crucial in fanning the protest flames—a movement that moved offline and into the streets during those eighteen days of uprisings (January 25 to February 11, 2011), where it was then propelled by people who were least familiar with such social networking sites as Facebook and Twitter.[87]

Facebook Invades Factional Politics

Members of both the April 6 Youth Movement and Kefaya were behind the creation of another popular Facebook group, one supporting Mohamed ElBaradei, the former head of the International Atomic

Energy Agency (IAEA), who returned to Egypt in 2010. In June 2010, activists, led by Wael Ghonim, a Google executive, created a Facebook page called "Kullena Khaled Said" ("We are all Khaled Said") in memory of a young man—his cell phone contained images of political brutality and drug use—who was beaten to death on June 6, 2010, by two secret police officers in Alexandria. This page attracted more than 1 million supporters and became the focal point for a number of large protests against state abuses in the summer of 2010. Ghonim, AbdelRahman Mansour, and many of their colleagues brought the Said case into the public consciousness by organizing several Silent Stands on June 18 and 25 and July 9, 2010, mainly organized at the corniche in Cairo and Alexandria by online activists, while also posting on the Kullena Khaled Said Facebook page. These online activists, as well as many bloggers, brought out more than 8,000 people on June 25, 2010, when Dr. ElBaradei, who at the time was running as a presidential candidate, took part. It was evident that the fear barrier was broken and virtual activism had been transferred into real-world action.[88]

Solidarity with the Said cause transcended national borders, as groups from Tunisia and Yemen began creating Facebook pages in support of Egyptian online activists. Said's Tunisian Facebook page drew more than one thousand members within two days of its launch.[89] The triggering event for the 2011 uprisings in Egypt happened some 1,300 miles away in Tunisia, when Mohammad Bouazizi set himself on fire on December 17, 2010. On January 4 he died and shortly thereafter, on January 14, Tunisian president Ben Ali fled to Saudi Arabia.[90] What happened in Tunisia encouraged and enabled Egyptians to follow suit. Ghonim took the Egyptians to task by posting on the Said Facebook page on January 14, 2011, the following message: "Today is the 14th ... January 25 is Police Day and it's a national holiday.... If 100,000 take to the streets, no one can stop us.... I wonder if we can?"[91]

The interaction of organized groups, networks, and social media was crystallized in nonviolent anti-Mubarak protests that removed long-reigned autocrats from power on February 11, 2011. These protests, some experts contend, showed that Egyptian society, much like Western societies, has transformed away from traditional groups and media—such as TV, radio, and newspapers—and toward more loosely structured "networked societies" or "network individualism," whereby there is less group control and more individual autonomy.[92] There is no denying that social media provided affordable access to social movements by curtailing the costs of mobilization and organization, while accelerating the dissemination of information. Young men and women in Egypt were able to use social networks, the Internet, and mobile phones "to access large and diversified networks, reach beyond physical and social boundaries, and exploit more resources to potentially bring about social change."[93] Yet it is important to be aware of the euphoria about social networking. The fact remains that Twitter alone is unlikely to generate successful uprisings. Though new media tools have a catalytic role, as experts remind us, it is the symbiosis between offline activity and online activism that is critical to how protests achieve their goals.[94]

In the cases of Iran and Egypt, the governments resorted to Internet crackdowns, shutting down Internet and cell phone communications, before starting a violent crackdown against protesters. According to one source, an American company—Boeing-owned Narus of Sunnyvale, California—had sold Egypt (Telecom Egypt, the state-run Internet service provider) Deep Packet Inspection (DPI) equipment that could have been used to help Mubarak's regime track, target, and crush political dissent over the Internet and mobile phones. The same company is selling this spying technology to other regimes with lamentable human rights records. Before DPI becomes more widely used, both abroad and at home, the US government must establish transparent and legitimate guidelines for preventing the use of such surveillance and control technology.[95]

Arab Hip-Hop Culture

Although Egyptian revolution has yet to become a subject of art, and it is too early for artists to map out the characteristics of current occurrence with any clarity,[96] a new generation of Muslim playwrights and filmmakers is turning these events into an art form, proving that the pen is more potent than the suicide bomb.[97] Arab hip-hop culture and its relevance to the Arab Spring are the key to understanding newly emerging identities among the Arab youth. As in the rest of the world, hip-hop culture in the Muslim world, represented by rap music and popularized by graffiti on walls, has come to mobilize the youth's defiance against their governments and create a sense of solidarity—both inside their country and across the border—with those defying the status quo. Rap music has become a tool of venting long-standing and pent-up frustrations and grievances as people throughout the Arab world have sought to redefine their relationship with the state and their rights as citizens. Increasingly, hip-hop songs have become anthems of protests and rebellion against autocrats and extremists across the Arab world. Just as rap initially provided an alternative to gang violence for young blacks in the Bronx (New York City), as Robin Wright, a prominent American journalist, has observed, hip-hop culture has offered an alternative to suicide bombs and Molotov cocktails among Palestinians.[98]

Likewise, the lyrics of rappers have linked feelings and frustrations of diasporic communities with homelands. One observer notes that "it has been hip-hop that has become the most iconic and widespread soundtrack of the Arab Spring and, interestingly, it is having the double effect of helping to mobilize activists in the countries directly impacted by the pro-democracy movements while also solidifying links between Arab diasporic communities in the West with those still residing in the homeland."[99]

This dynamic became apparent with the popularity of protest songs by Chicago-based artist Khaled M. Libyan. By birth, Libyan is the son of a Qaddafi dissident whose father was tortured and jailed under the Libyan regime. Khaled's father died when he was nine. After protests broke out in Libya on February 17, 2011, Khaled M. Libyan released the haunting single "Can't Take Our Freedom," which reads like an open letter to both Qaddafi and the people of the MENA region: "Can't take our freedom and take our soul / can't take our freedom, take our soul / you are not the one that's in control / you are not the one that's in control / lā ilāha illallāh, there is no power greater than God / go ahead and divide your plans / at the end of the day you are just a man."[100]

The song powerfully employs the *shahada* and a common humanity to decapitate the Qaddafi regime while encouraging protesters from all over the Arab world to rise up against oppression. It also points to a strengthening of familial, political, and identity ties and interests between diasporic Arabs who have long lived abroad and younger generations who may have never visited the countries their parents originally migrated from. This sense of connectedness renewed by the song has prompted a collaboration of sorts between diasporic communities in the rewriting of history with those who never left the country of origin but nevertheless felt disenchanted and dispossessed by the repressive regimes under which they lived. Khaled's story, as a multilingual Libyan-American with a dual identity and global popularity, demonstrates that the Arab

Spring has become a multifaceted, globalized movement transcending the MENA region.[101]

Similarly, a young Tunisian rapper—known as El General, whose real name is Hamada Ben Amor—posted a song on his Facebook page and YouTube channel. The song was entitled "Raies le Bled" meaning the president of the country. It expressed through music a youth culture of defiance and outrage against prevailing socioeconomic ills, including unemployment, poverty, and social injustice in Tunisia, placing the blame squarely on the Tunisian government. El General's video was picked up by Al Jazeera, after which it went viral. The lyrics of this song quickly and forcefully resonated with many young people who lived under the repressive regime of Ben Ali for so long:

> Mr. President, today I speak to you,
> In the name of all who are suffering.
> People dying of hunger,
> They want to work to survive.
> Go down to the street and look around you,
> People are treated like animals.
> Look at the cops,
> Their batons beat everyone with impunity
> Because there's no one to say no,
> Not even the law or the constitution.[102]

Robin Wright summarizes it best: "The song had a transformative influence. It set the stage for the 'Jasmine Revolution' that broke out a month later. It did what many Tunisians dared not do—speak out."[103] Western media labeled such peaceful democratic uprisings throughout the region as the Jasmine Revolution in keeping with the geopolitical nomenclature of "color revolutions" that have transpired in Georgia and Ukraine in the previous years. What singled out the uprisings in Tunisia, however, was that Bouazizi's self-immolation, together with the powerful lyrics of a young rapper, became two young men who, in Wright's words, "had transformed political activism in Tunisia—and in turn the entire Arab world."[104]

In Yemen, Hagage "AJ" Masaed, known as the godfather of Yemeni hip-hop, places a high premium on hip-hop music, arguing that it can be "a tool to effect social change." One of the battles he has taken on is education and trying to keep young Yemenis in school. "Youth listen to me. I'm putting out positive messages in hip-hop form. They like what I'm doing and I'm flipping it in Arabic and in English," said Masaed. "The schools, the tools / You have to believe / If we live, learn, love / Defeat enemies," are a few of the lines from his song "Biladee" (in English, "My Country"), which advocates for education to combat terrorism. It continues, "too many followers we need more leaders to lead ... so no terrorists please."[105]

Palestinian hip-hop rappers, such as Tamer Nafar, have expressed their rage with a microphone—not a weapon—and have repeatedly condemned extremism and violence by both Israelis and Palestinians, even as their songs have explained the context of civil disobedience and suicide bombings in 1987 and 2000 Intifada uprisings, respectively. For a new generation of Palestinians, hip-hop has filled a social and communications void, capturing the popular sentiment that has largely turned against violence and jihadists.[106]

Moral Emotions, Solidarity, and Identity

Although technology and social media tell us how and when the Arab Spring happened, they tell us little or nothing about why, for example, Egyptians revolted in 2011. Poverty, unemployment, political repression, and a booming, educated youth population created a combustive scenario, but what sparked the revolts was emotional and moral identification with Bouazizi's self-immolation in protest against the humiliation and suppression to which he was subjected. This act of self-homicide or self-sacrifice stirred the emotions of a younger generation that seeks freedom. Throughout the Arab world, the demonstrative value of this form of resistance translated into a potent and emotional showing of grassroots democracy.

The unprecedented global interconnectedness has extended the scope of emotional identification at the level of humanity and increased the sense of moral responsibility for people at risk in other societies.[107] Of particular relevance to the study of human rights and world politics is the examination of the psychological and emotional dimensions of social conduct and moral interaction. The critical investigations of global norms have underscored the importance not only of material interests but also of moral ideas and emotions such as fear, pity, sympathy, empathy, cruelty, and compassion.

This focus on collective moral emotions has provided an important counterweight to traditional views that norms exercise little influence on world politics.[108] Changing attitudes to violence, suffering, and solidarity have created greater sensitivity toward such emotions as embarrassment, guilt, shame, and disgust. "At the heart of this approach," Andrew Linklater writes, "is the suggestion that the most basic forms of solidarity between strangers are grounded in the shared sense of vulnerability to mental and physical suffering and in the related capacity to enlarge the scope of ethical concern to include the members of all other social groups."[109]

Some scholars have argued that ethical principles can be grounded in the moral emotions such as sympathy, compassion, and solidarity, challenging Kantian understandings of the relationship between reason and morality as being excessive rationalism.[110] The capacities for empathizing and sympathizing with suffering others are in fact the foundations on which all moral emotions and codes rest.[111] Other analyses of global norms have begun to focus on the role of the personal and emotional—both individually and as a community—as central in interpretation of research and thinking, especially as these relate to risk, fear, awe, exposure, and celebration.[112] Suspicious of rationalistic approaches to politics, Edmund Burke notes that "reason alone cannot help us understand the political world because humans are not simply rational creatures. Human nature is a mix of the social and the individualistic, the emotional and the rational."[113]

Bouazizi's act of self-destructive defiance symbolized the resistance by ordinary people. This act evolved from a popular and peaceful uprising in Tunisia to a complicated series of popular revolts, military interventions, civil strife, geopolitical realignments, and global dissent.[114] The solidarity that bonded Arabs across the large swath of Arab lands—manifested in the belief that the fear barrier, or the so-called wall of fear, has been shattered—posed a formidable challenge to political regimes in the region. The emerging identities shaped by these new media and bloggers became increasingly synonymous with protest and protester.[115] But what really prompted change in the region was when Egyptians began to empathize with the Tunisian youth's pain and difficulties. Egyptian online activists viewed developments of early 2011 in Tunisia as immensely positive as the Tunisian army had refused to point their weapons at their people.

Egyptian online activists began to post opinions and publish photographs and images that depicted a sympathetic and emotional interaction between the Tunisian people and the Tunisian army. One posting in Egypt struck at the heart of this emotional bond:

> The Tunisian army set an example of patriotism.... An army where officers and soldiers learn to defend their homeland and their countrymen cannot possibly fire at their own people and kill them.... During the funeral procession of one Tunisian martyr killed by the police's bullets, one of the army officers stood in respect for the martyr.[116]

Some activists skillfully appealed to and exploited the emotional aspects of zealous soccer fans known as "ultras," inviting them to unite for a much greater cause:

> To the ultras of Ahly, Zamalek, Ismaili, and Itihad soccer teams.... If you exert the same effort you do for any soccer match on the 25th of January, you will help Egypt change.... Let us all be ultras of Egypt.... Let us all take action and take to the streets.... Who among us is an ultras member and prepared to cheer for Egypt?[117]

A similar attempt to appeal to the Egyptians' emotions proved to be successful:

> To everyone who cried in tears on the day Egypt lost at the World Cup (and I was one of them), we must now cry in tears that Tunisia gained the Cup of Liberty.... Liberty is much more important than a soccer match.... Dignity and humane treatment are much more important than the World Cup.... We must reclaim our rights and this is why we must all take action on Jan 25.[118]

The rise of a new, popular pan-Arabism, premised on the notion of unity and solidarity, directed against corrupt and inept regimes was perhaps the greatest revelation of the uprisings. Not since the 1950s has a unifying slogan ("The People Want to Overthrow the Regime") so powerfully captured the imagination of people in the MENA region. This widespread pan-Arab identification has given masses of ordinary people a newfound feeling that they themselves could take control of their destiny.[119] One observer has characterized this younger generation as having a deep sense of ownership over the change they have generated, a feeling of connectivity with the rest of the world, and a striking sense of global citizenship. This perspective concludes that "the language they use and the mechanisms of revolution they employ are better understood as global phenomena rather than as characteristics unique to the Arab world."[120]

That said, it is important to acknowledge the limits to emotional appeal. The video campaign *Kony 2012* produced by the California-based NGO, Invisible Children, has grabbed the attention of many people by spreading a central message: arrest African warlord Joseph Kony for atrocities perpetrated in northern Uganda. While it has successfully raised awareness about this human tragedy, this video has left out the history of conflict in that part of Africa. What we need, one expert notes, is committed humanitarian NGOs and aid workers who have the knowledge of structural causes of poverty, conflict, and disease around the world. It is important to "publicize who (elites, corporations, financial institutions, etc.) controls resources, land, and water in order to expose targets for change. Helping people understand complex, interconnected causes is the key to engaging them in an effective, sustainable campaign."[121] Aid workers must run from anything advertised as a silver bullet—such as the *Kony 2012* campaign, micro-credit, and mosquito nets—for solving conflict, poverty, or disease in Africa or anywhere.[122]

In sum, the expression of youthful Arab identity as nonextremist has been facilitated by a merger of youth identity and social media identity, prompting a so-called counter-jihadist identity. This emerging identity has been further boosted by young Arab voices that have attributed the enlargement of democracy and civil society to nonviolent democratic change and civil disobedience. Together with evolving Arab popular culture in relation to employment, migration, and political protests, new identities have developed the space necessary for creative resistance to tyranny while defying traditional notions of apathy, indifference, and passivity. The empowerment of these young voices in the context of the Arab Spring could potentially pave the way for the formation of open and democratic societies in the region. Although growing evidence indicates that economic problems and rising demands for democracy and human rights have created new norms for behavior in the Arab world by outmoding the region's authoritarian regimes, we should not be so quick to dismiss youthful identity as a useful perspective, especially given the way young people's support for new forms of peaceful resistance has made the ruling regimes' programs and strategies obsolete through defining new norms for acceptable government behavior.

Conclusion

Throughout the MENA region, the rising political consciousness, in part a reaction to a sense of social disempowerment and fueled by pressing socioeconomic problems, has in recent years built a consensus around a narrative that demands a new social contract, one that is aimed at achieving human dignity, civil rights, and social justice through a method of nonviolent civil disobedience. The concept of "the people" has become a new marker of identity for millions of the people in the region, providing an impetus for participatory politics and moving toward the achievement of a humane standard of living. This call was initially rejuvenated by Iran's Green Movement, which met with resistance from the regime's brutal clampdown on its citizens. The Islamic Republic's crackdown was repeatedly exposed in the glare of the global media as well as social networking sites.

In both Tunisia and Egypt, the authoritarian populist social contract had been torn apart after many decades of mismanagement and corruption, fueled largely by neoliberal economic programs in the 1980s and 1990s that greatly undermined the legacy of supporting workers and peasants. The resulting unemployment and youth bulge marked the emergence of a new identity encapsulated in the political slogan, *Ash-sha'b yurīd isqāt an-niẓām* ("The people want the fall of the regime"). The concept of "the people" demanding the removal of the regime deeply resonated among the educated and urbanized younger generation that reclaimed its political and rightful space long neglected by Mubarak's regime.

The youth's call for a peaceful democratic change was helped and in many ways facilitated by satellite TV, the Internet and social networking sites, and hip-hop culture—notably rap music and art—that laid the groundwork for participation in contentious politics. In both the Green Movement and the Arab uprisings, women came out in massive and unprecedented numbers as demonstrators and protesters. Women in Egypt, Tunisia, Libya, Syria, and Yemen have viewed these protests as renewal of a sense of equality denied them by either conservative forces in society or corrupt and repressive regimes. The moral identification—manifested in solidarity against suffering and invoked by suppression and humiliation—has stirred the emotions of a generation of young Arabs that aspires for freedom and grassroots democracy, seeks to shape its future, and struggles to regain personal agency.

Chapter 5
US-IRAN RELATIONS

From the Green Movement
to the Arab Spring

To many Middle Eastern specialists, the link between Iran's Green Movement and the Arab Spring is palpably apparent. They argue that some of the first use of cell phones and other new media—especially Twitter—in the Middle East was connected with the 2009 Green Movement. Facilitated by a constant digital interaction via instant messaging and social network services such as Twitter, Facebook, and YouTube, the Green Movement drew immediate attention to human rights violations and political violence in Iran. If nothing else, these protests clearly manifested as the normative diffusion of human rights language into the everyday politics of Iran. Despite the regime's attempts to override the resonance of human rights norms by invoking considerations of security, sovereignty, and cultural exceptionalism, public demands for individual freedoms and rights have been on the upswing.[1]

This chapter attempts to put into perspective the purported link between Iran's Green Movement and the Arab Spring. To better understand the broader implications of such a link for US-Iran relations, we begin by exploring the genealogy and evolution of competition—in both ideological and geopolitical terms—between the two countries. We will then shift our focus to US-Iran relations, arguing that Obama's reelection is likely to pave the way for bilateral talks between the two. It is worth noting that since the 2011 Arab uprisings, the US-Iran rivalry over ideological, normative, and policy considerations has assumed a new twist given the resurgence of Islamic groups via the ballot box. Iran has also been a trendsetter for the MENA region as its reformist Green Movement is seen as a potent prelude to the unfolding Arab Spring. How the Arab Spring will affect US-Iran relations in the coming years merits full discussion. So does the question of the US-Iran rivalry's broader implications for the MENA region.

A Historical Overview

Iran's foreign policy since 1979 has been motivated by four goals: independence, territorial integrity, noninterference, and regional leadership. By contrast, US foreign policy toward the MENA has emphasized different and sometimes conflicting goals, supporting authoritarian but pro-West regimes on one hand, and promoting democracy—alongside secular modernization and gender equality—on the other. The latter has frequently clashed directly with the Islamic Republic's preoccupation with Islamic law as the source of human dignity and gender identity.

By emphasizing pragmatism, economic nationalism, and an Asian identity, Iran has identified globalization with Western sources and agents, all the while underscoring the importance of a regional identity that rejects outside intervention and the imposition of external human rights standards. While the US has led globalization in all its forms (socioeconomic, social, ethical, and cultural), Iranian leaders have placed their geopolitical considerations and Islamic identity over and above the strict adherence to democratization and human rights.

The revelations of prisoner abuse, including indefinite detention without trial, after 9/11 at Abu Ghraib, Guantánamo Bay, and Bagram Air Force Base have strengthened the hands of Islamic groups not only in Iran but throughout the MENA region. Many experts have pointed to the undeniable fact that high-ranking US officials knowingly authorized the gross abuse of numerous prisoners, often as part of enforced disappearances or secret detention, despite legal bans. "While some lower-level persons exceeded instructions," David P. Forsythe writes, "the push for widespread abusive interrogation was instigated, authorized, and (badly) managed from the very top."[2]

This reality, when combined with the fact that US officials as well as Western human rights scholars and activists have often viewed Islamism as a countervailing force to the rise of human rights movements and democratic institutions, has severely undermined US attempts to instill democracy in the region.

The First Missionaries

US-Iran relations can be traced back to the 1830s when Americans traveled to Iran as the first missionaries.[3] During the Naseredin Shah period, direct contact with Americans helped to create a navy force for Persia in the Bushehr port. Later in the 1870s, a group of American physicians helped establish Urmia University's College of Medicine. By the early twentieth century, relations between the two countries became a major force for Iranians to modernize their economy and liberate it from British and Russian influences.

During the Persian Constitutional Revolution (1905–1911), Morgan Shuster was appointed treasury general of Persia to counter Russian and British interests in Iran. Under pressure by both Russia and Great Britain, Shuster resigned. The British proved instrumental in carrying out the 1921 coup that brought Reza Shah Pahlavi to power. World War II and the emergence of the United States as the dominant player on the global scene marginalized the British role in Iran. The abdication of Reza Shah and his son's ascension to power in the early 1940s heralded a new era in US-Iran relations, one that was marked by fast-paced modernization.

Oil Nationalization and the Coup

During the early 1950s, Iran's democratically elected nationalist prime minister, Mohammad Mossadeq, rose to an unprecedented popularity, forcing the Reza Shah Pahlavi into exile. Mossadeq's rise to power and parliament's approval of nationalizing the Anglo-Iranian Oil Company (AIOC) thrilled Iranians but outraged British leaders.[4]

Prime Minister Mossadeq was removed from power in 1953 by a CIA/MI6-engineered coup (known as Operation Ajax), which was conducted mainly from the US Embassy in Tehran. US officials helped organize street demonstrations and protests to overthrow Mossadeq and return the Shah from his brief exile. The 1953 coup ended Iran's fledgling attempts at democracy, giving rise to a modernizing, royal dictatorship that, a quarter of a century later, set off an anti-American revolution that brought militant Islamic groups to power. The Shah eliminated all constitutional obstacles to his absolute power. He repressed opposition newspapers, political parties, trade unions, and civil groups.[5]

The real tragedy of American-Iranian relations stemmed from the fact that United States policymakers depended solely upon the Shah's view of the domestic situation that overlooked blatant signs of popular disenchantment and unrest, which ultimately led to the Islamic Revolution. Many US foreign policymakers were caught by surprise at the Khomeini revolution and by the extent of hatred toward the United States. In the long run, US intervention in Iran paved the way for the eventual rupture of US-Iranian relations in the 1979 Islamic Revolution.[6]

US-Iranian relations were premised largely on maintaining stability in the Persian Gulf. The Shah received unconditional US support as a pillar of US foreign policy in the region. President Richard Nixon developed a strategy of cooperation with dictators such as the Shah to be the guarantor of US interests in the Persian Gulf region. Despite the pressure on the Shah to open up the country's political space, Jimmy Carter's presidency viewed the Shah as an ally and thus a source of stability that had to be backed up by US foreign policy.

The Shah's aggressive modernization and Westernization projects alienated cultural and religious elites in a country where religious values were deeply influential. Moreover, modernization under the Shah was intimately linked to economic growth and industrialization. Oil-induced growth boosted Iran's gross national product (GNP) per capita from $108 in 1957 to $1,660 in 1978.[7] The pace of economic growth reached its most dramatic peak in Iran's history between 1970 and 1978, when the annual average GNP was 13.3 percent—by far the world's highest figure.[8] Meanwhile, the agricultural sector faced many setbacks as a result of the Shah's at-any-cost industrialization program. The Shah's land reform programs, under pressure from the Kennedy administration, altered the class structure in Iran's countryside, creating a new rural bourgeoisie, a new rural propertied class, a new proletariat, and a new landless class that relied on its labor for survival.

The Iranian Revolution

From 1960 to 1970, the GDP contribution from the agricultural sector dropped from 29 percent to 9 percent, the largest decline among Middle Eastern countries during that period. High economic growth rates during the 1960s and the 1970s resulted in a narrow distribution of income. The Shah's continued reliance on oil revenues made such growth rates feasible.

At the same time, social mobilization in Iran contributed to higher rates of education, literacy, communication development, and urbanization. The newly mobilized, politically relevant segments of the population had a high propensity for political participation. These social strata were composed of elements of the middle class, the urban working class, and the jobless labor forces in cities. The latter group proved to be highly politicized during the 1979 Iranian Revolution, even as the revolution was not rural overall.

The state reduced religious authorities' spheres of influence, culminating in a crisis of legitimacy that weakened the Shah's regime in the late 1970s. The regime deprived the clerics of their economic and ideological status as well as their control over two areas in which their social influence had been dominant—law and education. The only opposition group allowed to operate was a secular group, the Committee for Defense of Freedom and Human Rights. Established in Tehran in 1977, this committee was the first independent human rights organization in Iran's history. Its membership included Shahpur Bakhtiar and Mahdi Bazargan. The latter became the Islamic Republic of Iran's first prime minister.

The Shah's distraction from civilian politics and his close ties to the army and the United States alienated him from certain segments of the Iranian population. His notorious security apparatus (known as SAVAK), in the absence of any viable secular opposition, caused deep resentment against the regime among the vast majority of Iranians. This fact, along with the failure of urban guerrillas to develop the mass base necessary to promote an effective guerrilla war, gave the clergy a unique opportunity to direct the revolution. By the late 1970s, the Shah's violent attempts to curb revolutionary fervor had proved ineffective. The conservative forces, spearheaded by Ayatollah Rouhollah Khomeini, overwhelmed pro-Shah forces and toppled the monarchy.

The Khomeini Era (1979–1989)

Intent on restoring power to the common person and on reinstating the social solidarity of early Islamic communities to urban life, neo-Islamic populism under the Khomeini regime aimed to terminate foreign economic and cultural domination. In the early years of the revolution, the government of Mahdi Bazargan struggled to define its foreign policy. When the Bazargan government tried to approach the US delegation in Algeria, it was heavily criticized at home by the clergy. The November 4, 1979, hostage crisis, in which revolutionary students stormed the US embassy in Tehran and took its fifty-four diplomats and staff hostage for fourteen months, effectively disrupted any diplomatic relations that existed between the two countries.

The ensuing Iran-Iraq war (1980–1988) further intensified US-Iran relations. Many Iranian experts held the view that the Iraqi invasion of Iran was largely instigated by the United States. In 1986, the Reagan administration "reflagged" Kuwaiti and other tankers that shipped oil from the Middle East to the West. This meant that the tankers would be defended by the US Navy. As the war was drawing to a close in 1988, the USS *Vincennes* mistakenly shot down an Iranian airliner, killing 290 passengers.

In a secret deal in 1987, the Reagan administration supplied Iran with arms—including missiles—and funding to win the release of American hostages in Lebanon and to support the Contras fighting a civil war in Nicaragua, support the US Congress had banned. When this plot, which became known as the Iran-Contra Affair, went public, President Ronald Reagan rationalized it in the name of building support for the moderates within the Iranian regime.[9]

The challenge of revolutionary Iran in the Persian Gulf preoccupied US foreign policy. Several factors contributed to the establishment of the Gulf Cooperation Council (GCC) in the early 1980s: the Iranian Revolution, the Soviet invasion of Afghanistan, superpower competition, and the threat of spillover violence from the Iran-Iraq war.[10]

The publication of Salman Rushdie's *The Satanic Verses* in 1989 gave Khomeini the necessary ammunition to criticize the West as well as to unify the nation during a period strained by the losses in the war with Iraq. Khomeini issued a *fatwa* against Rushdie, placing a bounty on his head. The pragmatists were unprepared for dealing with the furor that erupted in the Muslim community more generally and in Iran more particularly in response to the publication of *The Satanic Verses*.[11]

During the 1990s, however, Iranian officials frequently said that their government had no plans to track down Rushdie and carry out the execution. On September 24, 1998, Iran's foreign minister, Kamal Kharrazi, announced the lifting of the death decree against Rushdie. Speaking to a press conference at the United Nations, Kharrazi stated, "The government of the Islamic Republic of Iran has no intention, nor is it going to take any action whatsoever to threaten the life of the author of *The Satanic Verses* or anybody associated with his work, nor will it encourage or assist anybody to do so."[12]

Although the *fatwa* remains in force and may not change for some time to come, it has no official backing. In his visit to the United Nations in late September 1998, Mohammad Khatami, Iran's then-president, distanced himself from the *fatwa* by declaring the case against Rushdie "completely finished." Internationally, Khatami's decision was seen by many as part of his emphasis on civilized dialogue to bring Iran into the international fold. Internally, however, his position was not shared by Iranian conservatives, revealing the jockeying for power among different factions. Though many hard-liners continued to insist that the death sentence against Rushdie be carried out, President Khatami, who sought improved ties with the West, appeared determined to lay the *fatwa* to rest.

By the mid-1980s, the United States had imposed—although not as an official policy—a trade embargo on the Islamic Republic. Since the mid-1990s, however, US sanctions became a principal instrument for pressuring Iran as part of a declared policy of "dual containment" intended to contain both Iran and Iraq. The results have been mixed. The immediate effect of US president Bill Clinton's May 8, 1995, executive order banning trade and investment with Iran was a sudden fall in the value of Iranian currency and, subsequently, a formal devaluation of the rial, Iran's main form of currency. The 1996 Iran-Libya Sanctions Act (ILSA) under President Clinton continued the sanction policy against Iran's petroleum exports. Such unilateral sanctions proved ineffectual, as they pulled Iran and Russia together and drove a wedge between the United States and its European and Asian allies. In 1995, when Conoco's deal was canceled under the US embargo, the French oil company Total subsumed Conoco's role in developing the Sirri oil fields in the Persian Gulf.

Islamic Pragmatism

In the first decade after the 1979 Islamic Revolution, ideological confrontation and plain hostility characterized the tumultuous relations between the United States and Iran. After the death of Ayatollah Khomeini in 1989, this adversarial relationship was replaced with a period of pragmatism about how best to work with the United States. With the ascendancy to power of President Khatami, enlightened pragmatism and regional détente came to define Iran's foreign policy orientation. Even then, not much progress toward rapprochement was made.

With the passing away of Khomeini from the Iranian political scene, interfactional disputes and the primacy of the economy over Islamic ideology came to characterize Ayatollah Rafsanjani's two-term presidency (1989–1997). Little was done to normalize ties between the two countries as Rafsanjani's most visible programs concerned Iran's economy. Rafsanjani's economic liberalization programs emphasized foreign trade reforms and exchange rate corrections.

In a decisive victory on May 23, 1997, Khatami became Iran's new reformist president. Formerly a minister of culture and Islamic guidance (1982–1992), Khatami attempted to ease restrictions on private life and open the country to more commercial and cultural influences from abroad. US-Iran relations entered a relaxed phase when US secretary of state Madeleine Albright apologized for the US past actions in Iran and opened the door for rapprochement.

Throughout Khatami's two-term presidency, conservative clerics trumped his efforts to appoint a more open and democratic government or to pursue much-needed reform. Constrained by such obstacles, Khatami could not have initiated a rapprochement with the United States. His goal of normalizing ties with the United States never went far. The Clinton administration approached the normalization talks with a two-track strategy. On the one hand, it continued to insist that if the 1996 ILSA was to be suspended, Iran must end its efforts to gain access to nuclear weapons, must terminate its support for terrorism, and must forgo denouncing the Middle East peace process. On the other hand, it repeatedly expressed its readiness to enter into state-to-state talks with Iran.

For its part, Iran responded with demands such as ending the US military presence in the Persian Gulf, releasing Iranian assets the United

States had frozen after the 1979 revolution, repaying Iran the money under dispute at the Hague, and stopping attempts to overthrow its Islamic regime. These issues, along with the lack of political determination and commitment on either side to overcome the barriers to normal diplomatic ties between the two countries, have hindered progress toward normalization.

The Aftermath of September 11

The tragic events of September 11, 2001, significantly altered US foreign policy toward the region. President George W. Bush included Iran with Iraq and North Korea in the "Axis of Evil," as defined in his 2002 State of the Union address, and bolstered his anti-Iranian rhetoric, especially regarding Iran's nuclear programs and its alleged ties with Hezbollah, Hamas, and Islamic Jihad. It seemed as though any possibility of rapprochement between the United States and Iran was fatally lost. The United States attempted to put Iran's nuclear program on the front burner only after international attention was already rallying to respond to North Korea's looming nuclear threat.

In retaliation to the September 11, 2001, terrorist attacks, the United States invaded Afghanistan and subsequently Iraq. The latter invasion has placed Iranian rulers in a far better position to bargain with the United States. The toppling of the Taliban regime with assistance from Iran and other regional countries, including Pakistan, raised the possibility of strengthening US-Iran relations. Likewise, the war in Iraq brought Iran and the United States closer in the sense that stability in Iraq serves both countries' interests, and that Iran can be a stabilizing factor in the postwar reconstruction, as was the case in Afghanistan.

Yet at the same time, Iranians genuinely fear encirclement by the United States.[13] Rapprochement between the two countries could prove to be a vexing problem for US policymakers. Winning trade and investment concessions from the West would almost certainly reinforce clerical rule. Absent genuine democratic reforms, these trade ties could further deepen the rift between Iranian state and society. US-Iran rapprochement is likely to bypass Iranian civil society, which is one of the most vibrant, explosive, and developed examples of its kind in the Middle East and Persian Gulf.

The Return of Islamic Populism

In the 2005 presidential elections, Mahmoud Ahmadinejad, Tehran's former mayor, became Iran's new president. Iran's Islamic hard-liners swept into power after thousands of pro-reform candidates were barred from running in recent disputed parliamentary elections. The Bush administration seemed less enthusiastic about pushing for regime change in Iran, even as Iranian conservative clerics consolidated political control at home. Some observers insisted that Iran would be the next target of a US preemptive strike.

When the conservatives won a new majority, the real question became, would Iran and the United States work toward improving their relations? Undoubtedly, the sham parliamentary elections further deepened Iranians' social discontent with clerical rule and dealt a severe blow to Iranian reformers. US foreign policy faced a classic dilemma: take into account geopolitical factors, or promote democratic values.

No Iranian politicians should delude themselves into believing that considerations of power politics and the regional balance of power will be subordinated to democratic values enunciated in US foreign policy. In fact, pragmatic conservatives signaled that they were ready to bargain with the United States when the time was opportune. Likewise, the Bush administration found it necessary—if not desirable—to deal with Iran's power-wielding elites who could deliver on the Non-Proliferation Treaty (NPT), stabilization of Iraq, reconstruction of Afghanistan, narcoterrorism, al-Qaeda, and Israeli-Palestinian tensions. With regard to Iran's nuclear program, experts argued that the central problem was not nuclear technology, but rather Iran's foreign policy as a revolutionary state, with nuclear ambitions that collide with the interests of its neighbors and the West.[14]

As the Bush administration's policy toward Iran grew deferential rather than supportive of human rights, the future boded ill for many reform-minded segments of Iranian society and, by implication, for the rest of the countries in the Middle East. The persistence of the Bush administration in asserting a pragmatic agenda alone was particularly damaging to the youth, women, and reform-minded journalists and activists—in essence, the human capital so essential to any democratic reform in Iran.

For the most part, Washington inconsistently navigated between strategic choices and human rights policy, employing double standards in its approach toward Iran, criticizing the Islamic Republic's human rights record while working on normalizing economic and diplomatic ties behind the scenes. This policy proved detrimental to reformist movements in Iran. No dramatic breakthroughs in US-Iran relations seemed likely unless US policymakers viewed the new regional security structure as imperative to preventing Iraq from descending into chaos and partition.

Several key questions persisted: Will the United States take a tougher stance toward Iran in sticking to its democratic rhetoric? Or will it pursue a pragmatic course guided solely by geopolitical exigencies? Each of these courses held profound ramifications for the future of democracy in Iran. Policymakers in both countries faced unprecedented challenges and tough choices, as millions of Iranians viewed with both hope and uncertainty the shape of things to come.

Iran's Nuclear Program

Iran's nuclear program was launched in 1957 when the United States and Iran signed a civil nuclear cooperation accord as part of the US Atoms for Peace Program.[15] In 1960, Iran established a 5 MW research center at Tehran University. In his visit to the United States in 1964, the Shah laid out Iran's ambitious plan for nuclear power. Tehran's Nuclear Research Center became operational in 1967, when the United States supplied limited enriched uranium to Iran for fuel in a research reactor. In the following year, Iran signed the Nuclear NPT, which it ratified in 1970.

In 1974, Iran signed several agreements to purchase two 1,200 MW pressurized water reactors from the German firm Kraftwerk Union to be installed at Bushehr and two 900 MW reactors from Framatome of France to be installed at Bandar-e Abbas. At the same time, the United States, under President Gerald Ford, pledged to assist Iran in operating a US-built reprocessing facility for extracting plutonium from nuclear reactor fuel, a process that entailed a complete nuclear fuel cycle. Under such conditions, Iran benefited from the competition between US and European nuclear energy companies—especially German and French firms—to assist it in launching its nuclear program.

After the 1979 Islamic Revolution, Iran and the International Atomic Energy Agency (IAEA) agreed to cooperate in the fields of nuclear reactor technology and fuel cycle technology. The IAEA, however, was forced to terminate the program under US pressure. It is worth noting that prior to the revolution, Iran had contracts with Germany, France, and the United States for a total of six nuclear power reactors and agreements to receive low-enriched uranium and nuclear training. After the revolution, Western countries canceled these nuclear agreements. The Bushehr reactors, which were not fully operative, were damaged by several Iraqi air strikes during the 1980s war with Iraq. With the end of the war with Iraq, Iran turned to Russia to complete the Bushehr projects. In 1995, Iran and Russia signed a contract to that end. Similarly, the US sanctions on Iran failed to prevent China from providing Tehran with a conversion plan and gas needed to test the uranium enrichment process.

By 2000, Iranian officials revealed the existence of two nuclear sites under construction in Natanz and Arak. Under the IAEA rules, Iran had no obligation to report the existence of these sites while they were still under construction. Iran's nuclear facilities are located in Anarak, Arak, Ardekan, Bushehr, Chalus, Darkhovin, Esfahan, Karaj/Karai/Hashtgerd, Kolahdouz, Lashkar Abad, Lavizan, Meysami, Natanz, Parchin, Sagend, Qatran, Tabas, and Tehran.

The IAEA reported in late 2003 that it had found no evidence that Iran had engaged in the act of diversion of fissile material to military use. The IAEA deferred a final decision on this situation pending further European diplomatic negotiations with Iran. With Iranians asserting their right to enrich uranium and Europeans convinced that Iran should forgo this process, diplomatic contacts produced no mutually agreed results. With the failure of the EU-3 (Great Britain, Germany, and France) diplomatic initiatives, the United Nations Security Council (UNSC) demanded Iran suspend its enrichment and reprocessing related activities.

Having secured no concessions from Iran, the UNSC threatened to put further sanctions on Iran. Two rounds of UNSC sanctions were subsequently imposed on Iran during 2006–2007, with increasing unwillingness on the part of China, Russia, and the EU to push for more intrusive sanctions. Russia's reluctance to impose further sanctions on Iran served to underline Moscow's independence from the United States. Meanwhile, the IAEA's head, Mohamed ElBaradei, stated on numerous occasions that he had seen "no evidence" that Iran was developing nuclear weapons.

The prospects for a military confrontation with Iran and placing further sanctions on the country receded with the release of the National Intelligence Estimate (NIE) report in the United States in December

2007. The report, which was composed by sixteen US intelligence agencies, emphatically concluded that Iran had ceased the military component of its nuclear program since 2003. This revelation exposed the extent to which the Iranian threat had been exaggerated. It has since become evident that the US diplomatic attempts to isolate Iran have also failed. The EU, Russia, and China resumed trade and commercial ties with Iran. Russia, for example, continued its efforts to help construct the Bushehr nuclear facility.

"Regime Change" or Sanctions

The talk of "regime change" via the military option was seen as counterproductive in Tehran, even as a genuine political settlement was not in sight. In the first place, the threat of regime change was not practical given the country's vast terrain and Iranians' nationalistic sentiments. An Osiraq-style attack, which was an air strike on an Iraqi nuclear reactor carried out by the Israeli Air Force in 1981, stood little chance of success in a huge country such as Iran, which had dispersed its nuclear power plants across the country. If used, this option would have undermined any confidence-building measure in the process of securing an eventual compromise. The fact remained that national policy regarding the nuclear program rested with Iran's Supreme Leader, Ali Hoseyni Khamenei, whose decisions reflected a view shared by many different players—military and otherwise. Ironically, the US presence in the region had enhanced Iran's sense of urgency for acquiring some form of strategic deterrence.

Secondly, Iran became the target of US mainstream media that refused to provide compelling reasons as to why Iran posed a real menace. The Bush administration supported a media propaganda campaign aimed at vilifying Iran under the assumption that Iran was trying to become a nuclear power. The option of imposing economic sanctions on Iran was also risky in part because not everyone was willing to participate in enforcing them and partly because they would have deprived international markets of no less than 3 million barrels of oil per day.

Moreover, sanctions, some experts rightly observed, would only hold back in the short run a nuclear assembly line, should Iran's clerical rulers decide to proceed. Iranian officials had raised the question all along concerning why other nuclear equipped countries are not subject to such sanction threats. They have said that they would withdraw from the NPT if faced with military and economic threats. Withdrawal from the NPT was, however, unlikely and it would prove to be too costly for a country where industrial infrastructure was (and continues to be) heavily dependent on production machinery and industrial components imported from EU countries.

The Nuclear Dispute

Looking back at the nuclear dispute, several questions appear to have shaped the political debate over Iran's nuclear program: Were Iran's nuclear ambitions economic/energy related, or were they strategic and security related? What were the possibilities, and what were the likelihoods? With conservative forces in control of the Iranian parliament (Majlis) and presidency, Iran's leaders seemed to have equated promoting their nuclear program with the country's national security. Some experts have portrayed Iran's nuclear program as part of its struggle to evade Western dominance, a struggle it has been waging since the end of the nineteenth century.[16] After a long period of negotiation with the EU-3, Iran chose to restart enriching uranium in 2007. For all practical purposes and intents, the EU-3 negotiations were forestalled.[17]

The Iranian government argued that it had suspended its activities on a voluntary basis and that it had a legal right to develop its nuclear program for peaceful purposes according to Article 4 of the Nuclear NPT. This article stipulates that member states pledge not to seek a weapons capability and that they are entitled to acquire the means of generating nuclear power for civilian purposes. It should be noted, however, that the NPT contains ambiguous language. It, for example, does not guarantee signatories the "right" to enrich uranium. It only supports "the benefit of nuclear technology" for peaceful purposes.

In addition to justifying Iran's nuclear program on legal grounds, Iranian officials pointed to pure and simple economics, arguing that while Iran's GDP was likely to grow by 6 percent, its young population's demand for power consumption was projected to grow at 7 percent annually. Iran's capacity, experts note, must nearly triple over the next fifteen years to meet projected demand. At the same time, Iran's daily consumption of 1.5 million barrels of oil per day means the country loses $75 million per day. More to the point, Iran had argued that with diminishing water resources, the use of hydroelectric technology as means to generate power had become less viable. Nuclear energy, Iranian officials have insisted—and continue to emphasize today—seems to be the most economically viable method of energy production, hence Iran's plan to generate 7,000 MW of nuclear power by 2020 through the construction of twenty nuclear power plants.[18]

In the latest rounds of negotiations (in April, May, and June 2012 in Istanbul, Baghdad, and Moscow) under the P5+1 process—also known as E3+3 talks with Iran—(involving Great Britain, France, China, Russia, the United States, and Germany), Iranian officials said that the issue of the fuel cycle was not an absolute position but that it was open to negotiation. Iranians were bargaining to get a better deal and in the end they would turn out to be flexible and accommodating. Given the history of the standoff, it is unlikely that Iran will accept a deal that ends its uranium enrichment and brings no relief from the painful sanctions imposed on Iran. While unequivocally recognizing Iran's right to enrich uranium for peaceful purposes, Western countries have insisted they are not inclined to trade away their key leverage at this stage. Whether Iran will eventually capitulate under the weight of sanctions, one expert notes, the US president and his closest advisers might have concluded that "a negotiated solution tends to be more durable than a solution imposed on a prostrate foe."[19]

It is worth noting that regional and global political considerations had compelled the Europeans to resolve this matter peacefully and avoid further diplomatic tension with the United States over Iran, and possibly another US or Israeli military incursion in the region. Economic difficulties, experts remind us, will lead to a further dissolution of European resolve to confront Iran's nuclear program.[20] Though opposing the unilateral sanctions strategy adopted by the United States and the EU, both Russia and China have supported softening sanctions in response to concrete Iranian measures to reassure the international community.[21]

The best, most realistic prognosis for a negotiated compromise is that these talks deliver a partial enrichment freeze in return for partial sanctions relief. Given the complexity of US domestic politics and the 2012 presidential election cycle, a calibrated European initiative to ease or delay its own sanctions was crucial to making real progress, or simply to fostering more talks.[22] A compromise can be reached, according to some Iranian experts, whereby Iran can maintain a right to enrich uranium up to 5 percent in its own facilities, and at the same time it issues an official statement in which Tehran will declare its readiness to halt 20 percent uranium enrichment.[23] Ultimately, however, as Western analysts admit, the true nature of Iran's nuclear program is neither legal nor technical, but rather political.[24]

The Green Movement

The 2009 elections, Iran's tenth presidential election, placed incumbent Mahmoud Ahmadinejad against political rival Mir Hossein Mousavi, who had served as Iran's prime minister from 1981 to 1989, under the Supreme Leader Khomeini. Mousavi reemerged into the political limelight in 2005 as a reformist, and he became the leader of the Green Movement. Mousavi chose green, the color of Islam, as his campaign color, because he claims to be one of the descendants of the prophet. A high voter turnout led to the extension of voting time. Shortly after midnight on June 13, 2009, the official Islamic Republic News Agency announced that Ahmadinejad had won the election with 69 percent of the votes. The ensuing days and weeks were filled with massive protests throughout Iran. Mousavi claimed large-scale voting fraud, releasing a statement to the effect that the people's movement "would not surrender to this charade." An appeal was submitted to the Council of Guardians, the appointed twelve-member council that possesses enormous influence in the Islamic Republic of Iran, to recount the votes. The council recounted the votes, amid protests from the opposition that many million ballots were missing, and subsequently announced that Ahmadinejad had won the election.

This result further galvanized the opposition that by now included Islamic reformists (and former political authorities of the Islamic Republic of Iran), human rights activists and lawyers, university professors, a wide array of NGOs, and large numbers of young people with secular ideas. In spite of the Islamic Republic's intense efforts to portray the movement as an *enqalob-e makhmalee* ("Velvet Revolution") financed and directed from the outside (i.e., the West), evidence suggests that the Iranian people were well aware of the movement's homegrown origin. The movement was not formulated along strict ideological lines: it was neither a class struggle against a populist government nor a secularist uprising against religious rule. Instead, it represented a post-Islamist democracy movement to reclaim human rights and dignity. The protesters asked not only,

"Where is my vote?" but also asked to live a dignified life free from fear, moral and political surveillance, corruption, and arbitrary rule. Essentially indigenous and nonviolent, this movement aimed at restoring the civil liberties promised but not delivered by the 1979 Islamic Revolution. Many Iranians were no longer resigned to the undemocratic aspects of the Islamic Republic's political system, which, over the previous thirty years, had declined rather than progressed.[25]

The Green Movement was fully aware of the means of political suppression at the disposal of the Iranian government, so its leaders and followers opted for a method of nonviolent civil disobedience. If nothing else, some scholars note, this was the closest Iran has come to creating a civil rights movement since the 1979 Iranian Revolution. Similar to the civil rights movement in US history, Iranians sought to address larger economic inequalities through social demands. Many experts are of the opinion that the Islamic Republic had prepared the way for its own demise by educating its people. Iran had become a middle-class society imbued with rising expectations and demands for political freedoms. A quick glance at the demographics behind the resurgence of Iran's Green Movement in 2009 explains why educated young women were at the forefront of this reformist movement. In the 1970s, toward the end of the Pahlavi monarchy, nearly 5 percent of college-age youth went to college. By 2009, the figure had reached 31 percent. Female students outnumbered male students in secondary schools (1996), primary schools (1999), and higher education (2001).[26]

The Green Movement was eventually suppressed by a combination of coercive means at the regime's disposal. The leaders were placed under house arrest. Protesters were attacked and killed in the streets, or imprisoned and tried on charges of treason against the regime. Media freedoms were severely restricted for international as well as Iranian journalists. The regime painted the protesters as a minority of pro-Western urban elites, out of touch with the majority of Iran's population in the provinces. The regime also staged pro-Ahmadinejad rallies that, unlike protest rallies, were allowed to be televised.

Iran and the Arab Spring

As many in the Arab world view the turmoil in the MENA region with both hope and apprehension, some ruling elites in the region are wary of the domino effects of these developments. They have begun to use counterrevolutionary tactics and strategies. Others, such as Iranian officials and state-run media, portray the antigovernment uprisings in Tunisia, Egypt, and Libya as a rejection of the secular and corrupt pro-West regimes in the region. For the Islamic Republic of Iran, any changes emerging from these unrests would be preferable to the status quo. There are two bases for this view: (1) any future democratically elected government in North Africa is likely to challenge the conventional US foreign policy in the region on the premise that democratic governments tend to be nationalist in their political orientations; and (2) although the emerging regimes are unlikely to follow Iran's theocratic model and governance, they may look for ways to engage Iran, if for no other reason than to bolster their bargaining position vis-à-vis the international community while at the same time gaining access to Iran's lucrative energy and trade contracts.

With the withdrawal of Western companies from Iran's market due to the 2010 US sanctions, the first companies that have sought to bypass sanctions for their own interests were oil firms and producers of oil and gas equipment from Eastern Europe, mostly from Hungary, Belarus, and Romania.[27] Other countries, known as "black knights" because they could not compete with the Europeans previously, have strived to increase their presence in Iran. These include, but are not limited to, Turkey, Venezuela, Ecuador, and Brazil.[28] Turkish minister for foreign trade Zafer Caglayan, for example, has stated that, by 2015, Iran and Turkey will have increased their trade volume by $30 billion. He has stressed the fact that the US sanctions against Iran would not present an obstacle to that goal.[29] Likewise, some Latin American countries have pursued a similar strategy in recent years, taking up the Islamic Republic's lucrative contracts in various sectors including energy, armaments, security, and even media.[30]

There is no doubt that Islamic groups or parties will form part of the new governments in the region, but whether or where they will gain dominance remains to be seen. Experts hold that Iran is likely to benefit from a change in the status quo, but only in the predominantly Shia countries, such as Bahrain in the Persian Gulf region and Lebanon in the Levant (the eastern Mediterranean). In general, however, they assert that "revolutions, once successful, tend to be nationalist rather than internationalist."[31] Two core questions are raised in this context: How will the Iranian regime gauge the consequences of the uprisings in the

MENA region? And what are the implications of the Arab Spring for US-Iran relations?

The debate regarding the impact of Iran's Green Movement on the Arab Spring continues. The Green Movement that followed the disputed presidential elections in June 2009 may have arguably been a potent prelude to the unfolding Arab Spring throughout the MENA region. To the extent that the resistance sparked among Iranian youth by the Green Movement was informed and motivated by modern, concrete human rights demands, the similarity between the two and the influence of Iran's Green Movement over the Arab Spring cannot be overlooked. In both cases, the human agency underlined the protest movements.[32] The Arab Spring may have in turn energized the Green Movement but the house arrest of Mousavi, coupled with an effective strategy of targeted arrests of activists, has meant that the organizational capacity of the movement has markedly declined.

Both opposition leaders and the Iranian government have praised the uprisings in Egypt, albeit for different reasons. The leadership of Iran's Green Movement—working under virtual house arrest in Tehran and dismissed by government officials as powerless "leaders of sedition"— have welcomed the Egyptian cause, even calling for demonstrations on February 14, 2011, to express "solidarity with the public movement in the region, especially the freedom-seeking uprising of the peoples of Tunisia and Egypt against tyrannical governments."[33] Meanwhile, Iranian officials have embraced the popular protests bursting across the Arab world as epitomizing the popular revolt that ushered in the Islamic Republic nearly three decades ago.[34]

Some Iranian politicians, such as Majlis (parliament) speaker Ali Larijani, have declared Iran's support for the popular uprisings in Tunisia and Egypt, as well as the rest of the Arab world, describing them as a spark for similar movements throughout the Middle East region.[35] Earlier, Larijani had referred to the uprisings in Egypt as part of a pan-Islamic movement. He described them as the revolution of the free-hearted, which has transcended nationalistic trends.[36]

The core argument here is that as a social movement, these uprisings will carry destabilizing consequences for Iran's theocratic regime and its ruling elites. They seem to be consistent with Iran's 2009 Green Movement—in fervor and intensity as well as in the adoption of ICTs aimed at mobilizing peaceful democratic change. But it is equally important to decouple the ICTs factor from the regime's ability to contain, deter, and even confront the opposing forces. Though the regime holds military sway and has its own ICTs, it has weakened ideologically.

Domestically, as experts warn, Iran's regional strength has been overshadowed by an ailing economy and the inability of parliament to implement financial transparency in the Ahmadinejad administration. The latter has slashed $20 billion worth of subsidies for fuel, electricity, and natural gas. Subsidies for other basic food supplies are slated to be phased out by March 2014. Instead the government will give cash handouts to all citizens who have registered to receive them. Disbursing money to all citizens will become unsustainable because mounting inflation and a sharp decline in oil sales have curtailed Iran's cash reserves. Iran's middle classes—the main force behind political reform in recent years—are likely to be hit hard by these policies. Their increasing economic hardship will probably reduce their will to continue to fight for political reform.[37] Yet there is no denying that the 2009 Green Movement has profoundly affected Iranians' political culture. The movement may be dormant, if not dead, and how it will manifest itself in the future remains uncertain.

Mohamed Morsi, when he was an Egyptian presidential candidate and a Muslim Brotherhood leader representing the Freedom and Development Party, was quoted as saying, "The Muslim Brotherhood opposes a religious state because Islam is against it."[38] Yet, in some ways, as Charles Kurzman points out, the successful uprisings of the Arab Spring replicated the Iranian Revolution of 1979 more intimately than the Green Movement of 2009. They succeeded in toppling authoritarian regimes, while the Green Movement failed to do so. They caused the collapse of these regimes through general strikes, which the Green Movement never managed to trigger. In both Tunisia and Egypt, labor strikes further fueled contentious movements of popular protest. The result was that authoritarian president of Tunisia, Ben Ali, fled the country on January 14, 2011. In Egypt, wildcat strikes were so widespread they threatened the country's food security, precipitating the downfall of the Egyptian president Mubarak on February 11, 2011.[39]

Iran and the Collapse of the Moderate Camp

The 2011 turmoil in the MENA region has caused the collapse of the so-called pro-West, moderate camp (Saudi Arabia, Jordan, and Egypt), resulting in the emergence of new coalitions and strategic alliances.[40] Egypt, experts agree, will be tied down for a considerable period of time, getting its house in order and sorting out civil-military relations in this new era.[41] These uprisings have undermined the Kingdom of Saudi Arabia's public posture and prestige. Moreover, Shia revivalism has intensified since the overthrow of Saddam Hussein in 2003 and has returned to Bahrain's political scene with a vengeance. The recent popular Shia expressions of discontent with the al-Khalifa family in Bahrain pose a major challenge to the ruling family. These tensions have broader regional implications, such as intensifying the existing Shia-Sunni divide.

With Shia comprising approximately 10 percent of the Saudi population in eastern provinces, the unrest in Bahrain is seen by many Persian Gulf Arab states—especially Saudi Arabia—as having the potential to pose a serious menace to the region's stability, hence Saudi Arabia's decision to send troops to Bahrain to maintain the status quo there. Saudi Arabia's preoccupation with Bahrain and its own declining role in the region could mean that there will be a perceptible shift of influence in the Middle East from the traditional Arab heartland to two countries that were once on the sidelines of regional politics: Turkey and Qatar.

What brings Turkey and Qatar together is twofold. First, their reactions to any possible military strikes against Iran: both Turkish and Qatari high-ranking officials have said that "there will be no act of aggression from their countries against Iran."[42] Second, both have vested interests in maintaining normal and friendly relations with Iran. That said, the crisis in Syria has created a tension between these two countries and Iran. Syria has become a conundrum without easy solutions.

Turkey, by providing a buffer zone for the Syrian opposition groups, has positioned itself diametrically opposite of Iran. Likewise, Qatar's support for Hamas-Fatah reconciliation efforts has made Qatar a key player in the region, while interposing it in what has until recently been a privileged Tehran-Damascus-Hamas connection. Aware of its deficiency in hard power, Qatar has been energetic in enhancing its soft power by positioning itself in high-leverage reconciliation efforts. This frees Qatar from Saudi Arabia's overshadowing influence in the region. With the same goal in mind, Qatar maintains cooperative relations with Iran—Saudi Arabia's regional rival. Iran and Qatar also share one of the world's largest natural gas fields.

Turkey's broader foreign policy objectives overlap with Qatar's ambitious mediation efforts. The Turkish objective of creating a broad region of free trade and unbridled movement of goods, people, and ideas is well-served by Qatar's mediation in the region. Turkey, in pursuit of political and economic goals, continues to seek neighborly relations with Iran too. This enhances their cultural affinity and Islamic identity. Iran has on the other hand sought prestige in the Arab world by embracing the Palestinian cause. To fulfill this mission, they have cooperated with Syria to arm and support both Hezbollah and Hamas. They are keen on maintaining that prestige.

Iran is in a predicament because supporting their allies in Damascus may negatively impact their relations with the Arab world. Turkey is in a bind in that if it intervenes militarily in Syria, it could well be political suicide for the AKP government. To not intervene, on the other hand, is an admission of powerlessness in its own backyard. The contradiction in which Qatar finds itself is that as much as they want to take the side of the Sunni majority in Syria, they cannot afford to antagonize Iran. Since these three regionally ambitious states are each in a similar predicament, the possibility of three-way mediation to resolve the Syrian crisis should not be ruled out.

Furthermore, a more representative future government in Egypt, some scholars remind us, will probably be more cautious and skeptical of US attempts to form a common front between Arab countries and Israel against Iran.[43] This is manifested in the negotiating role played by Egypt's new government between different Palestinian groups in the West Bank and Gaza and its subsequent recognition of the pro-Hamas Muslim Brotherhood—both of which indicate that Egypt's evolving foreign policy could have important implications for the region's politics.[44]

According to some scholars, Egypt's preoccupation with its transitional problems for years to come will favor Turkey and Iran. This may bring the two together in important ways. Iran's combination of oil and natural gas reserves makes it a very important player in the energy market both currently and well into the future—especially at a time when natural gas is expected to play a more prominent role as a source of energy.[45] In this regard, Iran's bilateral economic ties with Egypt could compete with Saudi Arabia's financial prowess in the region.[46] Turkey's soft power is largely a function of the legitimacy of its democratic political system and of the AKP's leadership at home. They present a model of EU candidacy and a workable synthesis of Muslim culture and economic growth. This is a model, some experts insist, that people in other Middle Eastern countries would like to emulate.[47]

Mixed Implications

Despite the Iranian regime's optimism, the uprisings in the MENA region suggest mixed implications for Iran. While the Muslim Brotherhood can be Iran's natural political ally in a new Egypt,[48] the extent to which such cooperation will be forged remains unclear. A younger, more moderate faction within the Brotherhood has accumulated greater influence. Some Brotherhood members, including Egyptian bloggers on the Internet, have expressed political views opposed to the Muslim Brotherhood's historical stance toward women and non-Muslims.

Just recently, for example, despite the Brotherhood's and other Islamist groups' heavy endorsement for the package of constitutional amendments in Egypt, several leading Brotherhood officials announced their rejection of the amendments. They blamed the Brotherhood for its "excessive enthusiasm in advising people to approve the amendments and distributing statements in mosques."[49] Some Brotherhood officials also favor cooperation with Egypt's secular reformist movement.[50] One prominent official announced recently that he intends to form a new political party, which will have open membership for all citizens, including Coptic Christians, and would cooperate with other moderate parties.[51]

Furthermore, as most analysts posit, the growing influence of Arab public opinion on the actions of Arab governments and the absence of charismatic and strong leaders is likely to render it much tougher for the United States to pursue its traditional policies.[52] Nevertheless, it is important to understand that the new government in Egypt will be closer to Washington than Tehran for several reasons. First, the Obama administration and its Western allies dramatically facilitated the Egyptian revolution by compelling President Hosni Mubarak to step down. Second, the military, which remains secular, will oppose any efforts to create a religious political order. In this regard, Egypt's army is inclined to follow the example of Turkey rather than Iran.[53] Third, Egyptian civil society is developed and complex and has within it a persistent liberal strain.[54] While the Muslim Brotherhood's politics contain an Islamic tone, the organization may not play as crucial of a role as the army or other civic organizations in shaping Egyptian politics.

With respect to Israel, some commentators have noted that without Mubarak, Israel is left with almost no friends in the Middle East, given that Israel saw its alliance with Turkey collapse in 2010 over the aid flotilla affair.[55] Israel's raid on an aid flotilla, which sailed out of Turkey toward Gaza, ended in the deaths of nine Turkish activists on May 31, 2010. That undermined, at least in the short term, any goodwill toward Israel among the Turkish political elite—Israel's single most stalwart ally in the Muslim world. With the power shifting to the Arab people in the aftermath of these uprisings, Arab governments are unlikely to remain as silent and complicit as they have for some time as Israel takes land from the Palestinians, walling them in and pushing them out.[56] Peace for both peoples can only be found in the two-state solution with overarching security guarantees.

An equitable solution to the "Palestinian question" remains perhaps the central issue in the Middle East, and the Israeli-Palestinian conflict merits particular concern. Israel's military approach of forcing the Palestinians into submission has failed, as the unilateral withdrawal from Gaza and the subsequent siege of Gaza have demonstrated. As one international law expert notes, an equitable resolution of the Palestinian-Israeli problem in accordance with international law—rather than "facts on the ground"—is crucial to both the region's stability and a sustainable peace.[57] Israel's illegal behavior in the occupied territories runs counter to the UN Security Council's Resolution 242. It also directly conflicts with the values the United States is trying to advance in the region.[58]

The creation of a Palestinian state is the first step en route to resolving other issues. Israel cannot gain security by imposing a version of peace not acceptable to the Palestinian leadership. Only active and balanced involvement of the United States and the EU, coupled with active Arab leadership, can salvage the abortive peace process. An effective negotiation must begin with halting further building of settlements in the occupied territories, and a just solution must arise from providing security and justice for both sides.[59] The Islamic Republic of Iran and ambitious Islamic parties are certain to continue to exploit this issue to gain influence over newly emerging governments in the region.

It is important, however, to recognize that the uprisings are hardly, if ever, sectarian or religious in nature. Rather, they are part of concrete social struggles for liberation, led by disenchanted young men and women who seek human dignity and a decent life, one free from torture, hunger, discrimination, and extrajudicial killings. Similarly, uprisings in Bahrain seem to indicate secular motivations on the part of the majority Shia protesters there. The sect of the protesters describes who is protesting but the protests are not religiously motivated.

The Case for Diplomacy

EU diplomatic proposals have in the past failed to resolve the current squabble between Iran and the United States, but they have defused the tension between the two for a while. Meanwhile, the Europeans continue to argue that trade deals and technical assistance could have a moderating influence on Iran. Economic necessities and pressures for rebuilding the country, as experts say, will eventually compel Iran to engage with the West rather than pursue confrontation. According to Europeans, multilateral diplomacy and dialogue are the most reasonable ways of resolving such tensions.[60]

The US military debacle in Iraq had awakened some US policymakers to the fact that a military approach toward Iran is questionable at best and perilous at worst, especially at a time when the United States has withdrawn its combat forces from Iraq and plans to do the same in Afghanistan in 2014. The assassination of Benazir Bhutto in late December of 2007 fueled the speculation that further instability awaited the region more generally. Pakistan—a nuclear-equipped power with an army that had close ties with the Taliban regime in Afghanistan—took center stage.

Since the Bush administration's decision to label Iran's Revolutionary Guard Corps as a "terrorist organization," the call for a military strike to set back Iran's nuclear program has been frequently echoed in Washington and Tel Aviv. The Obama administration has pursued both threat and diplomacy vis-à-vis Iran by expanding the reach or scale of sanctions against Iran, more specifically targeting Iran's Central Bank. Knowing that economic sanctions will most likely harm ordinary people, the Obama administration has emphasized the utility of smart sanctions, targeting specific individuals on a blacklist by imposing a travel ban on them and seizing their assets. Many observers believe that smart sanctions are an effective way to ratchet up the pressure on the Islamic Republic.[61] Additionally, by accelerating a covert campaign of assassinations, sabotage, cyberattacks, spy flights, and encouraging defections, the Obama administration appears to offer an alternative to aerial bombardment. The United States, Israel, and Great Britain are allegedly involved in this covert campaign.[62]

Several nuclear scientists/technicians have thus far been killed in assassination attempts. An explosion, which destroyed much of an Iranian missile base near Tehran on November 12, 2011, killed at least seventeen people, including Major General Hassan Moghadam, described by Iranian state media as a pioneer in Iranian missile development and the Revolutionary Guard commander in charge of "ensuring self-sufficiency" in armaments.[63] Some legal experts note that killing Iranian scientists would violate a long-standing US executive order banning assassinations. The legal rationale for drone strikes against terrorist suspects—as in the case of war against al-Qaeda and its allies—would not apply here. Others are skeptical about sanctions and the covert campaign of assassinations and cyberattacks, arguing that these methods are unlikely to persuade Iran to abandon its nuclear program. On the contrary, they warn, such a covert campaign will provoke Iran to fight back.[64]

The idea of air strikes against Iran has been and continues to be open to skepticism on several accounts. To begin with, military strikes alone may disrupt Iran's nuclear program but would certainly make it difficult to isolate Iran, much less to change the regime. Broad sanctions against Iran may not be effectively applied in large part because of Iran's geography and vast oil reserves. A military attack from outside would enable Iran's leadership to win a broad base of popular support. A military attack—whether by Israelis or Americans—is likely to plunge the Persian Gulf region into chaos, sending oil prices through the roof.

A military strike will also inflame Iranians' nationalistic sentiments and cause them to rally around the government. Some observers have warned that such an attack is bound to radicalize the Arab world at a time when they are going through a delicate transitional period. It would ignite Hezbollah on the Lebanese border, bolster Hamas in the Gaza Strip, jeopardize US troops in the region, prompt further terrorism, and could trigger a regional war. Such costs and risks are likely to only cause a temporary setback in Iran's nuclear program of about two years.[65]

Iranians hold the key to solving many problems in the region. Although strengthened by the US invasion of Iraq, Iranians still have many incentives to continue working toward establishing a dialogue with the United States. Iranians can play a constructive role in rebuilding Afghanistan and Iraq. They may even be able to convince the United States of their long-term interests in maintaining regional stability if they make their nuclear programs more transparent. The fact remains that Iran will not abandon its nuclear program or its related enrichment plan, as they view such programs as a mark of power, prestige, and independence.

The West's insistence that Iran renounce this aspiration, including uranium enrichment on its own soil, looks increasingly unrealistic.

The Turkey and Brazil fuel-swap deal with Iran is an option worthy of contemplating as it keeps Iran's enrichment program under the 20 to 25 percent threshold. In May 2010, Turkey and Brazil talked to Iran on equal diplomatic footing and without preconditions. Iran signed on to the deal, which was similar to a US proposal only six months earlier that it had refused. Iran would ship 1,200 kg of low-enriched uranium to be held in escrow in Turkey, according to the arrangement, to be returned two years later as nuclear fuel. The Obama administration rejected the deal on the grounds that it was an Iranian tactic to buy time. This rejection was a snub to the Brazilians and the Turks.[66]

Are diplomatic solutions to US-Iran tensions a win–win scenario for both countries? Does a more positive dialogue represent an investment in long-term peace and stability throughout the Middle East? Iran is a Shiite-majority country that could cultivate close ties with Iraq's US-backed Nouri al-Maliki government. Yet, several facts reinforce Iranian leaders' sense of insecurity. First, Iran is not a member of any regional security pact. Second, the US presence in the region has increased Iran's sense of urgency to acquire some form of strategic deterrence. Finally, the talk of "regime change" through military force further alienates Iran's leaders. In fact, the more US military presence in the region increases, the more it reinforces the belief inside Iran that the best way to defend the country is to have a nuclear capability. Unless the United States pursues negotiations that address Iran's security concerns, tensions between the two will linger.

Washington has pushed Tehran to hand over suspected al-Qaeda members still in Iran—and has suggested that doing so would result in even better relations. In the past, Iran has supplied the UNSC with a list of more than 200 suspected al-Qaeda members, formerly based in Iran, who had been extradited to their countries of origin. Iran's approval of the formation of the Iraqi Governing Council and its proposal to form a trilateral commission to consult about the stabilization of Iraq could be crucial for the future of that country. The mutual security interests of the United States and Iran in restoring stability to both Iraq and Afghanistan have unexpectedly merged. Hamid Karzai, Afghanistan's president, sees Iranians' role as positive and vitally significant to his country's stability. Moreover, there is a growing consensus in Iran—in spite of its polarized politics—that dialogue with its neighbors, such as Iraq, Pakistan, Turkey, and Afghanistan, is the only way to enhance peace in the region.

In the long run, the campaign against terrorism is a campaign without military solutions. As with North Korea, the Obama administration must pursue a diplomatic track with Iran, while allowing economic sanctions to do what military means cannot accomplish alone—that is, containing Iran. The United States and Iran can arguably be inevitable allies—increasingly so as history progresses—in certain foreign policy arenas. Iran opposes al-Qaeda, prefers stability in Iraq, has been fighting drug trafficking from Afghanistan, and favors regional détente—all of these preferences coincide with US interests. Increasingly, experts, military or otherwise, argue that no single factor would more advance US capacity to redress the power balance in the Middle East than US-Iran cooperation. Given that there is no evidence of a nuclear weapons program in Iran and given that its leaders have not made a political or strategic decision to weaponize Iran's civil nuclear program, there is still room for diplomacy.

The Obama administration's quiet diplomacy and persistent two-year campaign to bring the Russians and Chinese into supporting the most serious round of economic sanctions ever passed by the UNSC, the EU, and the United States have placed enormous pressure on the Iranian oil industry and Central Bank. Iran's economy has endured tremendous losses, and this has pushed Iranian politicians to come to the negotiating table with a serious offer.[67] The key question for Iranian officials is finding a solution that will result in the relaxation of sanctions. The Obama reelection is likely to lead to a new approach toward Iran, fostering bilateral negotiations between Iran and the United States to curb Iran's nuclear program in exchange for easing economic sanctions if the latter is willing to make necessary concessions. This approach will offer an opportunity to pursue serious, direct negotiations that address Iran's security concerns, bearing in mind that bargaining is not appeasement.

Conclusion

A grassroots and indigenous movement, the Green Movement displayed deep divisions between Iranian ruling elites and rising resistance against rigid social and political conditions. But more important than the revelation of further cracks within the ruling establishment was the question of how to deal with a digitally mobilized youth. Although Iran's Green Movement was suppressed and silenced, its reverberations were felt throughout the region as pictures and images of resistance were instantly portrayed in the region via traditional and new media. Many experts have noted that the recent revolts in the Arab world against corrupt and inept regimes were more akin to the nonviolent demonstrations in Tehran than to the violent Basiji thugs who have unabatedly put down the revolts. Moreover, the worsening economic situation, high unemployment rates, and the oppressive political climate not only have intensified tensions within the Iranian regime itself, but also have further undermined the regime's legitimacy. As in the rest of the MENA, the Iranian regime is challenged by its demographic youth bulge—a young generation that tends to view rampant corruption as stripping them of their future.

Even today, and despite the fact that the street protests in Iran have noticeably vanished in the face of the government's machinations, the political divisions within the ruling elites—stemming largely from the dual authority that is inherent to the Islamic Republic's constitution—continue unabated. A new generation of activists now works behind the scenes to sustain the movement's momentum. Unlike the 1999 student protests, however, the Green Movement has expanded far beyond university campuses to encompass diverse groups and civil society organizations, including human rights activists, women, disgruntled clerics, and the unemployed. In sum, the struggle for democracy, the rule of law, and modern human rights have become integrated into the consciousness of the Iranians, as the Islamic Republic increasingly finds itself in a race against time.

The implications of US-Iran rivalry in the MENA region are many and varied, but none is more important than the value clash between two different identities and perspectives. In the Arab world, tensions are emerging between Arab republics, which are caught in messy transitions, and the monarchies of the Persian Gulf, along with Morocco and Jordan, which are advocating for the status quo or incremental reform. The shifting regional dynamics suggest that the United States and Iran will continue to compete over which country best embodies the values and aspirations of the peoples of the Middle East.[68]

The US interpretation of Islamism as a countervailing force to the rise of the human rights movement and democratic institutions is typical of such rivalry. Although the United States has fostered globalizing processes and their secular trends throughout the region, Iranian ruling elites have placed their geostrategic concerns and Islamic identity above the strict adherence to democracy promotion and human rights. More particularly, the US emphasis on secular modernization and gender issues has clashed directly with the Islamic Republic's insistence on Shari'a as the source of human dignity and gender identity. The Islamic Republic saw the Green Movement as a seditious plot engineered by foreign agents to overthrow the Islamic regime, all the while accusing the Western media of overhyping the Green Movement and its powerful oppositional prowess.

As sanctions are ratcheted up further on Iran, the most realistic prognosis might be a partial enrichment freeze in return for partial easing of sanctions. Talks on Iran's nuclear program may lead to an opening for further diplomatic negotiations between the two countries. Yet there can be no doubt that the nature of the US-Iran rivalry is political—not technical or legal. Some Iranian experts have noted that the main goal of the West is, indeed, regime change in Iran, and the nuclear dispute is a disguise for pursuing that goal. More specifically, they warn, "Americans are trying to use Iran's nuclear program as a pretext to go on with their large-scale plan for regime change in Iran."[69] In this fundamental sense, the true test of diplomacy will be if all parties concerned will offer serious political steps and compromises during the negotiations. Calling for further sanctions amid negotiations (the so-called two-track policy) may at first glance appear a proper way to moving talks forward. But this approach may prove counterproductive if Iranian negotiators are not offered tangible gains for sticking with the talks.

Chapter 6
THE ARAB SPRING

Regional Implications and Beyond

The rise of democratic forces against autocratic regimes across the MENA region brought new leadership to Egypt, Tunisia, Libya, and Yemen, and could result in yet more leadership changes in the coming years. Although it is too early to foretell the course of events in the post-upheaval period, it is important to bear in mind that revolutionary changes are typically slow to come by and usually take many years to take shape. What is evident is that the United States' traditional bargain with autocrats has unraveled and that the strategic interests of the United States are better served, at least during this historic period, by working with governments that genuinely reflect the will of their people.

The issue in focus here is how US foreign policy should adjust to these uprisings by concurrently supporting competing—and at times, even antagonistic—political forces in the region. Regional and global responses to these uprisings are also likely to impact oil prices, human rights conditions, and the US role in the region. The key question is, should the United States support these emerging illiberal democracies? The military is likely to play a key role for years to come, at least in Egypt, as it did during democratic transitions in South Korea, Indonesia, and Chile.[1] But without a deeper understanding of the historical context, it is impossible to gauge the scope of such changes and their long-term implications.

World War II ended with the decline of the European powers and a surge in US might. America inherited the legacies of European great powers: postcolonialism and nationalist resistance movements. Instead of embracing independence or emancipatory movements, the United States pursued the old bargain of working with autocrats to the detriment of their people's democratic aspirations. One major culprit was oil. The history of the postwar period demonstrates that many nationalist leaders in the MENA region fell into disfavor with the United States over the issue of oil.[2] Thus, to better understand the region's place in US foreign policy, it is critical to take a hard look at the *economics* of intervention.[3] US petroleum politics often resulted in repeated intervention with tense and uncertain outcomes. For the ensuing six decades, US foreign policy toward the MENA region became embroiled in myriad paradoxes. The United States frequently found itself faced with the all-too-familiar foreign policy dilemma: whether to stand firmly behind authoritarian but pro-West regimes, or to support the aspirations of the region's peoples for basic human rights, meaningful economic or justice opportunity, and political reforms.

The recent explosion of concerns about the rising cost of living in the perpetually underdeveloped MENA region during the current global economic meltdown is forcing social change. Whereas in some parts of the MENA region criticisms of inept government policies, rampant corruption, and the military's widespread graft have formed into calls for revolt, in other parts they have led to calls for more autonomy to pursue the goals and aspirations brought into focus by rising levels of education and globalization in the region.[4]

Some of the oil-rich countries of the MENA region have attempted to defuse similar tensions by paying off their people in various ways.[5] But especially for those countries that do not produce oil, a combination of modernizing youth and tough economic times has driven an unprecedented wave of change.[6] In the wake of these uprisings, two key questions follow: How will US foreign policy respond to the MENA's rapidly changing social and political landscape? And how can the people properly capitalize on the opportunities presented by such uprisings?

It is notable that change and transformation in the MENA region have resulted from bottom-up, antiestablishment popular movements that have exposed the flaws of some US foreign policies and will most likely call into question other US policies in the region in the coming years. To flesh out this argument, this chapter situates US foreign policy in four periods: (1) the period of 1945–1989, known as the Cold War era; (2) the period of 1990–2001, the era of political liberalization and opening, also known as the post–Cold War era; (3) the period of

2001–2010, known as the post-9/11 era; and (4) the period of uprisings (2011–ongoing), which today is referred to as the "democracy era."[7] To assess the way US foreign policy is affected by regional developments in the aftermath of uprisings in the MENA region, the rest of this chapter will focus on the cases of Libya, Bahrain, Syria, and Turkey.

The Cold War Era (1945–1989)

The end of World War II marked an era of dwindling European power and a surge of US influence in the world. During this period, the United States employed the full panoply of instruments ranging from financial and military aid and trade and investment, to engineered coups and military interventions, and support of friendly but repressive regimes throughout the world.[8] These instruments were seen as pivotal to the maintenance of stability against revolutionary challenges that were always suspected of serving Soviet strategic goals. Security concerns led the Unites States to support right-wing dictatorships and military juntas in the name of anti-Communism, marginalizing—and even excluding—human rights.[9]

During the Cold War era, the United States acted as the sole extra-regional hegemonic power on the basis of its military preeminence in the MENA region, guaranteeing the persistence of pro-West but dysfunctional and corrupt regimes. Many of these regimes owed their political longevity and power to their readiness, albeit tacitly, to adhere to the US line on foreign affairs.[10] Looking back on a half century of US foreign policy in the MENA region, it is obvious that a slew of contradictory measures propped up unpopular regimes, caused disillusionment, prolonged the plight of the people, and produced deepening confusion regarding who was a US ally or enemy.

During the second half of the twentieth century, the US foreign policy toward the Middle East centered on protecting oil flows from the region, supporting Israel and the region's pro-West but authoritarian governments, and maintaining political stability, not just to keep the status quo, but largely to deter, contain, and, if necessary, confront Communism. This list later expanded to include other objectives such as combating terrorism, brokering a truce between the Palestinians and the Israelis, and preventing the spread of weapons of mass destruction. In pursuit of these objectives, the United States relied on the use of force, covert intervention, economic and military assistance, arms sales, military presence, and diplomacy. The continued support for the monarchies in Saudi Arabia and the smaller Persian Gulf states proved critical, especially when they faced threats from outside their borders.[11]

During this time, the MENA region was plagued by numerous conflicts, both intra-regional (such as the Arab-Israeli wars, the Iran-Iraq war, the Soviet invasion of Afghanistan, and the Iraqi invasion of Kuwait), and inter-regional (such as the civil war in Lebanon and the subsequent stationing of the US marines there in the early 1980s, Iran's Islamic Revolution, and growing Islamic radicalism and associated terrorism). In response to this long list of destabilizing events, the United States continued to build up its military presence in Saudi Arabia and the Persian Gulf, especially after the Shah's regime in Iran collapsed in 1979.[12]

Consequently, the region became home to some of the world's most repressive regimes, an oppressive Israeli occupation, human rights abuses, economic disparities, unelected governments, and corrupt political systems. The Arab defeats in the wars with Israel and the failure of parliamentary democracy to make ruling elites and military institutions electorally accountable precipitated a deepening sense of disillusionment and crisis in many Muslim societies, culminating in the resurgence of political Islam by the late 1970s.[13] This resurgence came to be seen as a potent backlash against the failure of secular states and secular ideologies, such as liberal nationalism and Arab socialism.[14]

Access to oil figured prominently in US foreign policy in the MENA region. The Western world believed they would gain more access to the region's oil resources by working with dictators than with accountable, democratic regimes. The 1953 coup in Iran is a notable case in point. The CIA and British agents, in collaboration with Iranian army generals, engineered a coup against the nationalist and constitutionally elected prime minister of Iran, Mohammad Mossadeq, who nationalized the Anglo-Iranian Oil Company. He was deposed and the Shah was restored to power shortly afterward. US foreign policy between 1953 and 1978 stressed a special relationship with the Shah and his inner circle, while largely disregarding the needs and demands of the Iranian people. Increasingly, US presence and interventionist policies became integral parts of the domestic politics in Iran.[15] When, in the late 1970s, President Carter's concern for human rights had to be balanced against US support for the Shah's repressive regime, the policy of having it both ways boomeranged, precipitating the fall of the monarchy.

Indeed, the quest for oil and security continued to compel the United States to support autocratic regimes in the region. The implications for human rights and human dignity were dire. One study reveals dismal human rights conditions of five Arab states—Morocco, Egypt, Jordan, Kuwait, and Saudi Arabia—often considered "US friends in the region." The United States, according to this study, exerted little or no political and diplomatic pressure on these governments to adopt liberal reforms.[16] The most glaring example of this willful blindness was Saudi Arabia, which was (and still is) by far the closest US Arab ally in the region, yet has one of the poorest human rights records in the Middle East. Human rights and democratic principles were clearly subordinated to US strategic, military, and commercial ties with the Saudi government.[17]

The United States does more trade—largely in oil and weapons—with Saudi Arabia than any other country in the MENA region, including Israel, and depends on close Saudi cooperation in its counterterrorism efforts in Yemen. For his part, Saudi king Abdullah has shown a degree of support for uprisings in the region, from arming the rebels in Syria to reconciling with the new Islamist leadership under the Morsi administration in Egypt.[18] Similarly, Saudi Arabia has helped nurture an Islamic revival across Tanzania, where Islamic extremists have sought a foothold. In Zanzibar alone, Saudis invest more than $1 million annually in Islamic universities, *madrasas*, and scholarships to study abroad in Mecca.[19] Saudis' main aim—spreading Shari'a (Islamic) law—appears contradictory to the Western world's goal of containing extremism as well as maintaining regional stability in Africa at a time when the international community is determined to curb the revitalization of extremist potential.

The Post–Cold War Era (1990–2001)

The post–Cold War era was fraught with challenges and contradictions for US foreign policy. In Afghanistan, for example, the secular state-building project was abandoned following the Soviet withdrawal in 1988. Still in the Cold War mind-set, the United States remained focused on confronting and deterring Communism. In fact, throughout the 1990s, the United States had no reconstruction plan for post-Soviet Afghanistan. As a result, chaos and poverty prevailed throughout the country. Afghanistan was abandoned to the Taliban and their friends.[20]

Osama bin Laden was the price the United States paid for victory over the Soviet Union in Afghanistan.[21] With the active encouragement of the CIA and Pakistan's ISI (Inter-Services Intelligence), the *mujahideen*—Muslim guerrilla warriors, also known as freedom fighters, who engaged in the war to expel Soviet troops from Afghanistan—played a significant role in dislodging Soviet forces from Afghanistan throughout the 1980s. The CIA supported Pakistan's ISI, which directed the Taliban's rise to power in Afghanistan by the mid-1990s. The actions of the Taliban at that time largely served the US geopolitical interests.[22] The drug trade in the region, according to one observer, was also used to finance and equip the Bosnian Muslim Army and the Kosovo Liberation Army.[23]

The unresolved Israeli-Palestinian conflict continued to complicate US foreign policy in the region during this era. The MENA's oil-producing nations were under pressure to keep supply lines open. Many of these governments, which depended on the United States for military protection, faced a populace increasingly agitated over the Palestinian issue. The second Intifada, which erupted in September 2000, generated concern among a significant number of governments and business people in the Middle East who regularly dealt with the United States and Europe.[24] Nevertheless, the United States continued to support both Israel and the region's corrupt and dysfunctional regimes, further alienating reformist social movements, and discrediting its foreign policy in the region.

Rolling back Iraq's invasion of Kuwait opened an opportunity to unleash a series of negotiations between the Israelis and the Palestinians under the Oslo talks. The United States found itself on the horns of another dilemma: brokering a truce while maintaining partisan diplomacy toward Israel. Those talks were dead on arrival. The collapse of the peace process and the continuing plight of the Palestinians under occupation pointed to a contradictory US policy. Any hope of successful mediation in the Israeli–Palestinian conflict was unrealistic. Failed US diplomacy bred further radicalism not only among the Palestinians inside the occupied territories but also throughout the Muslim world. The Israeli prime minister, Ariel Sharon, could not see where the conflict was going. Chair of the Palestinian Liberation Organization (PLO) Yasser Arafat had no means to stop terrorism; he was rapidly losing control of popular politics to more radical elements. Meanwhile, the United States' unqualified and unconditional support for Israel made it difficult for the United States to challenge Israeli defiance on such contentious issues as settlements in the occupied territories.

The Palestinians saw a double standard at work here: the right of return for Soviet Jews was upheld by the United States, whereas the return of Palestinian refugees was not guaranteed. For many Palestinians, the US diplomatic initiatives made no difference to their lives under occupation. As a result, they continued to lose faith in US diplomacy, even as they came to grips with the reality that active and sustained US engagement was crucial to the resolution of the conflict. This mentality, in turn, created conditions among the Palestinians that assured extremist elements had moral and material support. Because of America's reliance on the region's oil, there was arguably an incentive for the United States to help in the resolution of the dispute. But other economic and geopolitical interests often overshadowed this incentive. With the United States playing the dual role of the main mediator of the conflict as well as the chief diplomatic, financial, and military supporter of Israeli occupation forces, US policy was mired in a critical paradox.[25]

September 11, 2001, and the "War on Terror"

In the Cold War mind-set, US policymakers focused on confronting and deterring Communism. During the post-9/11 era, that fixation was replaced with a preoccupation with militant Islam. In the aftermath of the terrorist attacks of September 11, 2001, US domestic law enforcement's scrutiny of Muslims raised the concern that the war against terrorism would be seen as a war against Muslims.[26] US foreign policymakers were explicitly aware of this danger while they designed policies to confront violent movements among Muslims.

The events of September 11, 2001, and the ensuing "war on terror" have had the effect of further securitization and the militarization of international politics. As a result, a growing preoccupation with "security" and "fear" is bound to affect how governments manage immigration, citizenship, and national security matters. In most cases, security and geopolitical concerns have supplanted rights spaces, thus privileging the dynamics of hegemony over the emancipatory potential of human rights practices. The declaration of the war on terror since the 9/11 attacks on the United States has spurred a debate among politicians, diplomats, and army officers over how the military should wage war against global terrorists. Furthermore, the US detention policies, as well as the abuse of prisoners both in Iraq's Abu Ghraib and Cuba's Guantánamo Bay, and the practice of extraordinary rendition launched by the CIA after 9/11, considerably damaged the United

States' image. This practice involved secretly flying captured terrorist suspects to some countries—including Syria, Jordan, Egypt, Morocco, and
other Arab states—for interrogation by local intelligence services, a practice
that regularly involved torture. Achieving counterterrorism goals this way
carried risks and complexities. These practices placed the United States and
its European allies in a precarious position with respect to the rights and
protections enunciated in the Geneva Convention.[27]

2011 and the Democratization Era

The collapse of the repressive but pro-West regimes in Tunisia and Egypt
following the 2011 uprisings has complicated—if not undermined—the
reliance upon similar authoritarian regimes that have served as an essential pillar in the campaign against terror. Western intelligence agencies,
particularly the CIA and Britain's Secret Intelligence Service, MI6,
collected much invaluable information on al-Qaeda, its allies, and their
operations, through the cooperation of friendly yet repressive regimes
across the Middle East.[28] This reality has promoted new thinking about
different ways to combat terrorism.

   The fallout from the wars in Afghanistan and Iraq, as well as the
poor justification for them, has indeed posed a huge setback for efforts to
build a new normative consensus around the notion of military intervention. The West needs to search for new ways of countering terrorism, as
the Islamic bogeyman has lost its meaning and relevance to the "Global
War on Terror." It is worth noting that the war on terror is now institutionalized and is likely to go on indefinitely in a "path dependence"
mode of operation in the coming years. The Obama administration has
stated clearly that the war on terror is not the lens through which US
foreign policy should look at its larger strategies in the MENA region.
Shifting that focus is the key to a new US foreign policy outlook. It is
within this context that rapprochement between the United States and
the Muslim Brotherhood could lead to better ways to contain Islamic
radical groups and their terrorist activities.

Failure of US Grand Strategy

The Bush administration's approach to the war on terror rested on a grand
strategy of military intervention, imposing democracy, and promoting

regime change in the Middle East. Instead of defeating terrorism, this strategy created confusion and poor policies. A reorientation of that strategy, as one expert notes, requires that the United States settles for a steady but grueling fight against al-Qaeda. It should ground its fight in a global normative prohibition against terrorism. Acts of terrorism should be seen as slavery and genocide, which are an outlawed type of social behavior that no state or even organized political group can support or endorse.[29] The central purpose in such a war, Doyle continues, must be to delegitimize terror as a tactic and to induce states to assume responsibility for combating terrorists within their borders. The war on terror, then, would be analogous to a worldwide global emergency rather than to a war. Otherwise, the prospects for victory in counterinsurgencies against terrorist groups are notoriously bleak.[30]

The problems with the US grand strategy in orchestrating the war on terror are manifold. Western governments that once expressed human rights concerns in their discussions with Middle Eastern regimes, more often than not praised Egypt and Tunisia for antiterror efforts and tended to cater to the demands of authoritarian regimes such as Uzbekistan. Western pressure on China to honor human rights—though never consistent—dissipated considerably. US policymakers turned a blind eye to Moscow's war in Chechnya. Likewise, the US strategic goal in East Africa was directed toward tracking al-Qaeda. This military emphasis accounts for why the Bush administration was reluctant to consistently push the Sudanese government to stop the genocide in Darfur. In these states, governments' antiterrorism policies stifled political dissent and undermined a wide variety of human rights protections.

There were several major problems with the strategy of promoting democracy in MENA countries in order to remove motivations for terrorism. The first was the fact that "transitions to democracy" or "consolidation" of democracies in these countries was difficult to achieve. The process was messy, unpredictable, and often faced a multitude of obstacles in policies and leadership.[31] The second was that elections in societies with deep sectarian and ethnic divisions and identities entailed grave risks and disastrous consequences. Finally, economic welfare did not necessarily lead to democratization, but it was as crucial to stability as elections were.

The rise of anti-Americanism also became part of each trade-off. It is worth noting that anti-American sentiments have arisen in reaction to the US invasion of Iraq, in part because there was no clear evidence of Iraqi logistic, financial, or intelligence support for al-Qaeda, and partly because this military adventure failed to establish a stable, democratic Iraq. If nothing else, the desire for a stable democracy was subjugated to intensifying sectarian tensions, rendering any future bargaining immensely difficult. Moreover, one of the unintended consequences of the US intervention in Iraq was giving the Iraqi Kurds the false impression that their cooperation with the United States was bound to lead to the fulfillment of their aspirations for autonomy initially, and nationhood ultimately. The Kurdish rights of self-determination are an issue that MENA states cannot escape. No country in the region is more concerned about this prospect than Turkey, which has the largest Kurdish population within the region, whose autonomous assertions also implicate the neighboring countries of Iran, Iraq, and Syria. Among Turks, feelings of alienation and bitterness toward the United States are growing dramatically.[32]

The Democratic Era: Uprisings in North Africa

As we have discussed above, the self-immolation of Mohamed Bouazizi— a Tunisian street vendor—in protest of the confiscation of his fruit cart and the harassment and humiliation that he suffered at the hands of local police prompted a nationwide uprising in Tunisia, sparking street demonstrations and riots throughout the country in reaction to Tunisia's economic decay, symbolized by Bouazizi's plight. Resentment and violence intensified following Bouazizi's death, leading then-president Zine El Abidine Ben Ali to step down on January 14, 2011, after ruling the country for twenty-three years. This uprising prompted a deep sense of empathy in neighboring Egypt, unleashing years of bottled-up resentment toward the Egyptian government. Following eighteen days of peaceful protests and demonstrations in Egypt, Hosni Mubarak's government collapsed. In both Tunisia and Egypt, a combination of similar factors paved the way for such uprisings: the sharp rise in food prices, high unemployment rates, especially among the youth, and widespread resentment directed at corrupt and repressive governments.

Some analysts have attributed these economic difficulties to neoliberal IMF and World Bank interventions in the region, arguing that privatization, falling real wages, and the accumulation of a great deal of wealth in the hands of the country's ruling families and their cronies have contributed largely to popular uprisings against widespread economic misery.[33] In Egypt, one observer notes, during the 1980s and 1990s, the United States and other Western countries encouraged neoliberal economic policies that provided state subsidies and other incentives for private investors to focus on such sectors as finance, real estate, construction, tourism, and raw material extraction and processing. These investors were given all sorts of incentives—including cheap land, cheap natural gas and oil, and tax and customs exemptions.[34] Although these reforms were followed by economic growth, they nevertheless failed to generate comparable employment expansion or wage increases, instead concentrating profits largely in the hands of large-scale foreign and domestic capitalists. By 2010, Egypt, like Turkey, faced good prospects despite the decline of the Gulf Cooperation Council members' foreign direct investment (FDI) in the region. The only missing part from the picture was how such liberalized development had caused considerable corruption and cronyism, as well as a vastly inequitable distribution of its benefits.[35]

Similarly, as one expert stresses, under Mubarak, neoliberal policies consolidated a regime that denied Egyptians the right to organize political opposition or hold political meetings. The implementation of neoliberal programs resulted in a frequent remilitarization of power, with control shifting away from ministries run by technocrats to provincial governors who were mostly appointed from the upper echelons of the military. Neoliberal economic reforms were accompanied and followed by the intimidation of human rights activists, civil society organizers, and journalists by closures, court cases, and imprisonment. Amid this atmosphere of fear and intimidation, US foreign policy was primarily concerned with the maintenance of the Mubarak regime and its privatization, trade liberalization, and deregulation programs.[36]

The new waves of protests in the MENA region also showed that the consequences of US foreign policy mistakes had eventually come to bear. Mubarak's regime, supported by the United States since 1981, was toppled when it became abundantly clear that it no longer represented the aspirations of the Egyptian people. Mubarak was seen as an autocrat who perpetuated the interests of a corrupt regime and as a ruler who owed his power to external support and foreign assistance, largely from the United States ($1.3 billion annually). US backing of the region's corrupt and dysfunctional regimes alienated reformist social movements and further discredited US foreign policy in the region. Nearly 20 percent of Egyptians live below the national poverty line, according to the World Bank, and nearly 40 percent of the population lives on $2 per day or less.[37] Moreover, uneven development has led to the emergence of an affluent class in predominantly lower-middle-class and poor cities such as Cairo and Alexandria. Since 1991, under IMF and World Bank guidance, Egypt has adopted myriad neoliberal policies. Privatization policies have consistently led to workers' strikes and demonstrations.

For the first time since the post–World War II period, across the MENA region, a shared and common Arab identity has swept the streets of the Arab world. These waves of uprisings challenge the orientalist construction of the Arab people as religious fanatics, regressive, apathetic, and resigned to their country's politics. This new narrative is neither about the United States and its regional wars and military interventions, or the Arab-Israeli conflicts, nor about military coups and assassinations. It is about the first modern Arab uprisings against poverty, unemployment, and general recession. It has no ideological or political leaders. This moment in history is not about social networking (Facebook and Twitter) and the power of technology—as the Western media wants us to believe; rather, it is about a genuine awakening in the Arab street and the Arab world, which have become more crowded and far more destitute than in years past. It is also about redefining regional political leadership and its rapport with the people in unprecedented ways.

It is time that our analytic gaze focuses on the causes of internal economic frustration and resentments toward Arab governments. As one analyst argues, for several decades, these countries have suffered triple crises—financial, climate change, and food—under the old policies of pre-packaged and trickle-down prescription of private-sector growth. A wide variety of problems emanating from inept and distorted economies, rising food and housing prices, slashed wages/prices and protections for workers and farmers, dropping standards of living in conjunction with diluted public welfare programs, and widespread restriction of rights and liberties have all crippled peoples' living conditions and destroyed their dignity. It is vitally important that we realize that the demands for popular democracy throughout the Arab world are rooted in social and economic justice.[38]

The Fallout from the Uprisings

Several far-reaching implications are likely to follow from these uprisings. First, we will witness the spread of solidarity and democratizing movements throughout the region. Another particularly important implication will be for a country like Iran, whose theocratic system grew out of a revolutionary movement. Yet another logical question is, will ending the bargain with autocrats lead to a push for a reasonable resolution of the Israeli-Palestinian conflict? And finally, the neoliberal policies of previous US administrations, which have led to economic difficulties and rising levels of unemployment for youths, will be seriously questioned.

Amid the growing celebration and joy of rebellion against tyranny, it is important not to get caught in a heady moment of jubilation, without asking the serious question: what will the new MENA region look like? For Egyptians, there is a long way to go to end the Mubarak regime's legacy. It is premature to say that the power vested in the government is moving to the people in the Second Republic. (The First Republic, which started in 1952, lasted until 2011 when peaceful democratic uprisings caused the downfall of the Mubarak regime. Between 1952 and 2011, all Egyptian leaders came from the military. The First Republic became synonymous with the rule of the army officers.) To begin with, we do not know the answers to several other questions that will most likely bedevil Egypt and its leaders in the coming months and years: Which system of governance will emerge from this revolution, another military leader or a civilian government? Which government can better cope with the economic reality of life in Egypt, given that some 40 percent of Egyptians live on $2 or less a day?[39] How can the developed world recalibrate its policies toward Egypt and use its leverage to nudge along this transition successfully? How will this popular revolution and the images of euphoria within the mass celebrations on Cairo's streets affect the rest of the Arab world?

No one can say with a modicum of certainty whether the face and political landscape of the region have changed irrevocably. By most accounts, other monarchies in North Africa and the rest of the Middle East may come under pressure very soon. The Egyptian experience could send out a strong message to the young monarchs of Morocco and Jordan. If democracy is going to be a reality in Egypt, the old structures of power must be entirely dismantled. We should be mindful of what comes next, keeping in mind the shape of things to come and the extent to which different groups (secular and nonsecular) will be fairly and justly represented in the formation of a democratic government. True, the Egyptian army decided *not* to go down with Mubarak, but will it be a midwife tending to the birth of democracy in Egypt?

If the Egyptian military *negotiates* the transition toward democracy with other groups in the interim period, positive results will follow. On March 4, 2011, then–prime minister Ahmad Shafiq and his cabinet resigned, and Ossam Sharaf was named the new interim prime minister. Interestingly enough, the two top winners in Egypt's first-ever free presidential election, held on May 23–24, 2012, were Mohamed Morsi, from Brotherhood's Freedom and Justice Party with 24.8 percent of votes, and former prime minister Ahmad Shafiq with 24.7 percent.[40]

On June 14, 2012, a panel of judges appointed by Hosni Mubarak threw the country's difficult transition to democracy into grave uncertainty with rulings that dissolved the popularly elected parliament, on the grounds that elected officials have inadmissibly allowed political parties to compete for seats designated for independents. This move, coupled with the fact that the same body allowed Shafiq to run for president, has reinforced the prevailing perception that the remnants of the old elite seek to block Islamists from coming to power.[41] The fact remains that with no constitution or parliament in place, the president's powers are likely to be determined by a military with power to arrest civilians for crimes as minor as traffic obstruction. Many activists who participated in the 2011 uprisings that toppled the Mubarak regime have called these elections a farce.[42]

After a weeklong delay in the official announcement of the result of the second round of elections (held on June 17–18, 2012), Morsi was declared the new president of Egypt on June 24, 2012. The Presidential Election Commission announced that Morsi had won 51.7 percent of the runoff vote, and Shafiq 48.3 percent.[43] Under an interim constitutional declaration, the SCAF retains the power to make laws and budget decisions until a new constitution is written and a new president is elected. The military council, with the tacit support of the Supreme Constitutional Court, has tried to insert specific provisions in the interim constitution to protect its power and immunity. The ongoing contestation of power among the generals, the Islamists, and the secular revolutionary groups notwithstanding, it will still be difficult to push the military, which has been the main force behind every regime since 1952, out of politics.[44]

Further compounding the electoral tension is the question of how much power the new president will actually wield given that previously the military council had full legislative authority. According to an interim constitutional declaration, the president has the power to declare war, but only with the approval of the military council. Many Egyptians, however, were in a jubilant and celebratory mood. Wael Ghonim, a former Google executive who played a key role in organizing the 2011 uprisings in Tahrir Square, posted his reaction to Morsi's victory on Twitter: "The first elected civilian Egyptian president in the history of modern Egypt. The revolution continues."[45] This optimism is shared by those activists—Islamists or otherwise—and secular revolutionary groups who insist that political gains can be incrementally achieved in Egypt. Since the 2011 uprisings, they note, popular demands have pushed the SCAF to make greater concessions and act more cautiously as it considers applying repressive means and measures. This is so because the military council feels it needs popular legitimacy more than the Mubarak regime.[46]

Morsi's victory, however, as many experts agree, will do little or nothing to reduce the intense polarization of Egyptian society, even as Morsi tries to downplay the Islamist orientation of his party, the Freedom and Development Party. This became evident when, on November 22, 2012, Morsi granted himself more power by issuing an order preventing any court from overturning his decisions, effectively allowing himself to run the country unchecked until a new constitution is drafted. Having been heartened by US and international praise for mediating a Gaza ceasefire on November 21, 2012, Morsi put himself above oversight and protected the Islamist-dominated assembly from an imminent threat of dissolution by court order.[47]

Morsi also ordered retrials and reinvestigations in the deaths of protesters during the 2011 uprisings against Mubarak—an order that could have certainly led to the reprosecution of Mubarak, who is currently serving a life prison term, and several acquitted officials who served under him. This decree fueled growing public anger and resentment toward the Morsi administration on the grounds that he and his Muslim Brotherhood were bent on confiscating too much power. Even though this edict divided Egypt, it certainly unified opponents. Critics argued that without forging a consensus, President Morsi was unlikely to bring stability and peace to Egypt.[48] Under heavy and widespread pressure from the public and his opponents, Morsi agreed on November 26, 2012, to scale back the sweeping decree he had issued earlier that raised his edicts above any judicial review. The agreement, which was reached with some of Egypt's highest judicial authorities, left most of President Morsi's actions subject to review by the courts, but preserved a crucial power—that is, protecting the constitutional council from being dissolved by the courts before it completes its work.[49]

It is worth noting that shortly after Morsi was elected, he came across as a pragmatic and level-headed politician keen on reducing the many uncertainties surrounding his presidency. In an interview with CNN, for example, Morsi said, "There is no such thing called an Islamist democracy. There is democracy only. . . . The people are the source of authority."[50] Morsi's victory has also raised questions about the future of Egypt-Israeli relations. Although Morsi avoided referring to Israel during his first address to the nation after his victory on June 24, 2012, he did stress, "we will preserve all national and international agreements."[51] This last message has somewhat alleviated the fears of many Israelis who have held a pessimistic view of the Arab Spring.

More immediately, Daniel Byman writes, the dramatic changes in the Arab world are likely to generate two security irritants for Israel: its confrontation with the Hamas government of the Gaza Strip and the status of the peace process. Under Mubarak, Byman argues, Egypt quietly helped Israel against Hamas, much to the latter's chagrin. Egypt mostly kept the Rafah crossing point between Egypt and Gaza closed, helping Israel in restricting the flow of goods and people into and out of Gaza.[52] The uprisings in Egypt and the rest of the Arab world, however, have shaken this fragile equilibrium between the two countries. Sympathy for the Palestinians living in Gaza, as well as popular support for their resistance to Israel, is high and widespread in Egypt. Where Israel sees a loss of an ally in Egypt, Hamas sees a potential friend over the horizon, especially if the Muslim Brotherhood gains increased leverage in Egyptian politics.[53]

Many challenges lie ahead for Egypt's new president. Leaving aside Egypt's sputtering economy and a wide array of other problems, Morsi will face specific governing challenges, especially in soliciting cooperation from parties who have been reluctant to work with the Muslim Brotherhood and dealing with an inept and bloating state bureaucracy bequeathed to him by Mubarak.[54] The army has pledged to end the state of emergency imposed since 1981, lift regulations on political parties and the press, and dissolve Mubarak's National Democratic Party. These changes notwithstanding, the army remains a key player—either overtly or behind the scenes.

The credibility of the army will soon be put to another political test: What is going to happen to the current group of senior commanders, who owe their privileged socioeconomic positions to the former president Mubarak and his regime? How are they going to deal with the demands of the majority of Egyptians who seek a fair distribution of the country's wealth and power? It is not yet clear, as one observer notes, whether the generals' understanding of "democracy" comports with the hopes so vividly expressed by the Egyptian people.[55] History has also shown us that revolutions typically begin with goodwill and a general sense of empowerment, but too often conclude with less than desirable—if not tumultuous—results. It will be interesting to see how the ensuing power struggle among the Egyptian ruling elite takes shape.

In the post–Arab Spring elections in both Egypt and Tunisia, Islamists' victories have raised concerns for US foreign policymakers. Yet, the threat of Islamists' ascendancy to power was somewhat exaggerated, as evidenced by the fact that the November 2011 elections in Tunisia effected an alliance of Islamists (the al-Nahda Party) with the Liberal Congress for the Republic and the left-of-center Ettakatoi Party with the intent of winning a majority (139 of the 217) of seats in the Parliament. The move toward the center by the al-Nahda Party is likely to subdue some worries that radical Islamists will take over political power. In Egypt, the Freedom and Justice Party—affiliated with the Muslim Brotherhood—has clearly disassociated itself from the al-Nour Party, which is spearheaded by Salafis. It is expected that Egypt's Freedom and Justice Party will serve as a model of a centrist Islamic party throughout the region.

Democratic transition in Egypt, however, is a bumpy road. An Egyptian court suspended the body chosen to write Egypt's new constitution on April 10, 2012. This decision has set back the Muslim Brotherhood because it opens up the likelihood that Egypt's new constitution would not be drafted before a new president is elected. Under such circumstances, the new president will take office with no clear job description, and he is also likely to have near-total power, a development that will surely bolster the military council's leverage in some important ways. The court ruling was based on the fact that the Islamic parliamentarians and their allies were poised to dominate the constitution writing, in large part because liberal, leftist, and other members of the constituent assembly had resigned to protest the fact that the constitution-writing body was not representative of Egypt. Experts believe that the court's decision may signal a move by the ruling military council to intervene in the democratic transition. Such a move could throw the transition into chaos.[56] In the following sections, we address some of these issues with an eye toward their broader implications for the region.

Solidarity and Rebellion in the Region

The democratic uprisings in North Africa demonstrate that maintaining order and stability can no longer be divorced from upholding human rights, human security, and social justice.[57] The young generation of educated men and women throughout the Arab world and beyond appears to be more open and sympathetic to a liberal, constitutional order. Increasingly, this generation has shown more interest in addressing economic and political grievances, including the issues of governmental competence, corruption, and growth, than in making grand ideological statements.[58] The leaderless uprisings in Tunisia, Egypt, Libya, and the rest of the Arab world attest to the fact that the time has come to end the bargain with autocrats.[59] The sudden and unexpected quality of these revolutionary movements has made them difficult to contain or deter. The old order, built around negotiation and collaboration with local autocrats, has fundamentally broken down. It is no longer cost effective to support dictators.

The strategy of pressuring nondemocratic Arab regimes to introduce reforms will produce positive results. There are, however, risks associated with promoting reforms, but those risks are far more manageable than the risk associated with continuing to support autocrats—a posturing that has become an unfortunate staple of US foreign policy. In the future, US support for political reforms will serve a dual purpose: it will contain further unrest and uprisings in the region; but more importantly, it can and will successfully reduce the capabilities of terrorist groups and organizations—both financially and socially—to operate and recruit. The triumph of a peaceful popular movement to rid Egypt of its long-time autocrat has been a nightmare for groups such as al-Qaeda. For the United States, this may be a time of great promise for the much-vaunted, ongoing "campaign against terror," but only through diplomacy and promotion of human rights can the final goal of a safer world be reached.

Throughout much of the post–World War II era, and especially since 9/11 and the war on terror, US foreign policy was fixated on refraining from direct interference with the way regional autocrats fashioned a *ruling bargain* with their own people. With demonstrations flaring around the region, we are beginning to understand the depth of the political and socioeconomic crises that have long been brewing beneath that formally placid surface. After uprisings in Tunisia, Egypt, and Libya come upheavals in Syria, Jordan, Bahrain, Morocco, Kuwait, Algeria, Iraq, Iran, the Palestinian Occupied Territories, and Yemen—and the distinct possibility of even more daunting challenges ahead. Of these, the three most interesting cases are the oil-rich nation of Libya, the tiny but rich kingdom of Bahrain, and the long-held authoritarian rule of the Assad family in Syria.

The Libyan Fallout

The uprisings in Libya were reactions to the uneven distribution of oil wealth and to repression in a police state, reflecting widespread frustration among Libyans who saw their immediate neighbors to the east (Egypt) and the west (Tunisia) achieve the freedoms they had long sought. With a population of just 6.4 million and a GNP per capita of $16,430, Libya is one of the region's wealthiest countries. The disparities of wealth in western Libya and Benghazi, however, have caused periodic revolts. Ultimately, the forty-one-year reign of Col. Muammar Qaddafi was overthrown by NATO forces amid burgeoning demands for the rule of law, basic rights, social justice, and a fairer distribution of wealth.

Not long ago, former president Clinton expressed deep regret to the people of Guatemala and El Salvador for the United States' support for right-wing military regimes during the Cold War. In 1999, the president was remarkably forthcoming: the United States must not repeat the mistake of backing repressive forces. Contrast that with the Obama administration's response to protests in Libya: the White House's initial silence was deafening. At least in the initial stages of the Libyan uprising, US foreign policy continued to be beleaguered by ambiguities and incoherent propositions. As we face a transformative moment in the lives of many people who have long endured tyrannical rule, there is a persistent need for new policies to take advantage of this unique opportunity to reconcile US strategic interests with democratic reforms. Certainly, government transparency and a more effective distribution of oil and aid money toward infrastructure and education are ideal places to start reform. Without such policies, the US government will be locked into supporting autocratic regimes, while disingenuously voicing support for the democratic aspirations of their people—a policy that has already continued for far too long.

If the United States wants to quell the threat of further unrest and instability in the region, now is the time to turn the page on the failed policies of the past. It is, however, too early to gauge the fallout from the collapse of the Qaddafi regime. Experts predict that two daunting challenges await post-Qaddafi Libya: (1) state building and (2) consensus building toward creating a unified civic identity. The leadership vacuum raises some concerns, as does the question of whether tribal or religious loyalties will be the primary political identity in the post-Qaddafi regime. Whether the National Transitional Council (NTC), which was under the control of semiautonomous militia commanders, can represent the collective will of Libyans during the interim process prior to establishing a new parliament and an elected government remains to be seen.[60] The NTC lacks a charismatic leader who can rise above the fray. While the NTC is likely to succeed in creating a new state, it will have trouble convincing all Libyans that this state represents a national consensus.[61] For this reason, although many MENA political leaders viewed the end of the Qaddafi era favorably, they had misgivings about outside intervention.

Some skeptics have pondered that Libya's future is presaged by the chaotic violence that engulfed Somalia after the toppling of the dictator Mohamed Siad Barre in 1991. The friction between the civilian and military arms of the revolution has been deepening since the initial stages of the February 2011 uprising. While the NTC has viewed the inclusion of defected old regime commanders and their forces as crucial for establishing a semblance of governance and smooth transition from revolution to reconstruction, the revolutionaries (*thuwaar*) and militia have come to see them as a fifth column riddled with Qaddafi loyalists whose aim is to deny them the ownership of the revolution for which they have risked their lives.[62]

Meanwhile, decrees such as the order to disband militias, which was to be implemented on April 2, 2012, remain largely ineffectual. In some places, such as Tripoli, where the government is intent on assuring its hold over the country's security, rogue militias continue to occupy key military installations in defiance of NTC demands that they leave.[63] Many reports indicate that the Libyan rebels have committed and continue to perpetrate flagrant human rights violations. The International Commission of Inquiry on Libya has, for example, reported that the Libyan rebels have committed "war crimes and breaches of international human rights law ... [such as] unlawful killing, arbitrary arrest, torture, enforced disappearance, indiscriminate attacks, and pillage."[64] Likewise, Amnesty International has confirmed that abuses of prisoners have taken place in a number of regions in Libya, many of whom have been reportedly tortured and killed at the hands of armed militia.[65]

Others, such as renowned international legal specialist Richard Falk, have observed that the fall of Qaddafi—unlike that of Hosni Mubarak, whose overthrow did not fundamentally change the power structure in Egypt—affords the victorious Libyan opposition a clean slate that may be more amicable to democratic nation-building. Libyans now enjoy a rare opportunity for genuine revolutionary transformation of their cultural, economic, and political life. Ironically, it could turn out to be helpful that Qaddafi left no institutional infrastructure behind.[66] Libya is not burdened by the institutional remnants of authoritarian bureaucracies such as Egypt's military.[67] But that also means that Libya must rebuild from scratch. This will prove challenging, especially when there is deep-seated bitterness amid victory. The challenges facing the country in the aftermath of the sordid killing of Qaddafi are numerous, of which the most critical ones include distributing the oil wealth justly, building a federal system that respects autonomous regions and smaller city-states, and curbing economic forces that may yet break Libya asunder.[68]

Though Iranian leaders, including President Mahmoud Ahmadine-jad, strongly denounced Qaddafi's crackdown against his own people, they were against NATO intervention there. Iranian ruling elites saw Qaddafi as a brutal ruler who played a double game with the West in recent years, dumping his nuclear program to shake off sanctions. Seen from alternative perspectives, Libya was either the latest dictatorship to fall to an "Islamic awakening" that would unite the Muslim Middle East against the Western colonialism, or it was a new foothold for the West to consolidate its economic and political domination over the region.[69]

The question some Iranians have raised is, would NATO have launched a campaign against Libya had Qaddafi possessed nuclear weapons? Less than a decade after ending his diplomatic isolation by abandoning efforts to acquire nuclear, chemical, and biological weapons, Qaddafi was attacked by NATO airpower. This scenario is not likely to convince Iranians to give up their nuclear program for future political gains. Some observers argue that while the former Yugoslavia, Iraq, and Libya were attacked, troublesome nuclear armed states such as North Korea and Pakistan have not been attacked since they have acquired the bomb. Qaddafi's forcible downfall, so it is assumed, will render acquiring nuclear weapons all the more justifiable to states that feel threatened by outsiders.[70]

With Qaddafi now gone, new groups, such as Berbers who are also known as Amazigh, are hoping for a better future with the right to express their heritage, culture, and identity. They also seek recognition of the sacrifices they made during Libya's bloody eight-month civil war. These rebel fighters, largely from the Nafusa Mountains southwest of Tripoli, consider themselves the original Libyans who have suffered decades of repression and discrimination at the hands of the Qaddafi regime. They make up only 5 to 10 percent of Libya's 6 million people. Amazigh predate the Arab settlers who brought Islam with them from east of the Mediterranean.[71] For these rebels the revolution will continue until their rights are constitutionally recognized. They fear marginalization as minority groups and are rightly concerned about whether the country's new leaders are serious about protecting their basic rights. A draft of the constitution prepared by the ruling NTC only mentioned Amazigh culture in broad terms, and when Libya's new interim prime minister, Abdurrahim al-Keib, appointed his cabinet in November 2011, none of his ministers were of Amazigh origin.[72]

As violence spread in the Arab world over a video on YouTube ridiculing the Prophet Muhammad on September 11, 2012, street protests in Benghazi led to the assault on the US diplomatic consulate there as well as the killing of US ambassador to Libya J. Christopher Stevens and three other Americans. Additional Libyan fallout with the embassy killings and their odd connection to media provocation have since gained much attention. Growing evidence points to the fact that Islamist militants armed with antiaircraft weapons and rocket-propelled grenades stormed a US diplomatic mission and that this was an organized—not spontaneous—assault. This evidence has raised questions about US foreign policy toward the region in the aftermath of the Arab Spring, as well as the way this incident will impact the upcoming elections in Libya. One key question, among others, is whether the United States should support Islamist groups in Libya during this transition period. Given that Islamists, as dominant political forces, are likely to play a dynamic role in the nation-building process in Libya, this question has invited an intense debate in Washington.

Bahrain's Lingering Tensions

Bahrain, a tiny island kingdom, is a new boiling pot where rhetoric and reality have clashed head-on. The revealing details regarding the pockets of poverty in Bahrain—a country of less than a million people, known for being the center of banking in the Persian Gulf region, and in fact one of the richest countries in terms of GDP per capita ($27,300, roughly on par with New Zealand)—should come as no surprise.[73] The Bahrain Centre for Human Rights (BCHR) has frequently reported that half of the Bahraini citizens are suffering from poverty and poor living conditions, with many being unemployed.[74] While some beneficiaries of social aid are unable to work, others are employed with meager incomes. This level of poverty, which is pervasive among the majority Shia population, has harbored deep socioeconomic and political resentment against the Sunni minority that rules with a tight grip.

Since 1783, Shiite Arabs in Bahrain have continuously lost their land and legal rights to Sunni Arabs. The Al-Khalifa family, which has ruled Bahrain for more than two hundred years, has conquered the islands and seems to have no sense of sharing identity with their local population. The Al-Khalifa family has averted public demands for a more participatory and accountable government since the 1950s. Promises for constitutional reforms since the 1970s have not been kept. Hamad ibn Isa Al Khalifa, the current ruler, also promised reforms when he came to power in 2002, but nothing came of it. Bahraini officials offer citizenship to anyone who is willing to serve in the army and police department, in an attempt to reduce the Shia demographic preponderance and to repress the majority Shia population.[75]

Standing between Bahrain and the rest of the Persian Gulf region, since 1995, has been the US Navy's Fifth Fleet at the naval base in Manama, the county's capital. Yet this security insurance has blinded the rulers to their responsibilities. Instead, they keep the wealth generated from common natural resources for a minority and leave the majority to suffer impoverished lives. The deployment of forces from Saudi Arabia and the United Arab Emirates to help secure the country for the Sunni ruling family will only further radicalize the more religious segments within the Shia majority. Absent local reforms, such tensions are certain to have broader regional implications, intensifying the existing Shia-Sunni divide. The United States and the United Kingdom have supported Bahrain's ruling family. The ruling family have allowed the United States to operate naval bases in Bahrain and assisted the United States in preserving the status quo.

Since the reverberations of Egypt and Tunisia reached Bahrain, pro-reform protests have been met with fierce and violent resistance in Pearl Square. The Bahraini regime's systematic and widespread crackdown on Shia communities has hardened the already institutionalized discrimination against the Shiite Muslim majority. Backed by the armed Saudi intervention, King Hamad bin Isa al-Khalifa declared martial law in March 2011. Al-Khalifa began a political process called the National Dialogue on July 2, 2011. It collapsed when Al Wifaq, Bahrain's largest legal opposition group, withdrew from the National Dialogue.[76] Ali Salman, the general secretary of Al Wifaq, notes that the situation is analogous to a tinderbox, ready to be ignited at any moment: "If we cannot succeed in bringing democracy to this country, then our country is headed toward violence. Is it a year or two years? I don't know. But that's the reality."[77]

It is worth pointing out another harsh reality: that Bahrain "stands as a singular example of the way venerable distinctions of ethnicity, sect and history can be manipulated in the Arab world, often cynically, in the pursuit of power."[78] Resentment has been increasingly brewing among Bahraini Shiites who see NATO's involvement in Libya and the US-directed sanctions against Syria as yet another double standard. No US official has called for sanctions against Bahrain, where the United States has its largest regional Fifth Fleet naval base.

The uprisings in the MENA region have been a setback for Iran's model for change and governance. One expert reminds us, however, that "Iran will be a beneficiary if reforms falter, particularly in Bahrain and Yemen."[79] That said, some experts note that the idea of Iranian involvement in Bahrain's uprisings has been exaggerated. Bahrainis are not taking their cues from Tehran; rather, their unrest indicates their own pent-up anger and frustration. The mainstream opposition party, Al Wifaq, looks to Arab religious leaders known as *marjas* rather than Iranian ones. This is evident in the Bahrainis' slogan "This nation is not for sale. Brothers, Sunni and Shia."[80]

The current rising public frustrations, as manifested by new waves of unrest and protests, are fueled largely by young Shia groups. Crying out for dignity and a decent life, these protests are rarely, if ever, motivated by sectarian and religious factors, although the escalation of the security crisis in Bahrain could potentially transform the nature of the protests into religiously motivated hostilities. A government-commissioned Bahrain Independent Commission of Inquiry, led by the well-respected Egyptian human rights lawyer M. Cherif Bassiouni, estimated that there are 400 political prisoners in jail.[81]

Others estimate that around 600 are detained there for political reasons.[82] On average, around fifteen villages are tear-gassed nightly. The Arabic language Al-Alam news channel has shown evidence of poisonous tear gas grenades being used. According to the BCHR, twenty people have died from tear gas inhalation since November 2011, many of them children or elderly people.[83] Twenty doctors have been imprisoned for treating prisoners during the pro-democracy unrest; ten of them have been given fifteen-year terms, two were sentenced to ten years in prison, and the rest to five.[84] The United Nations condemned these prison sentences that were issued by a Bahrain military court. Despite these persistent abuses and the widely recognized hunger strike of prominent human rights activist Abdulahi al-Khawaja, the planned April 20–22, 2012, Grand Prix event known as the supercharged Formula One (F1) car-racing circuit went off without incident.[85]

Syria: Where Is the Revolt Headed?

Genocidal state conduct under Syria's Bashar al-Assad has long called for international action to protect Syrian citizens caught in the middle of violent uprisings. Yet, for a variety of geopolitical reasons, not the least of which is the fact that military intervention in Syria will be unpredictable and complicated, the case for such action is unappealing. A combination of internal and external factors accounts for a lack of geopolitical consensus favoring military intervention. Internally, the disjointed Syrian opposition movement is hampered by a lack of organization and effectiveness, largely because rebel groups feature different factions with diverse agendas and loose organizational affiliations. Unlike Tunisia and Egypt, where labor movements and trade organizations played an important role in toppling the regimes in power, there exist no such trade unions independent of Syria's official trade union federation.[86]

Many experts argue that a military intervention is bound to make things worse for Syrian civilians, while also plunging Syria and its neighboring countries into a sectarian conflagration and simultaneously forcing the West and the region into a protracted civil war with no visible endgame in sight. Thus, no international actor is willing to encounter the risk of an unstable or fragmented Syria such as might follow the collapse of the regime. The fear of sectarian and ethnic tensions spilling over into neighboring countries, as well as a takeover by the Syrian Muslim Brotherhood, pits geopolitical realities against the ethical call for military intervention.[87] This dilemma is best captured by Richard Falk: "Just as doing nothing is unacceptable, mounting a military intervention is unrealistic, and hence, impossible."[88]

Under such circumstances, as Falk argues, determining what is the proper course of action appears to be far from evident. "The clarity of condemnation," Falk insists, "should not be confused with devising a prescription for action."[89] To begin with, military intervention does more harm than good, prompting more questions than providing answers. Falk emphatically rejects such acts, arguing that "military intervention rarely succeeds, violates the right of self-determination, and often expands the scope and severity of violence, especially if carried out from the air."[90]

Who Are the Opposition?

Myriad questions still surround the Syrian opposition. Who are they? Are they organized or disjointed? Are they affiliated with radical Islamist groups such as al-Qaeda? Can they be trusted? Absent clarity about the identity of rebel groups, there is no international consensus on how to work with the opposition and how to mobilize and legitimize a military intervention. It is widely agreed that the opposition to Assad's regime continues to suffer from two major weaknesses: its diversity and loose structure.[91] These problems have raised some doubts among Western supporters concerning the efficacy of the military intervention. The Syrian National Council, for example, which represents a key opposition group, is utterly fragmented. It is neither broad-based nor organized. Whereas in Egypt and Libya all the major and regional powers supported, either explicitly or tacitly, intervention, in the case of Syria there is no such consensus.

The fact remains that we know little about the opposition in Syria and to what extent its governance of the country would be based on the rule of law and respect for human rights. There are increasing reports about rebel atrocities as well as the role al-Qaeda operatives play in leading some of the rebel forces.[92] Much of the confusion surrounds US foreign policy and regional actors' role in supporting rebel groups with arms supplies. Considerable doubt has been raised about whether the White House's strategy of minimal and indirect intervention in the Syrian conflict is aiding a democratic-minded opposition or whether the opposition groups on the receiving end of the lethal aid are Islamic extremists. This confusion is reinforced by mounting frustration over the fact that "there is no central clearinghouse for the shipments, and no effective way of vetting the groups that ultimately receive them."[93]

The reports that Arab countries of the Persian Gulf, such as Qatar and Saudi Arabia, provide money and weapons to the anti-Assad uprising have raised serious questions about their endgame. Most of the arms shipped at the behest of Saudi Arabia and Qatar to supply Syrian rebels are going to hard-line Islamic jihadists, and not to the more secular opposition groups that the West wants to bolster. Thus far, the various rebel groups have failed to assemble a clear military plan, have lacked a coherent strategy for governing Syria afterward if the Assad government falls, and have quarreled too often among themselves, undermining their military and political effectiveness.[94] Meanwhile, international law experts have reminded us of the other side of these concerns: "Every government has the right to fight against its internal enemies, especially if heavily assisted by hostile external forces, although that right must be exercised within the framework of constraints imposed by international humanitarian law."[95]

Whether uprisings in Syria will morph into a revolutionary change remains the subject of much speculation. Whereas the Assad regime seeks gradual and negotiated reforms, the protesters are interested in regime change. In the meantime, there is a growing power vacuum in the embattled streets as the sorely divided exiled opposition fails to connect with the domestic protest movement.[96] Short of fueling what has the potential to become a full-blown civil war, economic sanctions seem to be a credible option to undermine the Assad regime. The hope is that economic hardship may eventually turn more of the Syrian people, including soldiers, against al-Assad.[97] Other diplomatic tools have failed to produce results. In December 2001, Syria agreed to allow 165 observers from the Arab League to monitor a deal, including ending the violence, releasing prisoners, and pulling the military out of the cities. That deal, however, failed to achieve a diplomatic solution when further violence erupted and many protesters were killed.

The Syrian government and United Nations officials have struck several deals covering how observers would operate and the responsibilities of the Syrian government. Yet the cease-fire has been repeatedly marred by lingering violence. Whether Syria's government will implement the UN-brokered peace agreements remains to be seen. UN reports indicate that more than 10,000 people have been killed in Assad's crackdown on protests in the year following March 2011. Syrian officials have said that foreign-backed "terrorists" have killed 2,000 soldiers and police.[98]

Syria's Regional and International Allies

Iran and Russia have developed strong ties to the Assad regime. Any military intervention could turn the situation into a proxy war and subsequently a protracted civil war with huge civilian casualties, reminiscent of a decades-long civil war in Lebanon (1975–1991) that resulted in more than 150,000 deaths and a million displaced people.[99] Arming the Free Syrian Army or declaring safe zones, Marc Lynch notes, will simply increase the duration of civil war in a country where the well-armed and fairly united Syrian military has a decisive edge. Such moves, Lynch continues, are likely to cause frightened Syrians to embrace, however grudgingly, the regime.[100]

Since the 1979 Islamic Revolution, but more specifically during the Iran-Iraq war (1980–1988), Iran and Syria have forged a new alliance that has been—and continues to be—based on geostrategic considerations rather than religion. Syria was the only Arab country that sided with Iran during that war. Iran, in turn, became a reliable supplier of energy to Syria, while the Arab countries of the Persian Gulf offered various economic inducements to Syria to bring it back into the fold. For Iran, the Syrian connection bolsters its regional status and power. Likewise, the current alliance with Iran puts Syria in a position to enhance the "price it can demand from the West in exchange for making peace with Israel or ensuring quiet in Lebanon."[101] This alliance with Iran has subsequently become known as the "axis of resistance," along with Hezbollah and Hamas, since the 1980s. The US invasion of Iraq in March 2003 reinvigorated that alliance.

Since the March 2011 uprisings in Syria, however, maintaining this alliance has become costly for Iran as it has led to its further isolation while jeopardizing its most important Arab ally. Some experts argue that the Iranian policymakers would prefer that Assad remain in power, but for long-term geopolitical considerations, they will settle for preserving Syria's governing elite and security structure should Assad fall. "Any change in Syria's governing elite," they point out, "increases the likelihood that Damascus will adopt regional policies more in line with those of its Arab brethren, such as support for Sunni political forces in Iraq. It could also lead to Syria becoming a full-fledged Saudi client."[102] Others, however, argue that even if a new government replaces the old regime in Syria and finds it politically and economically advantageous to sustain this alliance, it would be difficult for that government to maintain special relations with Iran as it did in the past.[103]

Iranians have insisted that the Syrian opposition is by no means a popular force, as the Sunni majority fears the Salafi minority. Iranians have criticized Kofi Annan's plan: "It never clarified in what way the crisis in Syria is supposed to hit its end. It was also silent on the future power structure in the country and specifications of the transition period." Iranian officials have noted that the United States and other regional players are bent on turning the Arab Spring into a conflict between Shias and Sunnis. To Iranians, the Syrian government and army have a firm grip over the country. It is highly unlikely, Iranians note, that Russia and China will reach an agreement with the West over Syria. Iranians see forging a reliable anti-West front consisting of Russia and China as a strategic goal.[104] In recent months, however, Iran's new position has shifted to "neutrality," partly because Iran fears alienation from the Sunni majority in the region, given that Hamas has broken away from Damascus.

Russia and China, albeit for different reasons, have on several occasions blocked Western-backed UN Security Council resolutions on Syria that aimed at placing more pressure on Syrian president Bashar al-Assad to step down. China's relations with the Middle East are undergoing a major shift, in large part due to the "Energy First" policy. China's diplomacy is transforming from "responsive diplomacy" (*fanying shi wwaijiao*) to "proactive diplomacy" (*zhudong shi waijiao*). Chinese officials seem to pursue three objectives: First, China as a net importer of oil has to secure strong, stable ties with oil-exporting countries. Secondly, China has problems in Xinjiang, where the local population is of Turkic origin and of Muslim religion, and thus has to make sure that Islamic countries of the Middle East do not become safe havens for anti-Chinese groups operating in the region. Finally, as Washington plays the Taiwan card to put pressure on Beijing, in return Beijing could be playing the Syrian card to secure concessions from Washington.[105]

Adopting a position of neutrality, Chinese foreign minister Yang Jiechi has said that China favors a period of political transition in Syria, while expressing Beijing's opposition to forceful military intervention. Jiechi's remarks strike a cautionary note: "Any solution should come from the people of Syria and reflect their wishes. It should not be imposed from outside."[106] Like Russia, China is wary of calls for change escalating into foreign intervention. In 2011, China joined Russia in approving a UN Security Council resolution on intervening in Libya to prevent further bloodshed and attacks on civilians, but later suggested NATO powers had exceeded the UN mandate by expanding a bombing campaign that proved decisive in toppling Muammar Qaddafi.[107]

Russia's interests in Syria, by contrast, are deeply commercial and strategic. Russia's naval facility at the Syrian port of Tartus, which is Russia's sole remaining naval base on the Mediterranean, is of enormous military-strategic significance. Its loss would mean negative consequences, including the actual loss of political influence in the region. Commercially speaking, present and future contracts to sell arms to Damascus, one expert notes, amount to a total of $5 billion. Having lost $13 billion due to international sanctions on Iran and $4.5 billion in canceled contracts to Libya, Russia's defense industry is facing financial difficulties. In addition to arms exports, Russian companies have major investments in Syria's infrastructure, energy, and tourism sectors, worth $19.4 billion in 2009.[108]

From a strategic standpoint, other experts remind us that the real reason why Russia resists strong international action against the Assad regime is that it fears the spread of Islamic militancy and the diminution of its great-power status in a world where Western nations are increasingly undertaking unilateral military interventions. Many Russian observers believe that the 2011 Arab uprisings have completely destabilized the region, paving the way for the Islamists' ascendancy to power. The Kremlin sees regime change as the recipe for radicalizing global Islam, and as a policy that does not necessarily bring about peace, as evidenced by the cases of Iraq and Libya. Attempts to overthrow the Assad regime by supporting the opposition will prove counterproductive, for such policies will most likely turn the Syrian crisis into a proxy war of leading powers.[109] In Moscow, according to most observers, secular authoritarian governments, such as Syria, are viewed as the sole realistic alternative to Islamic dominance.[110] The active support from Saudi Arabia, Qatar, and Turkey's Islamist government for rebels in Syria, they conclude, further heightens Russia's suspicions concerning the Islamist-led revolutions in Syria and, for that matter, in other uprisings throughout the Middle East.[111]

The Obama Administration

The bloody uprising in Syria has thrust the Obama administration into an increasingly tough and complicated position as the conflict shows signs of evolving into a full-fledged civil war. Former US secretary of state Hillary Clinton frequently accused Russia of sending attack helicopters to Syria to defeat anti-Assad rebels. Meanwhile, opposition forces have received more powerful anti-tank missiles from Turkey, with the financial support of Saudi Arabia and Qatar. Despite the fact that the fears of Arab Spring contagion have given Saudi-led counterrevolution and regional diplomacy an added urgency to contain protests close to its shores in Bahrain, the Saudis have relentlessly supported rebels and their armed struggle against Bashar's regime in Syria.[112] Many observers have noted that the shipment of these heavier weapons to both sides of this conflict would likely plunge Syria into a bloody civil war.[113]

Given the unintended consequences of the military intervention in Syria, Turkey and the United States face a multitude of challenges. Turkey's leaders have in recent years shown that they are keen on playing a much more constructive role in the region's stability. They have shown themselves to be unlikely proponents of military engagement if it means Turkey has to provide the bulk of military operations. If NATO commanders, however, seek a military solution based largely on the compelling evidence that the Assad regime has used chemical weapons against the rebels, Turkey has little choice but to play an active role in the implementation of this plan. This will prove to be a drastic departure from Turkey's often-stated preference to exert its soft power to induce incremental and peaceful change.

This perspective, however, does not entirely gloss over the fact that external intervention and support for rebels—both inside and outside the country—have raised fears that the unrest in Syria will most likely broaden into a regional war. Thus far, the United States has pledged $60 million in nonlethal aid for the opposition, as well as $385 million in humanitarian aid. Nonlethal aid alone, however, will not cause a drastic change in the opposition's favor, but the United States appears hesitant to provide rebels with weapons or to intervene militarily. This hesitancy stems from the fact that there is no way to ensure that weapons stay out of the hands of anti-US militant Islamists fighting alongside the opposition, nor that the intensely sectarian conflict would not be followed by an even more violent, chaotic period.[114] Ultimately, seeking a solution to the crisis in Syria requires Iran's active participation in any conceivable regional agreement. Iran's regional policies still matter—possibly more so than in the past—insofar as they support the regional consensus with Egypt and Turkey that NATO-initiated international military intervention must be avoided.

Future Scenarios: No Good Options

There can be no doubt that the potential collapse of the Assad regime will have profound implications for the regional as well as transregional balance of power. This will be the detriment of Iran's position, leaving it virtually alone among an array of bitter rivals, such as Saudi Arabia and Israel, not to mention competitors such as Turkey and Egypt. Iranians fear that any major change in Syria will likely undermine Iran's connections with its "resistance proxies" such as Hezbollah in Lebanon and Hamas in Palestine.[115] In the meantime, the fear of a Sunni Islamist takeover after the collapse of Assad's regime in Syria looms large. A military attack on Syria by NATO—à la military intervention in Libya—is risky if not unlikely.

Several possible scenarios, according to the region's experts, can be visualized. One scenario is that leftist and secular groups spearhead a revolutionary mass movement. The other is that Islamist groups may take over the movement. This possibility could divert the movement toward a religious civil war. Shortly after the revolt broke out, a small group of Syrian people began chanting, "The Alawites to their grave, the Christians to Beirut."[116] Yet another scenario might be a military coup replacing the present political leadership with one that would be unburdened by an alliance with Iran and Hezbollah.[117]

This last scenario continues to preoccupy Tehran as the Islamic Republic sees its influence decline in such circumstances. Although the future is uncertain, one thing is clear: the Islamic Republic runs the risk of a popular backlash in Syria and in the Arab world if President Assad continues his heavy-handed suppression of protesters. Indeed, shortly after the initial round of violence, an unconfirmed video of the Syrian protests posted on the Internet showed Syrian protesters chanting, "la Hezbollah, la Iran," meaning "no Hezbollah, no Iran."[118] Will the Syrian protesters be able to force President Assad to relinquish some or all of his power? Will the Islamic Republic's position in Syria be undermined by the ensuing power vacuum?

These questions are being answered by continued violence, despite a UN-brokered cease-fire on April 12, 2012, led by Kofi Annan along with the UN Security Council peace plan. This included the full contingent of a mere 300 inspectors that were deployed by the end of April 2012, and practically failed to produce results.[119] On June 27, 2012, Annan announced the creation of an "action group," composed of the UN Security Council's five permanent members, representatives of the

European Union, the Arab League, Qatar, Kuwait, Turkey, and Iraq, as well as Ban ki-moon, the UN secretary-general. Conspicuously absent from the list of the nations invited were Iran, the staunch regional ally of President Bashar al-Assad of Syria, and Saudi Arabia, a prominent supporter of Assad's opponents. The aim of this group is to "identify the steps and measures to secure full implementation of Annan's six-point plan" and to bring "an immediate cessation of violence in all forms."[120]

Many observers, including Annan, have warned that the turmoil, which began as a peaceful Arab Spring opposition movement against President Assad in March 2011, could potentially plunge Syria and its neighboring countries into a sectarian conflagration. The outcome of this new initiative will depend on, among other things, whether the United States and Russia can bridge their differences over Syria. While the United States has insisted that President Assad step down, Russia, the main military supplier to Assad's government, has disapproved of any solution in which political change in Syria is imposed by outside powers.[121] Some experts argue that, despite the fact that a decision to intervene in Syria is complex and daunting, the escalating atrocities, the continued stalemate, and the remote likelihood for a negotiated settlement in the current state of conflict, as well as the strategic benefits provide sufficient grounds for the United States and its allies to act.[122] Yet other observers, while warning against foreign military intervention in Syria, note that Syrians themselves will have to win this struggle. The international community is unlikely to act as it did in the case of Libya. Military intervention is too tough in Syria. Moreover, the political will in the West to do so is noticeably lacking, at least for now.[123]

Turkey and the New Middle East

In the midst of the new regional developments and challenges facing US conventional foreign policy in the MENA region, the NATO ally and EU candidate, Turkey, has emerged as the new regional power determined to position herself firmly on the side of change in the Arab revolts. Rachid Ghannouchi, the leader of the al-Nahda Party in Tunisia, an Islamic reformist party, has openly said that his movement, "admire[d] the Turkish case."[124] Likewise, Ashraf Abdel Ghaffar, a leader of the Muslim Brotherhood of Egypt, has said that his organization viewed "the AKP [as] a model for Egypt after Mubarak."[125]

Even if the Muslim Brotherhood plays a significant role in Egypt's political life, it is safe to say that the new government might eventually end up following the Turkish model: blending a secular constitution with a pronounced sociopolitical Islamic identity. In terms of foreign policy, Turkey has pursued new relationships with its immediate neighbors based on a regional détente and tension-free relations. The new governments of North Africa may very well follow that path. If they do, Iran's regional policies would still matter more so than in the past. One interesting issue to follow is the Iran-Turkey relationship. To what extent will it continue to bear diplomatic and economic fruit? Will the two countries continue to build their ties, or alternatively engage in competition for influence in the reshaped region (as Iran and Saudi Arabia are most likely to do)? One observer notes that in much of the Arab world where the United States appears in retreat, Europe seems ineffectual, and countries like Israel and Iran are unsettled and unsure owing to their internal developments, Turkish officials have a vision for what may emerge from the uprisings and turmoil. For a region long ruled by seemingly impotent leaders submissive to American and Israeli demands, Turkey's prime minister Recep Tayyip Erdoğan comes across as independent and forceful.[126]

In recent months, Turkey and the United States have adopted a similar position vis-à-vis Syria, condemning Bashar al-Assad and the spread of violence there. This is partly due to the fact that the Turkish government intends to establish itself as a regional power, and partly because of the brutal way Assad has stifled the unrest in his country. Since 9/11 and the US problems in Afghanistan and Iraq, and with the improved position of Iran in the region, the United States has come to view Turkey and its Islamist-rooted party (the Justice and Development Party—AKP) as a counterbalance to Iran, Lebanese Hezbollah, Hamas in Gaza (now a Turkish ally), Saudi-supported Salafists, and al-Qaeda and Islamic Jihad. Both the United States and the Arab countries of the Persian Gulf and the rest of the Middle East recognize and welcome Turkey's role as counterbalance to Iran.[127]

In June 2011, the AKP won reelection by a landslide, giving Erdoğan a third term. AKP has presided over stellar economic growth (8.9 percent in 2010—the second-fastest growth rate in the Group of 20) and has weakened the hold of the military, which had ousted four governments in the forty years prior to the AKP's rise to power in 2002.[128] As Turkey's Islamist-rooted party has increased its influence, Prime Minister Erdoğan has taken a tougher stance against Israel, which he accuses of oppressing the Palestinian people and disregarding international law. The Turkish-Israeli rift can be traced back to January 2009, when Turkish premier Erdoğan publicly criticized Israeli president Shimon Peres for the Gaza war against Hamas. Subsequently, an Israeli raid on a Gaza-bound aid flotilla in May 2010 killed eight Turks and one Turkish-American. In September 2011, a UN report called on Israel to apologize to Turkey for the deaths of flotilla activists. Israel refused and Turkey cut diplomatic ties with Israel.[129]

Although Turkish-Israeli relations have progressively deteriorated, they have had no bearing on Turkish relations with the West.[130] For the most part, Turkey's strategic importance to the West has remained intact, placing the Turkish government in a desirable bargaining position. With the second-largest military in NATO, Turkey has agreed to the deployment of a radar station crucial to NATO's planned missile defense system—known as a missile shield—on its soil.[131] Some Iranian commentators see this development as Washington's new strategy to strain Tehran-Ankara relations. They argue that since Turkey's negative vote on international sanctions against Iran, Washington has attempted to undermine the deepening of relations between Iran and Turkey.[132]

Other Iranian analysts have downplayed the significance of the NATO missile shield in Turkey, arguing that strong economic relations and cultural commonalities between the two countries will prevent this problem from causing friction in Iranian-Turkish relations in years to come.[133] From the viewpoint of Western analysts, especially those who see Turkey as being a counterforce to Iran and its regional aspirations, Turkey has maintained a balancing relationship with Iran, on the one hand trying to protect it from tougher Western sanctions, but simultaneously allowing installation in its territory of a NATO missile shield clearly directed at Iran.[134]

For its part, Turkey as a "balancing power" and an ally of the West can also serve as a model for Islamic and secular governance in the region. Some analysts see the goal of this balancing act as one that is aimed at breaking the Iran-Syria alliance. They argue that if Turkey succeeds in promoting change in Syria, it would then play a decisive role in the Arab-Israeli peace process and in the entire Islamic world.[135] Turkey, they point out, "has utterly eclipsed Iran as the leader of the Arab street."[136] Others assert that the old Israeli model—cutting deals with the region's kings and autocrats, while getting Washington to lean on Turkey's generals—will no longer bear fruit.

Yet at the same time, as many analysts point out, Turkey is rapidly discovering the limits of its regional influence and "zero-problem policy" while supporting the Syrian opposition inside Turkey. By the fall of 2011, as experts remind us, Turkey's decision makers decided that it was not prudent to pursue the "zero-problem strategy" with illiberal neighbors such as Syria. This drastic policy shift "marked the beginning of the reassertion of democracy promotion at the expense of the zero problems doctrine."[137] The crisis of refugees from Syria has also pushed Turkey toward seriously contemplating a buffer zone at the border—a zone that may turn into a safe haven for the Syrian opposition.[138] Since Erdoğan's call for Assad to step down, Turkey has hosted the Syrian opposition and the Free Syrian Army (FSA), while calling for an end to regime violence. Turkey's role in the "Friends of Syria" group, a group of fourteen countries that includes France, the United States, Saudi Arabia, and Qatar, is very telling.

Yet Turkey is reluctant to endorse military intervention for fear of getting entangled in a sectarian civil war, which would become a war of regionally sponsored proxy armies. Such a scenario could easily implicate sectarian and ethnic groups from Lebanon to Iraq.[139] Whether Turkey can manage to pursue its zero-problem policy toward its neighbors while at the same time maintaining its strategic ties with the Western world remains to be seen. For the time being, pursuing this multipronged policy appears to be a daunting task fraught with uncertainties and tough choices. Finding an effective way to deal with the complexities of Syria's political developments poses the most difficult challenge for Turkey since the beginning of the 2011 Arab uprisings.[140]

In sum, there is a consensus among experts of the region that as the views on the Arab public begin to shape their governments' foreign policies more and more, the space available for US policies and influence is likely to contract.[141] US policies toward Iran will be particularly affected by this reality. Though the future balance of power in the MENA region remains uncertain, one thing is evident: to take full advantage of the region's geopolitical transformation, the Iranian ruling elite might see the need to make domestic and foreign policy adjustments. Thus far they have chosen to treat their local but "loyal" opposition (the Green Movement) with repressive measures. This political opportunity will be recklessly squandered if Iran's leaders defend democracy and civil liberties for "others" while denying their local opposition the very same freedoms that their Arab counterparts have so painstakingly won—and this is exactly what they have done so far.

The dynamics of peaceful democratic changes in Tunisia and Egypt, as well as violent rebellion—backed by NATO forces—in Libya, have given Turkey the upper hand in establishing itself as a regional power. A combination of youth, technology, and a push for human rights in the 2011 uprisings in the MENA region, à la Iran's Green Movement, has put the Islamic Republic of Iran and its ruling elites on the defensive. Viable political opposition is no longer the preserve of Islamic groups. On the contrary, the success of protesters in discarding despotic rulers highlights the very fact that there is an activism and a democratic ideology aimed at peaceful democratic change that is an alternative to radical Islamism.[142] Although it is still too early to say for certain what the fallout from these uprisings will be for Iran in the coming years, it seems clear that the region's model of authoritarian regimes with narrow social bases has become unsustainable.

The Rise of Islamists: What That Means for US Foreign Policy

The 9/11 terrorist attacks on the United States served only to sharpen the differences between reform-oriented Islamists and extremists, which has given rise to the emergence of a new brand of Islamist political actors (the so-called neo-Islamists) who have rejected violence as a means of opposing dictatorial regimes and the West while encouraging their members to participate in electoral processes. Egyptian Islamist leaders, however belatedly, condemned such acts. Khairat el-Shater, deputy president of the Muslim Brotherhood in Egypt, in a letter to the editor of the *New York Times*, condemned the breach of the US embassy premises by Egyptians, calling these attacks "illegal under international law" while noting that "The failure of the protecting police force has to be investigated."[143] Shater expressed the hope that the relationship between the United States and the new Egypt in the post-Mubarak era can survive the tragic events, admitting the fragility of new democracies during difficult transition.[144]

In Tunis, where the US Embassy was assaulted on September 14, 2012, by protesters, the reformist Islamist party that governs the country, al-Nahda, condemned these attacks and violence more generally. The party warned that such violence, which left at least three dead and twenty-eight injured, undermines the country's progress toward democracy after decades of authoritarian rule in that country. In an e-mailed statement that condemned both the film that incited the protests and the ensuing violence in Tunis, the youth wing of al-Nahda noted, "We call on the youth and on all Tunisians to maintain vigilance and unity in order to prevent all attempts at sowing divisions and halting the revolution."[145]

There can be no doubt that extremists seek to exploit the pervasive anger and resentment caused by this video for political reasons, trying to disrupt the democratic agenda and hijack elections won by reform-minded Islamists in the aftermath of the Arab Spring. As the fledgling democracies of the MENA region struggle to cope with the uncertainties unleashed by the Arab Spring, such outrages are likely to erupt and drag the region into similar violent situations from time to time.[146] Even though it is the case that extremists appear bent on achieving by violence what they could not have gained via ballot box, it is equally true that the outpouring of outrage against the video had built up over a longer period of perceived denigrations of Muslims and their faith by the United States and its interventionist policies in the region, which are detailed extensively in the Arab news media: the invasion of Iraq on a specious excuse; the reprehensible images of abuse from the Abu Ghraib prison; the burning or desecrations of the Qur'an by US troops in Afghanistan and a pastor in Florida; detentions without trial at Guantánamo Bay in the name of war on terror; the denials of visas to well-known Muslim intellectuals; the death of Muslim civilians as "collateral damage" in drone strikes in Afghanistan and Pakistan; and also political campaigns against the prospect for the application of Islamic law inside the United States.[147]

Increasingly, however, reform-minded Islamists and Muslim intellectuals argue that the "Islamist radical reading of Islam does not reflect the totality of the religion."[148] These Islamists call into question the appeal of violence, arguing that the militants have failed to provide constructive solutions and strategies. The extremist strategy has backfired, and Islamic militancy in all its forms and variations has proved "costly, unproductive, and ultimately unappealing."[149] Contrary to popular belief, the Muslim Brotherhood is not really new, although their ability to act within the Egyptian political sphere certainly is. Though the Brothers and their parties have successfully maintained a moderate base of support, their access to mechanisms of democratic political redress has occurred fairly recently. Since the 1980s, the Brotherhood has—whenever legally permitted—consistently participated in legislative and city council elections despite tremendous government repression. While keen on participating in democratic processes, as Samer Shehata reminds us, the Brothers are not liberal democrats, as some of their views on women's rights, individual freedoms, and minority rights reflect the limits of their liberalism.[150]

A decade later, peaceful, democratic uprisings in the Arab world have given the reformist Islamists the upper hand by dramatically changing the momentum in their favor. Since the Arab revolts of 2011, Islamist parties have won elections in Tunisia, Egypt, Morocco, and Kuwait and may soon emerge as dominant political agents in other countries affected by the popular uprisings in the Arab world, such as Libya, Yemen, and Syria.[151] In the case of Syria, Islamist and other national parties differ over the future form of the government (an Islamic or secular state) and the Islamization of laws. Moreover, while some parties favor the creation of a no-fly zone, enforced by NATO or Western air forces, others strongly resist foreign military intervention in order to maintain Syria's sovereignty.[152]

The decisive victory by the Muslim Brotherhood's FJP in the 2012 parliamentary elections in Egypt and the election of Morsi, affiliated with FJP, as the first civilian president of Egypt, as well as the election of the al-Nahda Party in Tunisia in October 2011, all seem to confirm an Islamic trend. These Islamists, who tend to blend religious and cultural authenticity with pragmatic political strategies, are bent on transforming politics by writing new constitutions and determining what kind of executive power—presidential or parliamentary systems—should govern their countries. It is worth noting that even reformist groups such as the Tunisian al-Nahda Party tend to offer reform in a conservative package. Absent institutions that guarantee protections, as one expert argues, creeping social conservatism and political competition could push the leaders of the al-Nahda Party to the right—that is to abuses of minority rights of the women, Jews, Christians, and others that can be eventually justified not on Islamic grounds but according to the majority rule.[153]

In order to understand the rise of Islamists after the Arab Spring, one must understand the nature of adaptability in Islamist parties, the wider reach of their welfare programs, and the political pragmatism of their agenda. The Islamists' adaptive approach—that is, coming to terms with the political process as the means to end conflict and move into dialogue with other groups in order to forge a centrist alliance—can be seen in the Muslim Brotherhood's evolutionary change from pan-Arabism, to violent confrontation with the regimes in power, to eventually providing their social welfare and aid programs.[154] This is particularly true of the Muslim Brotherhood in Egypt, whose leaders have argued that "Egypt's long-term political future would not be decided on the battlefields of the insurrection, but by the newly-elected constitutional bodies."[155] In Tunisia, coalition-building with liberals and secular forces has led to less ideologically charged democratization. Al-Nahda president, Rachid Ghannouchi, has laid to rest the fears of investors by endorsing the "free market."[156]

For decades, authoritarian regimes and secular modernizers across the Arab world have offered their people one stark choice: "It is either us or chaos." Following the removal or expulsion of the dictators from power, Islamists have entered the political fray amid myriad uncertainties. Voters wonder how these new leaders will deal with women's rights and free speech, and the extent to which Islamic law (Shari'a) will inform social affairs and lawmaking. In Egypt, for instance, the leaders of the FJP have frequently denied taking drastic actions, such as banning alcohol or bikinis, which—while against their moral/ethical code—could drastically undermine Egyptian tourism. With Egypt mired in economic struggles, the new Islamists appear more motivated by an ethos centered on problem-solving and stability rather than pushing a traditionally conservative ideology.[157] Increasingly, for the pragmatic Islamists at the helm, adopting radical or orthodox Islamic policies in the future would result in a significant drop in income from both tourism and much-needed foreign direct investment (FDI).[158] Moreover, the fear of an Islamization of the political and societal realms in Egypt is likely to alienate women, many of whom are wary of their civil rights and gender equality, and the Christian minority of Copts, whose foremost concern is religious equality.

The Obama administration appears to be acutely aware of the fact that persistently high unemployment, especially among women and young people, could weaken Morsi's government and cause further instability in Egypt and beyond. Because of the centrality of Egypt in the Arab world, stability or instability there is likely to spread throughout the region. This accounts for a shift in US policy from economic assistance to the promotion of growth and business. In addition to the debt assistance, the US support for a $4.8 billion loan, which is being negotiated between Egypt and the IMF, as well as $375 million in financing and loan guarantees for American financiers who invest in Egypt and a $60 million investment fund for Egyptian businesses all seem intended to bolster Egypt's transition to democracy.[159]

In the wake of an emerging new Arab order, US foreign policy toward the MENA region faces many challenges. These challenges entail a unique opportunity that turns on a drastic shift in US foreign policy toward consistent and meaningful engagement with Islamists. This is a difficult task in light of the fact that most Islamists—regardless of their ideological strands and willingness to have diplomatic ties with the United States—want to diminish US influence in their countries.[160] Given the United States' continuing unpopularity among Arab countries and given that political activists and politicians seem to display serious disagreements with the US policies in the region it is important that US foreign policymakers adopt a different approach toward the region. Most crucially, because current trends indicate that Islamists will play a bigger role after the fall of the autocrats—largely through the ballot box—it is critical that US foreign policymakers seek a political dialogue with Islamists, one that is designed to strengthen pragmatic elements and policies of Islamist groups.

One way to do so is to nudge Islamists toward integrating Islam as both a political and ecumenical body into the new democratic systems. The Islamist agenda and practices can be similarly used as a force to promote regional identity and harmony. For example, Turkey's prime minister Erdoğan has taken a position on religion that seems to bear out this method of dual track inclusion: "The Turkish state in its core is a state of freedoms and secularism." This view in the midst of the Arab Spring is immensely reassuring, even as the Western world's fear of unintended consequences flowing from these uprisings in terms of the region may not be entirely baseless. Regardless, Erdoğan's message illustrates the positive role that Islamists can and should play in absorbing the dynamics of change in international relations.

The Islamists' disenchantment with the policies of Western powers toward the Palestinian issue merits particular attention. Despite the fact that Arab people have been preoccupied with their domestic agendas and problems, as one observer indicates, the issue of how the West—and particularly the United States—deals with the Palestinian problem will remain a major concern. The West's continued lackluster support for the rights of Palestinians to statehood, independence, and self-determination will further widen the gap of representation and any notion of freedom within the reconfigured Arab world.[161]

US policymakers must also reconsider their old policy of prohibiting diplomatic contacts with Hamas in Palestine and Hezbollah in Lebanon, both of whom are included on the US State Department list of foreign terrorist organizations. In Afghanistan, the United States has periodically shown a willingness to engage with even violent and ultraconservative Islamists, such as the Taliban.[162] Diplomatic engagement with Islamists will have positive results, including having a moderating impact on their ideology, promoting understanding of their political preferences and strategies, and serving as an effective risk management strategy for the West.[163] There are no simple ways to predict the influence of Islamists on international relations, and it is hard to generalize about such a role beyond certain publicly accepted facts. To the extent that Islamists continue to be a marker of identity, their influence on the world stage and global politics cannot be overlooked or underestimated.

Conventional views and thinking about the MENA region have consistently overlooked the role that popular will and individuals can play in bringing about change. A younger generation of Islamists now questions the instrumentalization of faith for the pursuit of power. To them, the Taliban in Afghanistan and the regime of Omar al-Bashir in Sudan are prime examples of exploitation of religion for political gain. These Islamists have opened up space for the variety of understandings of the text, advocating reflexive dialogue and meaningful peace to encounter the long-term problems that their communities face.[164]

Perhaps most importantly, to ignore the rising popularity of Islam and its newly enunciated democratic leanings, or at worst to demonize actors that call for a unification, or at least an amelioration, of faith and freedom, risks radicalization, bigotry, and the disengagement of entire swathes of Arab society. To bridge the gap between a nominally secular—yet fervently religious—United States and an emerging reformist Islamic Middle East is the challenge of this stage of foreign policy. To fail in this endeavor will bring a return to the repressive "devil's bargain" that allowed for leaders—though secular—such as Mubarak and Ben Ali to retain power at the expense of freedom. To succeed will, by contrast, allow for a greater expansion of peaceful and respectful engagement between the West and the Middle East. The stakes are clear: the rise of Islamism in politics is ongoing and the challenge for US policymakers will require new methods of remaining engaged with newly emerging Arab democracies in the region as well as thinking about politics, society, and the role of the Islamists within the context of the evolving Middle East and North Africa.

Looking Ahead: Consequences for US Foreign Policy

A quick glance at the US foreign policy toward the Middle East since World War II demonstrates the need for change in the face of the region's different set of realities. During 1945–1989, US foreign policy in the MENA region promoted stability and the preservation of the status quo, reinforcing repressive rule in the Arab world. The period of 1990–2001 saw the end of the Cold War, shifting the balance in favor of expanding civil society and political openings in some parts of the MENA region. With the 9/11 terrorist attacks on the United States, however, US foreign policy reverted back to supporting repressive regimes in a bid to secure their cooperation in the global war on terror.

Although the 2001 US invasion of Afghanistan aimed at confronting and removing the Taliban, which harbored the al-Qaeda terror network, the subsequent 2003 invasion of Iraq intended to destroy weapons of mass destruction and to promote democracy under the rubric of strategic transformation of the region. But what American troops could not bring to Iraq, a determined mass of Tunisian and Egyptian protesters successfully brought to their respective countries, unleashing an unprecedented wave of protests in the region and breathing new life into the heavily suppressed democracy movement in Iran. The younger activists who took to the streets to expel despots in the name of national empowerment, human dignity, social justice, and democracy have created new political dynamics that have thrown into question the old US policy toward the region.

In the MENA region, populations' aspiration for basic human rights, articulated in universal terms, is emblematic of a yearning for the same basic civil and political liberties that Westerners have historically sought for themselves. These concrete demands for human rights and dignity call for a new US foreign policy—one that is predicated on promoting the counter-narrative of peaceful democratic change rather than relying solely on the "global war on terror." To avoid the tactical mistakes of the Bush administration, the Obama team has shown an obvious aversion to military intervention and putting US boots on the ground in order to effect regime change. Some experts view this cautious approach or an underlying conservatism about direct military intervention as a positive development.[165] Taking this new foreign policy approach is not a sign of weakness; it is a sign of strength, even as we face a growing threat of terrorism across the globe. This US foreign policy adjustment needs to be accompanied by security reforms and effective local governance in targeted countries, both of which will likely unfold over the long term, occasionally interrupted by reversals and periods of rough transition and conflict.

Aware of the problems facing the realization of universal human rights, Western scholars have too often expressed skepticism toward the worldwide spread of these norms, arguing that although the human rights discourse has achieved a pivotal place on the global political agenda in recent years, it has *not* succeeded in making the transition from the transnational sphere to the local sphere, especially in non-Western, traditional societies.[166] The promise of democratic change sweeping across the region challenges this argument, illustrating that the Arab world is now much more politically mobilized, and that the habit of deference to authoritarian rule has been broken.[167]

As the entire region experiences an Arab awakening, the political parlance is changing. Ordinary Arabs themselves have achieved a sense of collective empowerment and are at the heart of this revolution for dignity.[168] Eating bread is no longer enough. The belief in dignity and liberty has fostered the spirit of revolt, resistance, and solidarity in the region. These uprisings are not only political demands for democracy, but direct popular reactions to widespread economic despair, rising food prices, and high unemployment rates, especially among the youth. These revolts are a clear expression of people's rejection of the neoliberal policies imposed by the IMF and World Bank. The IMF's claim to promote "socially inclusive growth" in the aid and loan packages to the countries of the region, especially Egypt and Tunisia, has lost its appeal. In June 2011, the Egyptian government rescinded its initial acceptance of an IMF loan worth $3 billion.[169] It remains to be seen whether or how the Egyptian leaders will determine a coherent and sustainable alternative program to such loan packages in the coming years.

The message of the Arab awakening for the Western world was and is clear: the old policy of unmitigated political support for unpopular and corrupt governments in the region is unsustainable. It has become increasingly clear that US strategic interests dovetail nicely with democratic, rather than autocratic, governments. Defending revolutions in North Africa but protecting other undemocratic regimes in the Middle East is reminiscent of the old US strategy that has usually preserved the status quo. How to properly adjust policies on the basis of these new realities will be the real test. There is a need to reflect upon the deeper causes of the revolution in North Africa, and to reexamine the policy approaches that have so far yielded no solution to the lingering problems of political unrest and change. The old US policies condemned Americans "to endless crises and conflicts in the Middle East, consuming more and more of our blood, treasure, and time as the years passed in return for a volatile oil market and worsening anti-Americanism. It was not a very good deal for us."[170]

Several questions come to mind in the face of the collapse of the Arab world's old order. Will tribal or sectarian violence erupt, presenting formidable challenges to the stability of pro-West regimes and the region more generally? How would these upheavals affect Arab-Israeli tensions in the region? Will social movements and uprisings find ways to institutionalize their presence and pressures? Will this process of transition be punctuated by reversals and periods of conflict over the role of military in the political system? Will Islamists gain political power? What kind of Islamists will govern and how?

Regarding the last two questions, experts argue that political Islam is here to stay and that Islamist parties are likely to proliferate—a development that is bound to compel non-Islamist parties to adopt policies and positions more intimately aligned with the conservative sentiments of voters across the region.[171] Regional experts have argued that Islamists' strength lies in three features: (1) they are closely tied to their local communities; (2) they have a cohesive internal organization; and (3) they hold a realistic, albeit undeclared, strategy for engaging with new power relations and new centers of power—both domestically and internationally.[172] Given these realities, they note, the revolutionary, secular, and liberal forces must fight simultaneously on three fronts as they face the counter-revolutionary forces, the theocratic state project, and undesirable—if not entirely hostile—international and regional opposition to the rise of true democracy in the region.[173]

For the United States, the challenge will be to move from ad hoc contacts to a more strategic dialogue and perhaps ever stronger relations, focusing on a discussion of overlapping interests and peace with Israel.[174] Whereas before the Arab Spring, the United States was reluctant to resolve its "Islamist dilemma," it now finds coming to terms with the rise of Islamists inevitable.[175] Combating the anti-Islam trend at home, which has marked US domestic politics since 9/11, is crucial if American leaders are keen on finding ways to engage effectively with a region struggling to peacefully incorporate its Islamists through democratic ways and means. The United States can ill afford to disregard the empowered new Arab publics. The engagement and communication with Arab public opinion, in the words of Marc Lynch, professor of political science and international affairs at George Washington University, "should be considered as seriously as the 'war of ideas' was after 9/11."[176] "Arab publics," Lynch notes, "have a hypersensitivity to double standards, particularly on the Palestinian issue. Why do all peoples have the right to democracy except Palestinians, they ask, and why is there a responsibility to protect Libyans but not Gazans?"[177]

The Israeli air strikes against Hamas organizations and leadership infrastructure since the war on Gaza broke out on November 14, 2012, demonstrated the region's altering geopolitical landscape in the post–Arab Spring era. Reactions to these attacks clearly showed that Gaza was no longer as isolated as it once was. Many countries in the region openly criticized death and destruction inflicted on both sides, while displaying support for the Palestinians living under siege in Gaza and—by extension—for Hamas. Several key Arab policymakers, including Egypt's prime minister, the foreign ministers of Qatar, Tunisia, and Turkey, as well as a delegation from the Arab League, visited the Gaza Strip. The cease-fire brokered by Egypt on November 21, 2012, led to, among other things, the lifting of the Gaza blockade. Whether this truce will endure is difficult to foretell, but it certainly underlined the necessity of jump-starting the stalled Israeli-Palestinian peace talks.

It remains to be seen how these evolving situations come to pose new challenges to the region and its global interlocutors. Given that the political landscape of the MENA region has changed, new rulers are likely to be more receptive to public opinion, which is less subservient to Western governments' geopolitical considerations. Perhaps this is the price to pay for the democratic polity that the United States and the European Union claim they wish to see.[178] It will be compensated by the productive energies of renewed nations in place of the current restless and jobless youth of the Arab world and Iran. It is a net gain to the United States and the European Union (EU) if Arab young people are prosperous and politically liberated.

The current, fluid political ambiance in the MENA region presents a unique opportunity to the Western world to adopt a new approach toward the region. The United States might be forced into an untenable situation—that is, not wanting to advocate regime change in Saudi

Arabia, but feeling a need to press for democratization there. One can see how even the best intended, prudent policies can later backfire, especially when the United States needs a state that is not amenable to reform. The introduction of the UN Truth and Reconciliation Commission in parts of the region to nudge along a democratic transition might be a good place to start. Unambiguous support for democratic movements in the region will most likely undermine extremist groups, allow the younger generation to seek an active role in shaping their society, and cause the obsolete institutions of power to crumble, opening the way for new politics and social forces.

Managing instability by using the old tricks of fueling sectarian tensions or supporting illegitimate and repressive regimes in the name of stability is fraught with risks. Both US values and interests will be best served if US allies and friends in the region are accountable to their own people, legitimate in their political standing, and transparent in enforcing the rule of law. There are no full guarantees that democratic movements in the MENA region will be at all times consistent with US long-term strategic interests. But it is possible that the struggle for human rights and democratic movements will bring to the forefront of politics a new generation of politicians and policymakers in the region who will seek to pragmatically renegotiate the terms of international relations with the West. The time has come to underline the need for a more nuanced view of stability in the Middle East. The pursuit of a security template that suspends basic civil liberties is not only morally bankrupt, but also has become politically imprudent. How do we avoid naiveté about the much-touted stability maintained by these autocratic but pro-West regimes? How would the emergence of illiberal democracies in the Arab world affect US foreign policy toward the region? How do we win the respect of the peoples in the Arab world more specifically and the Muslim world more generally? These are the key questions facing the MENA region for the foreseeable future.

Conclusion

Regime transition often presents crises of governability, rooted in the turbulence that permeates political and social change. This is especially true of transitions born of violent uprisings that typically involve disruptions to the state and economy. Even democratic transitions, which tend to produce legitimate authority and respect for the rule of law and human rights, result in upheaval, uncertainty, and counterrevolutionary resistance to reform.

Transitional periods and processes raise essential yet unresolved questions regarding the viability of the democratic process. A long view of history demonstrates that combating authoritarianism, deeply embedded patronage, endemic corruption, and the mismanagement of the economy in fledgling, frail democracies is no easy task, and that the possibility of backsliding into a new form of illiberal democracy or traditional authoritarianism usually remains. The struggling democracies of the post–Arab Spring era have found themselves entangled in such a historical trajectory.

The surprising success of a tech-savvy young population motivated by a strong sense of entitlement in dismantling—albeit not fully in some cases—decades of patronage, authoritarianism, and corrupt politics has significantly altered the political landscape of the MENA region. In Egypt, for example, the combination of a vast security apparatus, loyal army, and foreign aid failed to prevent the Mubarak government's downfall. Widespread and peaceful protests rocked the foundation of a state that was widely regarded as repressive, corrupt, distracted from civilian politics, and thus devoid of popular mandate.

Neoliberal economic policies of the 1980s and 1990s concentrated wealth in the hands of many business conglomerates and regime officials in the MENA region, exacerbating wealth disparities. When combined with demographic trends, such as high rates of population growth and "youth bulge," these inequalities intensified.[179] A broad consensus holds that inequality or social justice was among central causes for the Arab uprisings, hence the popular demand for greater equality in the future.[180]

In recent years, modern communication technologies and social media have become new tools of revolt against widespread corruption, social injustice, and political repression, rendering leaderless protests a real possibility. But more importantly, these modern technologies have produced a profound shared identity and liberation narrative, bringing together people of every political stripe and social class and invoking the pan-Arab consciousness as never before. Today, many parts of the region face antigovernment protests and dissent by a young generation frustrated with the lack of employment opportunities, economic collapse, absence of basic freedoms, and the prospects of an uncertain future.

Although it is premature to forecast any drastic or wide-ranging changes, it is clear that old regimes can no longer provide security, maintain order, deliver social justice, and fulfill their people's long-delayed democratic aspirations. This paradigm shift points to an entirely new context where ruling elites cannot return to the ways of the past even if they so desired. Egyptian culture, once heavily influenced by state centralization, subsidies, and censorship, has liberated itself from the omnipotent state power. The revolution has disrupted this precedent, as centralized, statist notions of cultural production have foundered. The state is no longer in a position to censor and repress emerging subcultures as in the past.[181]

Egyptian president Mohamed Morsi witnessed this shift firsthand when he faced a vociferous opposition to the nation's draft constitution in late 2012. Morsi's blatant attempts to shore up executive power came under great scrutiny. This change of paradigm has equally exposed the glaring contradictions of the Western governments that have over the course of the last half century supported corrupt but pro-Western regimes in the Middle East for mainly strategic reasons, while at the same time claiming to have espoused democratic governance wherever possible.

Significantly, the 2011 peaceful democratic uprisings have deflated the notion that Middle Easterners are apathetic, passive, and estranged from modern human rights norms and standards. A cohort of youth throughout the Arab world has effectively utilized modern communication tools to open up a new public space, allowing them to actively participate in politics and hold their governments accountable. Since the Arab uprisings erupted, even despite high tensions and uncertain political situations, the fear factor has diminished. Subsequently this has resulted in bringing about the vaunted "Arab Street" opposition forces as diverse as human rights activists, intellectuals, bloggers, labor unions, liberal and Islamist groups, feminists, and the cultural elite.

In the past several years, we have witnessed protesters driven by movements for human dignity, economic security, and social justice, renewing a heated and healthy debate over the best way to respond to the demands of modernity and social change. Without a doubt, governments throughout the region have realized that engagement with young people is essential to solidifying these fragile democracies. The human rights community should take comfort from the fact that the single most important aspect of these most recent democratic struggles is their indigenous and local roots. The Middle East engagement with human rights, as one expert notes, is increasingly being shaped by Middle Eastern actors and their lived experience of injustice and repression. These engagements are deeply political and mundane, rendering human rights claims a more inspiring, meaningful, and emancipatory force in the region.[182]

Yet the fact remains that the young men and women who sparked these revolts face tough times and many uncertainties, not the least of which is the absence of a sustainable economic and political order. Despite the limits of social change through the Internet and social media, there is still plenty of room for optimism if these young people can effectively direct their efforts toward the proper channels in the newly emerging politics of the region. This vast, young, and digitally engaged population provides a unique reservoir of human capital that—if properly used—can be a major driving force for economic and political change in the region.

Clearly, sustainable economic development and effective implementation of policies and programs capable of capturing this youthful momentum and energy within a democratic framework will remain a major challenge for the foreseeable future in many parts of the MENA. But perhaps for now the single most serious challenge facing the youth movement is the lack of the right political structure to drive democratic changes forward. Without having the requisite political infrastructure—that is, institutions and organizations—in place, the youth movements lack an effective means to engage in the strategic decision-making process at the top of state organizations.

An alternative view holds that the spontaneous nature of street protests can be an asset for such youth movements. That possibility, along with the decentralization of information in the Internet age, renders repressive governments vulnerable to wider public criticism and unrest. Governments have often proven feeble and incapacitated at coping with such spontaneous uprisings.[183] As the MENA region moves toward further modernization and globalization, its major urban areas cannot escape becoming an arena for dissent and social change. This trend can be attributed to the critical nexus between social media, traditional media, and urban spaces, especially at times of mass popular uprisings and protest.[184] While the underlying political and socioeconomic conditions are widely regarded as major contributing factors to the eventual eruption of mass uprisings, the role of proximate factors, such as social media and communication technology, should not be overlooked.

It is also worth noting that the young people's energy, optimism, and enthusiasm are crucial to shaping a new social contract. Ahmed Maher, the founder and the general coordinator of the April 6 Youth

Movement in Egypt, and his young cohorts display unequivocal enthusiasm for continuing the revolution. A conversation with Maher in Cairo convinced me of his drive and determination. Maher confidently spoke of the growing potential for change in Egypt in coming years, all the while insisting that no one can change Egyptians' core identity, which has been forged largely around the dynamics of liberty, faith, art, music, and other cultural markers.[185] This view is consistent with various surveys that have shown that Arabs do not care exclusively about religion. Internal security and economic issues regularly rank as top concerns for Egyptians and Tunisians.[186] Although this degree of optimism is not usually shared by many of the region's experts, most Egyptians seem to believe firmly in the new modes of resistance, activism, and politics.

One such Egyptian is Omaima Abou-Bakr, professor of English and comparative literature at Cairo University, who notes that today's fledgling Arab democracies face colossal challenges and a vast array of problems. More precisely, in the case of Egypt, Abou-Bakr points out that "resistance continues in the post-Mubarak Egypt and that the transition process will be rewarding but slow. This process, however sluggish, is likely to produce a desirable democratic outcome for the vast majority of Egyptians over the longer term only if peaceful democratic means and processes are employed to effect change."[187] The history of constructing democratic orders and maintaining postrevolutionary stability tells us that the process of political development in both Western and non-Western contexts has almost always been messy, tumultuous, and time consuming. The growing pessimism in certain quarters about the Arab Spring—though understandable—is surely misguided. In the words of one expert, "stable liberal democracy usually emerges only at the end of long, often violent struggles, with many twists, turns, false starts, and detours."[188]

To be sure, Egyptian people have invested heavily in the transition process and are prepared to deal with all of its attendant uncertainties, although questions persist about the pace of change and the extent to which such a transformation is likely to provoke violence. It may very well be the case that the peaceful democratic uprisings in Tunisia and Egypt have created the wrong model by which to judge other uprisings in the region. Violence and further social discord are likely to occur over the issue of separation of power as well as the role of security forces and the military in the postrevolutionary period. If this is the case, one should not be dramatically troubled.

Consider, for example, the way the post-uprising stability has been marred by periodic violence in Tunisia, which had been known as the birthplace of the recent democratic uprisings in the MENA and as a country that had offered the best prospects of all the Arab countries for democratization. The assassination of Chokri Belaid—secretary-general of the Unified Democratic Patriots Party, general coordinator of the People's Front, and an outspoken critic of the Islamist party Al-Nahda—has led to a renewed outburst of violence the like of which has not been seen since the ouster two years ago of the autocratic leader, Zine El Abidine Ben Ali. This violent act and the tumultuous response pose a serious threat to the democratic process under way in Tunisia. Of the several questions that arise in this regard, the two most important ones are, Will Tunisia descend into chaos and further political violence in the coming years? And would further tumult affect Tunisia's neighboring countries?

In the final analysis, it is worth noting that the fight for democracy and the enunciation of the rights of the public constitute a noble purpose that at times requires human sacrifice. No one should be under the illusion that the struggle for democratic change and reform will be risk-free, nonviolent, and enduring in the coming years, but hope is a possibility that now more than ever appears present in the youthful longings of the region.

NOTES

Chapter 1

1. James L. Gelvin, *The Arab Uprisings: What Everyone Needs to Know* (New York: Oxford University Press, 2012), 24.

2. Anthony Tirado Chase, *Human Rights, Revolution, and Reform in the Muslim World* (Boulder: Lynne Rienner Publishers, 2012), 40–43.

3. Ibid., 174.

4. Michael C. Hudson, "The Middle East in Flux," *Current History* 110, no. 740 (December 2011): 367.

5. Lisa Anderson, "Demystifying the Arab Spring: Parsing the Differences Between Tunisia, Egypt, and Libya," in *The New Arab Revolt: What Happened, What It Means, and What Comes Next* (New York: Council on Foreign Relations, 2011), 321.

6. Ibid., 328.

7. BBC News Middle East, "Yemen's President Ali Abdullah Cedes Power," February 27, 2012, www.bbc.co.uk/news/world-middle-east-17177720.

8. Fouad Ajami, "The Arab Spring at One: A Year of Living Dangerously," *Foreign Affairs* 91, no. 2 (March/April 2012): 61–62.

9. Suzanne Maloney, "The Economic Dimension: The Price of Freedom," in *The Arab Awakening: America and the Transformation of the Middle East*, eds. Kenneth M. Pollack et al. (Washington, DC: Brookings Institution Press, 2011), 68.

10. Kenneth M. Pollack, "Understanding the Arab Awakening," in Pollack et al., *The Arab Awakening*, 2.

11. Rami G. Khouri, "The Arab Awakening," *The Nation*, September 12, 2011, www.thenation.com/signup/162972?destination=authors/rami-g-khouri.

12. See an interview with Ragui Assaad, "Demographics of Arab Protests," in *The New Arab Revolt*, 236–241.

13. Tarek Osman, *Egypt on the Brink: From Nasser to Mubarak* (New Haven: Yale University Press, 2010), 210.

14. Bruce Feiler, *Generation Freedom: The Middle East Uprisings and the Remaking of the Modern World* (New York: HarperCollins, 2011), 112–124.

15. Francis Ghiles, "A New Deal for Arab People," *Insight Turkey* 14, no. 1 (Winter 2012): 14.

16. Al Arabiya News, "More Men Unemployed Than Women in Libya: Report," March 18, 2012, http://english.alarabiya.net/articles/2012/03/18/201511.html.

17. Marwan Bishara, *The Invisible Arab: The Promise and Peril of the Arab Revolution* (New York: Nation Books, 2012), 78.

18. Al Arabiya News, "More Men Unemployed."

19. "Arab Youth Unemployment: Roots, Risks, and Responses," http://carnegie -mec.org/events/?fa=3158.

20. "Middle East Leaders Address Unemployment in Arab Spring Wake," *Bloomberg Businessweek*, October 21, 2011, www.businessweek.com/news/2011-10-21/middle -east-leaders-address-unemployment-in-arab-spring-wake.html.

21. Ibid.

22. Ibid., 48.

23. Ingo Forstenlechner and Emilie Rutledge, "Unemployment in the Gulf: Time to Update the 'Social Contract,'" *Middle East Policy* XVII, no. 2 (Summer 2010): 39.

24. Jon B. Alterman, "The Revolution Will Not Be Tweeted," *Washington Quarterly* 34, no. 4 (Fall 2001): 134.

25. Ibid., 135.

26. Clay Shirky, *Here Comes Everybody: The Power of Organizing Without Organization* (New York: Penguin, 2008), 304.

27. Rasha A. Abdulla, "The Revolution Will Be Tweeted," *Cairo Review of Global Affairs*, www.aucegypt.edu/gapp/cairoreview/pages/articledetails.aspx?aid=89.

28. Bishara, 91–92.

29. Daniel W. Drezner, "Weighing the Scales: The Internet's Effect on State-Society Relations," *Brown Journal of International Affairs* XVI, issue II (Spring/Summer 2010): 39–41.

30. Ibid., 37.

31. Michael S. Doran, "The Impact of New Media: The Revolution Will Be Tweeted," in Pollack et al., *The Arab Awakening*, 45.

32. See Clay Shirky's reply to Malcolm Gladwell, "From Innovation to Revolution: Do Social Media Make Protests Possible?" *Foreign Affairs* 90, no. 2 (March/April 2012): 153–154.

33. See excerpts from the interview with Nathan Gardels, editor of Global View-point Network. *Christian Science Monitor*, March 26, 2012, 34.

34. For further details on the history of Tahrir Square, see Nezar AlSayyad, *Cairo: Histories of a City* (Cambridge, MA: Harvard University Press, 2011), 245–254. AlSayyad writes that much like the pharaohs of ancient Egypt, who erased the names and histories of those who came before them, Nasser's administration changed the names of important urban landmarks and arteries. Ismailiya Square became Tahrir—or liberation—Square and King Fouad Avenue was renamed 26th of July Avenue, after the date of Farouk's abdication.

35. Alterman, 103–104 and 110–111.

36. Shibley Telhami, "Arab Public Opinion: What Do They Want?" in Pollack et al., *The Arab Awakening*, 13–14.

37. Alterman, 111.

38. Virginia Eubanks, *Digital Dead End: Fighting for Social Justice in the Information Age* (Cambridge, MA: The MIT Press, 2011), 31–32.

39. Doran, 39–46.

40. Malcolm Gladwell, "Small Change: Why the Revolution Will Not Be Tweeted," *The New Yorker* 86, issue 30 (October 4, 2010), www.newyorker.com /reporting/2010/10/04/101004fa_fact_gladwell.

41. Wael Ghonim, *Revolution 2.0: The Power of People Is Greater Than the People in Power: A Memoir* (Boston: Houghton Mifflin Harcourt, 2012), 190.

42. Guobin Yang, "New and Old Media Strengthen Democracy Together," Yale Global, June 2009, Atlantic-Community.org, www.atlantic-community.org/index /Global_Must_Read_Article/New_and_Old_Media_Strengthen_Democracy _Together.

43. Evgeny Morozov, *The Net Delusion: The Dark Side of Internet Freedom* (New York: Public Affairs, 2011), 307–308 and 313–319.

44. Sherry Turkle, "The Flight from Conversation," *New York Times Review*, April 22, 2012.

45. See Letter to the Editors, *New York Times*, April 26, 2012, A22.

46. Stephen R. Grand, "Democratization 101: Historical Lessons for the Arab Spring," in Pollack et al., *The Arab Awakening*, 24.

47. Philip N. Howard, *The Digital Origins of Dictatorship and Democracy: Information Technology and Political Islam* (New York: Oxford University Press, 2011), 156.

48. H. A. Hellyer, "The Chance for Change in the Arab World: Egypt's Uprising," *International Affairs* 87, no. 6 (November 2011): 1321.

49. David D. Kirkpatrick, "Islamist Victors in Egypt Seeking Shift by Hamas," *New York Times*, March 24, 2012, www.nytimes.com/2012/03/24/world/middleeast /egypts-election-victors-seek-shift-by-hamas-to.

50. Ibid.

51. Jason Brownlee, "Peace Before Freedom: Diplomacy and Repression in Sadat's Egypt," *Political Science Quarterly* 126, no. 4 (Winter 2011–2012): 688.

52. Tarek Masoud, "Liberty, Democracy, and Discord in Egypt," *Washington Quarterly* 34, no. 4 (Fall 2011): 126.

53. Michelle Dunne, "Libya's Revolution: Do Institutions Matter?" *Current History* 110, no. 740 (December 2011): 370–371.

54. Hussain Abdul-Hussain, "Arab Spring or Islamist Winter? Three Views," *World Affairs*, January/February 2012, 36–42.

55. Volker Perthes, "Europe and the Arab Spring," *Survival* 53, no. 6 (December 2011–January 2012): 73.

56. Ibid., 83.

57. Paul R. Pillar, "The Arab Spring and US Foreign Policy," *US/ME Policy Brief*, July 18, 2011, www.usmep.us/usmep/wp-content/uploads/2011-18-USMEPolicy -Brief1.pdf.

58. Kevin Cross, "Why Iran's Green Movement Faltered: The Limits of Information Technology in a Rentier State," *SAIS Review* 30, no. 2 (Summer–Fall 2010): 183.

59. Thomas R. Pickering, "Implications of the Arab Awakening for US Policy in Iraq, Iran, and Afghanistan," *US/ME Policy Brief*, July 18, 2011, www.usmep.us/usmep /wp-content/uploads/2011-18-USMEPolicy-Brief1.pdf.

60. See Anthony H. Cordesman's comments in Anthony H. Cordesman, Barak Barfi, Bassam Haddad, and Karim Mezran, "The Arab Uprisings and U.S. Policy: What Is the American National Interest?" *Middle East Policy* XVIII, no. 2 (Summer 2011): 8.

61. Ibid.

62. Alex J. Bellamy, *Global Politics and the Responsibility to Protect: From Words to Deeds* (Oxon, UK: Routledge, 2011).

63. Gareth Evans, *The Responsibility to Protect: Ending Mass Atrocity Crimes Once and for All* (Washington, DC: Brookings Institution Press, 2008).

64. Uri Dadush and Michele Dunne, "American and European Responses to the Arab Spring: What's the Big Idea?" *Washington Quarterly* 34, no. 4 (Fall 2011): 136.

65. Ibid., 139–141.

Chapter 2

1. Wael Ghonim, *Revolution 2.0: The Power of People Is Greater Than the People in Power: A Memoir* (Boston: Houghton Mifflin Harcourt, 2012), 59.

2. Bruce Feiler, *Generation Freedom: The Middle East Uprisings and the Remaking of the Modern World* (New York: HarperCollins, 2011), 117.

3. Council of Europe, "Training Course: New Media in Youth Work," European Youth Center, Strasbourg, Budapest, July 5, 2011, DJS/TC Media (2011), 1.

4. Pamela Ann Smith and Peter Feuilherade, "Now, the Media Revolution," *The Middle East* 427 (November 21, 2011): 38.

5. Quoted in Virginia Eubanks, *Digital Dead End: Fighting for Social Justice in the Information Age* (Cambridge, MA: The MIT Press, 2011), 31.

6. Alanoud Al Sharekh, "Reform and Rebirth in the Middle East," *Survival* 53, no. 2 (April–May 2011): 52.

7. Robert Kunzig, "Seven Billion," *National Geographic* 219, no. 1 (January 2011): 50.

8. Ibid.

9. Ibid., 52.

10. Ibid.

11. The Pew Forum on Religion and Public Life, "The Future of the Global Muslim Population: Projections for 2010–2030," January 27, 2011, http://pewforum.org /future-of-the-global-muslim-population-regional-middle-east.aspx.

12. Ibid.

13. Ibid.

14. Ibid.

15. United Nations Development Program, Regional Bureau for Arab States, *Arab Human Development Report 2009: Challenges to Human Security in the Arab Countries* (New York: UNDP, 2009), 35–36.

16. A review of Gilles Kepel, *Jihad: The Trail of Political Islam*, trans. Anthony F. Roberts (London: Tauris, 2002); available in Jeremy Harding, "Great Unleashing," *London Review of Books* 24, no. 14 (July 25, 2002): 6–9.

17. Ted Swedenburg, "Imagined Youths," in *The Journey to Tahrir: Revolution, Protest, and Social Change in Egypt*, eds. Jeannie Sowers and Chris Toesning (New York: Verso Books, 2012), 287–288.

18. "Middle East: Population Growth Poses Huge Challenge for Middle East and North Africa," *New York Times*, January 18, 2007, www.nytimes.com/2007/01/18 /news/18iht-oxan.0118.4250941.html.

19. Un-Habitat: Globalization and Urban Culture, "State of the World's Cities: Trends in the Middle East and North Africa," www.unhabitat.org/documents/media _centre/sowc/NorthAfrica.pdf.

20. Ibid.

21. NATO Parliamentary Assembly, "The Implications of the Youth Bulge in Middle East and North African Populations," January 25, 2011, www.nato-pa.int /default.asp?SHORTCUT=2342.

22. United Nations Development Program, *Human Development Report 2010* (New York: UNDP, 2010), 184–186.

23. NATO Parliamentary Assembly.

24. Ibid.

25. *Human Development Report 2010*, 184–187.

26. Brian Nickiporuk, *The Security Dynamics of Demographic Factors* (Santa Monica, CA: Rand, 2000), 2.

27. Ibid., 11.

28. Ibid., 19.

29. Ibid., 39.

30. Ibid., 40.

31. Elizabeth Leahy Madsen, "The Demographics of Revolt," *Population Action International*, February 15, 2011, www.populationaction.org/blog/2011/02/the -demographics-of-revolt.html.

32. Meaghan Parker, commenting on "The Security Demographic: Population and Civil Conflict After the Cold War," The Woodrow Wilson Center, *PECS News*, Spring 2004, www.wilsoncenter.org/topics/pubs/PECSnews.pdf, 4–5.

33. Ibid., 4

34. Madsen.

35. Ibid.

36. Jack A. Goldstone, "The New Population Bomb: The Four Megatrends That Will Change the World," *Foreign Affairs* 98, no. 1 (January/February 2010): 36.

37. Ibid., 37.

38. Ragui Assaad and Farzaneh Roudi-Fahimi, "Youth in the Middle East and North Africa: Demographic Opportunity or Challenge?" *Population Reference Bureau*, 2007, www.prb.org/pdf07/youthinMENA.pdf, 1–8.

39. Ibid., 1

40. Ibid.

41. "Arab Youth Unemployment: Roots, Risks, and Responses," http://carnegie -mec.org/events/?fa=3158.

42. Amal A. Kandeel, "Egypt at a Crossroads," *Middle East Policy* XVIII, no. 2 (Summer 2011): 40.

43. Ibid.

44. Ellen Knickmeyer, "The Arab World's Youth Army," in *Revolution in the Arab World: Tunisia, Egypt, and the Unmaking of an Era*, eds. Marc Lynch, Susan B. Glasser, and Blake Hounshell (Washington, DC: Foreign Policy, 2011), 125.

45. Assaad and Roudi-Fahimi, 6.

46. Edward Sayre and Samantha Constant, "The Whole World Is Watching," *National Journal*, February 21, 2011, www.nationaljournal.com/magazine/why-the -middle-east-s-youth-bulge-is-key-to-the-region-s-stability-20110221.

47. Ali Akbar Mahdi, "Lebanon," in *Teen Life in the Middle East*, ed. Ali Akbar Mahdi (Westport, CT: Greenwood Press, 2003), 145.

48. *Arab Human Development Report 2009*, 110.

49. Assaad and Roudi-Fahimi, 7.

50. Feiler, 115.

51. Ibid.

52. Sayre and Constant.

53. Kristen Chick, "Why Tunisia? Why Now?" *Christian Science Monitor*, January 31, 2011, 10.

54. Eric Goldstein, "A Middle-Class Revolution," in Lynch, Glasser, and Hounshell, *Revolution in the Arab World*, 66.

55. Charles Kurzman, "Cultural Jiu-Jitsu and the Iranian Greens," in *The People Reloaded: The Green Movement and the Struggle for Iran's Future*, eds. Nader Hashemi and Danny Postel (Brooklyn: Melville House, 2010), 8.

56. Ibid.

57. "Arab Youth Unemployment."

58. Abdeljalil Akkari, "Education in the Middle East and North Africa: The Current Situation and Future Challenges," *International Education Journal* 5, no. 2 (2004): 145.

59. Thoraya Ahmed Obaid, "Youth and Population in the Middle East: Expanding Opportunity and Hope," UNFPA, April 25, 2002, www.unfpa.org/public/News /pid/3748.

60. The World Bank, "Education in the Middle East and North Africa: A Strategy Towards Learning for Development," Human Development Sector, 2008, www .worldbank.org/education/strategy/MENA-E.pdf, 20.

61. Mounira M. Charrad, *States and Women's Rights: The Making of Postcolonial Tunisia, Algeria, and Morocco* (Berkeley: University of California Press, 2001), 218–219.

62. Ibid., 219.

63. Kurt Andersen, "The Protester," *Time*, December 26, 2011–January 2, 2012, 61.

64. Philip N. Howard, *The Digital Origins of Dictatorship and Democracy: Information Technology and Political Islam* (New York: Oxford University Press, 2011), 179.

65. Ibid.

66. Ibid.

67. Ibid., 197.

68. Tarek Osman, *Egypt on the Brink: From Nasser to Mubarak* (New Haven: Yale University Press, 2010), 210.

69. Ibid., 215.

70. Samuel P. Huntington, *The Third Wave: Democratization in the Late Twentieth Century* (Norman: University of Oklahoma Press, 1991).

71. Augustus Richard Norton, "Arab Revolts Upend Old Assumptions," *Current History* 111, no. 741 (January 2012): 15–16.

72. Dan Murphy, Nicholas Seeley, and Kristen Chick, "Arab Upheaval Begins to Settle," *Christian Science Monitor*, February 6, 2012, 12–13.

73. Interview with Dan Tschirgi, professor of political science, American University–Cairo, November 21, 2011, Cairo.

74. Interview with Mohammad Nassar, professor of literature, Al-Alsun University, November 23, 2011, Cairo.

75. Ibrahim A. Karawan, "Politics and the Army in Egypt," *Survival* 53, no. 2 (April–May 2011): 47.

76. Marc Lynch, *Revolution in the Arab World: Tunisia, Egypt, and the Unmaking of an Era* (New York: Foreign Policy, 2011).

77. Lauren E. Bohn, "Egypt's Revolutionary Narrative Breaks Down," *Foreign Policy*, January 26, 2012, www.foreignpolicy.com/articles/2012/01/26/egypt_s _revolutionary_narrative_breaks_down?page=0,1.

78. Steve Coll, "The Second Tunisian Revolution: A New Model of Change for a New Generation," US/ME Policy Brief, July 18, 2011, http://www.usmep.us/usmep /wp-content/uploads/2011-18-USMEPolicy-Brief1.pdf.

79. Francis Ghiles, "A New Deal for Arab People," *Insight Turkey* 14, no. 1 (Winter 2012): 20.

80. Abigail Hauslohner, "Egypt's NGO Crisis: How Will US Aid Play in the Controversy?" *Time*, February 9, 2012, www.time.com/time/world/article/0,8599,2106420,00 .html.

81. Thomas L. Friedman, "Defendant No. 34 Has Her Say," *New York Times*, April 25, 2012, A21.

82. Michael Jansen, "Tahrir Square, One Year Later," *Gulf Today*, January 27, 2012, http://gulftoday.ae/portal/cbbcf50c-26bb-456e-b997-94a2f748a0a0.aspx.

83. Interview with Negad El Borai, attorney at law, United Group, November 21, 2011, Cairo.

84. Eva Bellin, "Reconsidering the Robustness of Authoritarianism in the Middle East: Lessons from the Arab Spring," *Comparative Politics* 44, no. 2 (January 2012): 143.

85. Steven A. Cook, *Ruling But Not Governing: The Military and Political Development in Egypt, Algeria, and Turkey* (Baltimore: Johns Hopkins University Press, 2007): 138–148.

86. David S. Sorenson, "Transitions in the Arab World: Spring or Fall?" *Strategic Studies Quarterly*, Fall 2011: 44.

87. Kenneth M. Pollack, "America's Second Chance and the Arab Spring," *Foreign Policy*, December 5, 2011, www.foreignpolicy.com/articles/2011/12/05/americas_second_chance.

88. Ibid.

89. Phillippe Droz-Vincent, "From Fighting Formal Wars to Maintaining Civil Peace," *International Journal of Middle East Studies* 43, no. 3 (August 2011): 393.

90. For a reference to Robert Springborg in this context, see Lloyd C. Gardner, *The Road to Tahrir Square: Egypt and the United States from the Rise of Nasser to the Fall of Mubarak* (New York: The New Press, 2011), 196. See also Robert Springborg, "Economic Involvements of Militaries," *International Journal of Middle East Studies* 43, no. 3 (August 2011): 397–399.

91. Lourdes Garcia-Navarro, "Landslide Win for Egypt's Muslim Brotherhood," National Public Radio, January 21, 2012, www.npr.org/2012/01/21/145564771/landslide-win-for-egypts-muslim-brotherhood.

92. Heinrich Obereuter, "How Do Elections Contribute to the Working of Democracy? Elections in Media Democracy," www.civiced.org/pdfs/GermanAmericanConf2011/Oberreuter_MS-Bloomington.pdf.

93. Professor Bahgat Korany of American University–Cairo, underlined the reality of hybrid systems in an interview with me, November 25, 2011, Cairo.

94. Anthony Shadid, "Libya Struggles to Curb Militias as Chaos Grows," *New York Times*, February 9, 2012, A1–A6.

95. Stephen Farrell, "Demonstrations Whisper of an Arab Spring in Jordan," *New York Times*, February 9, 2012, www.nytimes.com/2012/02/10/world/middleeast/jordan-protests-whisper-of-an-arab-spring.htm.

96. Erica Chenoweth, "Backfire in the Arab Spring—Analysis," *Eurasia Review News and Analysis*, October 12, 2011, www.eurasiareview.com/12102011-backfire-in-the-arab-spring-analysis/.

97. Stephen Zunes, "Syrian Repression, the Chinese-Russian Veto, and U.S. Hypocrisy," February 7, 2012, www.fpif.org/articles/syrian_repression_the_chinese-russian_veto_and_us_hypocrisy.

98. Fabrice Murtin and Romain Wacziarg, "The Democratic Transition," *VOX*, October 5, 2011, www.voxeu.org/index.php?q=node/7062.

99. Howard, 26.

Chapter 3

1. Rami G. Khouri, "The Long Revolt," *Wilson Quarterly* XXXV, no. 3 (Summer 2011): 43.

2. Laryssa Chomiak and John P. Entelis, "The Making of North Africa's Intifadas," *Middle East Report, No. 259* 41, no. 2 (Summer 2011): 15.

3. Tarek Osman, *Egypt on the Brink: From Nasser to Mubarak* (New Haven: Yale University Press, 2010), 210.

4. Samuel Huntington quoted in Robin Wright, *Rock the Casbah: Rage and Rebellion across the Islamic World* (New York: Simon and Schuster, 2011), 10.

5. Claus V. Pedersen, "Youth Culture and Official State Discourse in Iran," in *Youth and Youth Culture in the Contemporary Middle East*, ed. Jorgen Baek Simonsen (Aarhus, Denmark: Aarhus University Press, 2005), 161.

6. Jeb Boone, "Yemen's Power Struggle," *Christian Science Monitor*, June 20, 2011, 8–9.

7. Peter Feuilherade, "Mediawatch: Arab Spring Transforms North Africa's Media Landscape," *The Middle East* 424 (July 2011): 28–29.

8. Ibid., 28.

9. Malcolm Gladwell, "Does Egypt Need Twitter?" *The New Yorker*, February 2, 2011, www.newyorker.com/online/blogs/newsdesk/2011/02/does-egypt-need-twitter.html.

10. Laurie Penny, "Revolts Don't Have to Be Tweeted," *New Statesman*, February 15, 2011, www.newstatesman.com/blogs/laurie-penny/2011/02/uprisings media-internet.

11. David Kravets, "What's Fuelling Mideast Protests? It's More Than Twitter," *Wired.co.uk*, January 28, 2011, www.wired.co.uk/news/archive/2011-01/28/middle-east-protests-twitter.

12. International Crisis Group, "Popular Protest in North Africa and the Middle East (II): Yemen Between Reform and Revolution," March 10, 2011, www.crisisgroup.org/en/regions/middle-east-north-africa/iraq-iran-gulf/yemen/102-popular-protest-in-north-africa-and-the-middle-east-II-yemen-between-reform-and-revolution.aspx.

13. Peter Beaumont, "The Truth about Twitter, Facebook and the Uprisings in the Arab World," *The Guardian*, February 25, 2011, www.guardian.co.uk/world/2011/feb/25/twitter-facebook-uprisings-arab-libya.

14. Ibid.

15. Ibid.

16. Charles Kurzman is quoted in Blake Hounshell, "Dark Crystal: Why Didn't Anyone Predict the Arab Revolutions?" *Foreign Policy* 187 (July/August 2011): 24.

17. F. Gregory Gause III, "Why Middle East Studies Missed the Arab Spring: The Myth of Authoritarian Stability," *Foreign Affairs* 90, no. 4 (July/August, 2011): 86.

18. Ibid., 86–87.

19. Khouri, 46.

20. Asef Bayat, "Arab Revolts: Islamists Aren't Coming!" *Insight Turkey* 13, no. 2 (Spring 2011): 13.

21. Nader Hashemi, "The Arab Revolution of 2011: Reflections on Religion and Politics," *Insight Turkey* 13, no. 2 (Spring 2011): 21.

22. Blake Hounshell, "So Much to Be Angry About," in *Revolution in the Arab World: Tunisia, Egypt, and the Unmaking of an Era*, eds. Marc Lynch, Susan B. Glasser, and Blake Hounshell (Washington, DC: Foreign Policy, 2011), 4.

23. Eugene Rogan, "The Arab Wave," *The National Interest* 113 (May/June 2011): 48.

24. Ibid., 56.

25. Chomiak and Entelis, 15.

26. Ibid.

27. Christopher Alexander, "A Month Made for Drama," in Lynch, Glasser, and Hounshell, *Revolution in the Arab World*, 47.

28. See Anthony H. Cordesman's comments in Anthony H. Cordesman, Barak Barfi, Bassam Haddad, and Karim Mezran, "The Arab Uprisings and U.S. Policy: What Is the American National Interest? *Middle East Policy* XVIII, no. 2 (Summer 2011): 5.

29. "Al Jazeera's Ayman Mohyeldin on Mideast Revolution, U.S. News, and Glenn Beck's Caliphate Theory," *Huffpost Media*, www.huffingtonpost.com/2011/03/23/al -jazeera-mohyeldin-glenn-beck_n_839346.html.

30. Ahmad Shokr, "The 18 Days of Tahrir," *Middle East Report, No. 258* 41, no. 1 (Spring 2011): 19.

31. Marc Lynch, "After Egypt: The Limits and Promise of Online Challenges to the Authoritarian Arab State," *Perspectives on Politics* 9, no. 2 (June 2011): 303.

32. Ibid., 303–307.

33. James Petras, *The Arab Revolt and the Imperialist Counterattack* (Atlanta: Clarity Press, 2011), 37.

34. Augustus Richard Norton and Ashraf El-Sherif, "North Africa's Epochal Year of Freedom," *Current History* 110, no. 736 (May 2011): 202.

35. Omar S. Dahi, "Understanding the Political Economy of the Arab Revolts," *Middle East Report, No. 259* 41, no. 2 (Summer 2011): 3.

36. Ibid.

37. Ibid., 3–4.

38. Ibid., 4.

39. Ibid., 5.

40. Petras, 33

41. Ibid., 35.

42. Ibid.

43. Ibid., 35–36.

44. Michel Chossudovsky, "Tunisia and the IMF's Diktats: How Macro-Economic Policy Triggers Worldwide Poverty and Unemployment," *Global Research*, January 20, 2011, www.globalresearch.ca/index.php?context=va&aid=22867.

45. Ibid.

46. Ibid.

47. "Revolution in Tunisia: Neoliberal Game Is Over," *Hamsayey.Net: Iran and International News Online*, January 15, 2011, http://hamsayeh.net/articles/235-turmoil -in-tunisia-rebellion-challenges-neoliberalism.html.

48. Hicham Safieddine, "Tomorrow's Tunis and Egypt: Reform or Revolution?" Socialist Project, E-Bulletin, No. 457, *The Bullet*, February 1, 2011, www.socialistproject .ca/bullet/457.php.

49. Lefty Coaster, "U.S. Press Ignores How Neoliberal Policies Are Driving Middle East Popular Uprisings," February 25, 2011, *Daily Kos*, www.dailykos.com /story/2011/02/25/949587/-US-Press-ignores-how-Neoliberal-Policies-are-driving -Middle-East-Popular-Uprisings.

50. Adam Hanieh, "Egypt's Uprising: Not Just a Question of 'Transition,'" Socialist Project, E-Bulletin, No. 462, *The Bullet*, February 14, 2011, www.socialistproject.ca /bullet/462.php.

51. Amal A. Kandeel, "Egypt at a Crossroads," *Middle East Policy* XVIII, no. 2 (Summer 2011): 39.

52. Hanieh.

53. Kandeel, 40.

54. Ibid., 41.

55. Hanieh.

56. Kandeel, 37.

57. Hanieh.

58. Bulent Gokay, "Neoliberal Western Policies Led to Uprisings," *Public Service Europe*, March 11, 2011, www.publicserviceeurope.com/article/99/ neoliberal-western-policies-led-to-uprisings.

59. Hesham Sallam, "Striking Back at Egyptian Workers," *Middle East Report, No. 259* 41, no. 2 (Summer 2011): 20–25.

60. Fareed Zakaria, "Why It's Different This Time," *Time*, February 28, 2011, 31.

61. Ali Akbar Mahdi, "Introduction: Teens, Islam, and the Middle East," in *Teen Life in the Middle East*, ed. Ali Akbar Mahdi (Westport, CT: Greenwood Press, 2003), 9.

62. Meral Kaya, "Turkey," in Mahdi, *Teen Life in the Middle East*, 226.

63. Malihe Maghazei, "Iran," in Mahdi, *Teen Life in the Middle East*, 29.

64. Bobby Ghosh, "Rage, Rap, and Revolution," *Time*, February 28, 2011, 34.

65. Ines Baune, "Youth in Morocco: How Does the Use of the Internet Shape the Daily Life of the Youth and What Are Its Repercussions?" in Simonsen, *Youth and Youth Culture in the Contemporary Middle East*, 128.

66. Brian Knowlton and Nazi Fathi, "U.S. Report Describes Worsening Human Rights in Iran and China," *New York Times*, March 11, 2010, www.nytimess.com /2010/03/12/world/12rights.html.

67. Shirin Ebadi and Azadeh Moaveni, *Iran Awakening: A Memoir of Revolution and Hope* (New York: Random House, 2006), 116.

68. Dina Shebata, "The Fall of the Pharaoh: How Hosni Mubarak's Reign Came to an End," *Foreign Affairs* 90, no. 3 (March/June 2011): 28.

69. Jack Donnelly, *International Human Rights*, 2nd ed. (Boulder: Westview Press, 1998), 161.

70. Charles R. Beitz, *The Idea of Human Rights* (New York: Oxford University Press, 2009), 1.

71. Ibid., 160.

72. David P. Forsythe, "US Foreign Policy and Human Rights: Situating Obama," paper presented at the International Studies Association, Montreal, Canada, 2011.

73. Alison Brysk, *Global Good Samaritans: Human Rights as Foreign Policy* (New York: Oxford University Press, 2009), 33–34.

74. Hans Peter Schmitz and Kathryn Sikkink, "International Human Rights," in *Handbook of International Relations*, eds. Walter Carlsnaes, Thomas Risse, and Beth A. Simmons (Thousand Oaks, CA: Sage, 2008), 530.

75. Ibid., 531.

76. Nadia Marzouki, "From People to Citizens in Tunisia," *Middle East Report, No. 259* 42, no. 2 (Summer 2011): 17–18.

77. Ibid., 18.

78. Robert Marquand, "Dignity Drives Arab Revolts," *Christian Science Monitor*, March 14, 2011, 10.

79. Shadi Mokhtari, "Cairo Optimism: The People Are Now Part of the Equation," *OpenDemocracy*, June 24, 2012, www.opendemocracy.net/shadi-mokhtari/cairo -optimism-people-are-now-part-of-equation.

80. Annia Ciezadlo, "Eat, Drink, Protest: Stories of the Middle East's Hungry Rumblings," *Foreign Policy* 186 (May/June 2011): 79.

81. Clayton Jones, "The Slap Heard Round the World," *Christian Science Monitor*, March 14, 2011, 31.

82. Bayat, 14.

83. Tom Malinowski, "Did Wikileaks Take Down Tunisia's Government?" in Lynch, Glasser, and Hounshell, *Revolution in the Arab World*, 61.

84. James Traub, "RIP, Engagement," in Lynch, Glasser, and Hounshell, *Revolution in the Arab World*, 171.

85. Fareed Zakaria, "How Democracy Can Work in the Middle East," *Time*, February 3, 2011, www.time.com/time/world/article/0,8599,2045888,00.html.

86. Bayat, 14.

87. Dale F. Eickelman, "Bin Laden, the Arab Street, and the Middle East's Democracy Deficit," *Current History*, January 2002, 36–39.

88. Jessica Stern, "The Protean Enemy," *Foreign Affairs* 82, no. 4 (July/August 2003): 27–40.

89. J. Dudley Woodberry, "Terrorism, Islam, and Mission: Reflections of a Guest in Muslim Lands," *International Bulletin of Missionary Research*, January 2002, 6.

90. Abbas Amanat, "Empowered Through Violence: The Reinventing of Islamic Extremism," in *The Age of Terror: America and the West After September 11*, eds. Strobe Talbott and Nayan Chanda (New York: Basic Books, 2001), 50.

91. John L. Esposito, *Unholy War: Terror in the Name of Islam* (New York: Oxford University Press, 2002), 147–160.

92. Graham E. Fuller, "The Future of Political Islam," *Foreign Affairs* 81, no. 2 (March/April 2002): 59.

93. Louay Y. Bahry, "The New Arab Media Phenomenon: Qatar's Al-Jazeera," *Middle East Policy* VIII, no. 2 (June 2001): 88–99.

94. Mohammed el-Nawawy and Adel Iskandar Farag, *Al-Jazeera: How the Free Arab News Network Scooped the World and Changed the Middle East* (Boulder: Westview Press, 2002).

95. Amy W. Hawthorne, "Promoting Religious Freedom in the Arab World, Post–September 11," Policy Watch no. 586, December 7, 2001, www.ciaonet.org/pbei/winep/haa05.html.

96. Michael Hudson, "The Crackdown in Bahrain: Notes from the Field," *Middle East Insight* 15 (March 18, 2011), www.mei.nus.edu.sg/wp-content/uploads/2011/04/Insight-15-Hudson.pdf.

97. Andrew J. Bacevich, "Last Act in the Mideast," *Newsweek*, April 11, 2011, 48–49.

98. Ibid., 49.

Chapter 4

1. Eugene Rogan, "The Arab Wave," *The National Interest* 113 (May/June 2011): 56.

2. Eduardo Navas, "After Iran's Twitter Revolution: Egypt," *The Levantine Review*, February 15, 2011, www.levantinecenter.org/levantine-review/after-irans-twitter-revolution-egypt.

3. David Kirkpatrick, *The Facebook Effect: The Inside Story of the Company That Is Connecting the World* (New York: Simon and Schuster, 2010), 296.

4. Ibid.

5. Ibid., 301, 333.

6. Blake Hounshell, "The Revolution Will Be Tweeted: Life in the Vanguard of the New Twitter Proletariat," *Foreign Policy* 187 (July/August 2011): 21.

7. Ibid., 20.

8. Ibid., 21.

9. Ray Takeyh, "The U.S. Must Empower the Green Movement," *Washington Post*, February 17, 2011, www.washingtonpost.com/wp-dyn/content/article/2011/02/16/AR2011021605286.html.

10. Jack Farmer and Peyman Jafari, "An Interview with Hamid Dabashi: Making a Stand with Iran's Green Movement," *Socialist Review*, June 2011, www.socialistreview.org.uk/article.php?articlenumber=11689.

11. Scott Peterson, "Iran Opposition Returns to Streets, Energized by Egypt," *Christian Science Monitor*, February 14, 2011, www.csmonitor.com/World/Middle-East/2011/0214/Iran-opposition-returns-to-streets-energized-by-Egypt.

12. Scott Peterson, *Let the Swords Encircle Me: Iran—A Journey Behind the Headlines* (New York: Simon and Schuster, 2010), 520.

13. Ibid., 522.

14. Ibid., 527.

15. Quoted in Matt Duss, "Iran's Second Islamic Revolution?" *Thinkprogress*, June 2, 2009, http://thinkprogress.org/security/2009/06/22/175502/irans-second -islamic-revolution/.

16. Mehdi Semati, "Media, the State, and the Pro-Democracy Movement in Iran," in *Negotiating Democracy: Media Transformations in Emerging Democracies*, eds. Isaac A. Blankson and Patrick D. Murphy (Albany: State University of New York Press, 2007), 153.

17. Abbas Amanat, "A Middle-Class Uprising," *New York Times*, June 16, 2009, http://roomfordebate.blogs.nytimes.com/2009/06/16/where-will-the-power-lie-in -iran/#abbas.

18. Asef Bayat, "A Wave for Life and Liberty: The Green Movement and Iran's Incomplete Revolution," in *The People Reloaded: The Green Movement and the Struggle for Iran's Future*, eds. Nader Hashemi and Danny Postel (Brooklyn: Melville House, 2010), 51.

19. Semati, 156.

20. Ibid., 157.

21. Philip N. Howard, *The Digital Origins of Dictatorship and Democracy: Information Technology and Political Islam* (New York: Oxford University Press, 2011), 5.

22. Ibid., 7.

23. Ibid.

24. Ibid., 10.

25. Hossein Bahsiriyeh, quoted in Danny Postel, " Counter-Revolution and Revolt in Iran: An Interview with Iranian Political Scientist Hossein Bashiriyeh," in Hashemi and Postel, *The People Reloaded*, 98.

26. Homan Majd, "The Green Movement Is a Viable Civil Rights Movement," in *Iran*, ed. Debra A. Miller (Detroit: Greenhaven Press, 2011), 133.

27. Ibid., 134.

28. Ibid., 138.

29. Hooman Majd, *The Ayatollah's Democracy: An Iranian Challenge* (New York: W. W. Norton, 2010), 45.

30. Genive Abdo, "Green Movement 2.0? How U.S. Support Could Lead the Opposition to Victory," *Foreign Affairs*, February 18, 2011, www.foreignaffairs.com /articles/67458/geneive-abdo/green-movement-20.

31. Peterson, *Let the Swords Encircle Me*, 572.

32. For more information on this subject, see Mahmood Monshipouri and Ali Assareh, "The Islamic Republic and the 'Green Movement': Coming Full Circle," *Middle East Policy* XVI, no. 4 (Winter 2009): 27–46.

33. Roger Cohen, "Iran: The Tragedy and the Future," *New York Review of Books* LVI, no. 13 (August 13, 2009): 8.

34. Ibid., 8.

35. Iason Athanasiadis and Barbara Slavin, "The Green Movement Is Growing," in Miller, *Iran*, 114–119.

36. Ibid., 117.

37. Nader Hashemi and Danny Postel, eds., *The People Reloaded: The Green Movement and the Struggle for Iran's Future* (Brooklyn: Melville House, 2010), xiv.

38. Robin Wright, *Rock the Casbah: Rage and Rebellion Across the Islamic World* (New York: Simon and Schuster, 2011), 111.

39. Elliot Hen-Tov and Nathan Gonzalez, "The Militarization of Post-Khomeini Iran: Praetorianism 2.0," *The Washington Quarterly* 34, no. 1 (Winter 2011): 53–54.

40. Mehranghiz Karr, *Eliminating Discrimination Against Women: A Comparison of the Convention on Elimination of All Forms of Discrimination Against Women with Iran's Domestic Laws* (Tehran: Parvin, 1999), 334.

41. Mohammad Zairmaran and Shirin Ebadi, *Modernity and Tradition in the Iranian Legal System* (Tehran: Gangedanesh, 1996), 247.

42. Shirin Ebadi, *History and Documentation of Human Rights in Iran* (Tehran: Roshangaran, 1994), 101–102, 119.

43. *Twenty-Four Human Rights Documents* (Ithaca, NY: Center for Human Rights Study, Columbia University, 1992), 181.

44. Pat Lancaster, "Dr. Shirin Ebadi," *The Middle East* 427 (November 2011): 30.

45. Ibid.

46. Monshipouri and Assareh, 27–46.

47. Thierry Coville, "An Economic Crisis after the Political Crisis in Iran," *Affairs-Strategiques.info*, July 27, 2009, www.affaires-strategiques.info/spip.php?article1735.

48. Central Intelligence Agency, *The World Factbook*, www.cia.gov/library/publications/the-world-factbook/geos/ir.html.

49. Ibid.

50. Morteza Aminmansor, "Iran, Inflation, and the Future of the Country," *News Central Asia*, January 16, 2008, www.newscentralasia.net/Articles-and-Reports/208.html.

51. Ali Mollahosseini, "Gender and Employment in Iran," *Indian Journal of Gender Studies* 15, no. 1 (2008): 161.

52. Christina Prifti, "Education in Iran: Towards a Second Islamization?" *Middle East Bulletin* 12 (July 2008): 10.

53. Association of Iranian Women in the UK, "Memorandum from the Association of Iranian Women in the UK," www.parliament.the-stationeryoffice.co.uk.pa/cm200203/cmselect/cmfaff/405/405we15.htm.

54. Mahmood Monshipouri, "The Road to Globalization Runs through Women's Struggle: Iran and the Impact of Nobel Peace Prize," *World Affairs* 167, no. 1 (Summer 2004): 3–14.

55. Wright, 155.

56. Mervat Hatem, "Gender and Revolution in Egypt," *Middle East Report, No. 261* 41, no. 4 (Winter 2011): 40.

57. Interviewed on November 19, 2011, in Cairo, Egypt.

58. Mona Eltahawy, "Why Do They Hate US?" *Foreign Policy*, May/June 2012, www.foreignpolicy.com/articles/2012/04/23/why_do_they_hate_us?page=0,3.

59. Hamza Hendawi, "Troops Charge Protesters in Pre-Dawn Raid," *The dailynewsegypt.com*, December 20, 2011, www.thedailynewsegypt.com/egypt/troops-charge-protesters-in-pre-dawn-raid.html.

60. David Kirkpatrik, "Mass March by Cairo Women in Protest Over Abuse by Soldiers," *New York Times*, December 20, 2011, www.nytimes.com/2011/12/21/world/middleeast/violence-enters-5th-day-as-egyptian-general-blames-protesters.html?pagewanted=all.

61. Ibid.

62. Hatem, 41.

63. Mounira M. Charrad, *States and Women's Rights: The Making of Postcolonial Tunisia, Algeria, and Morocco* (Berkeley: University of California Press, 2001), 218–219.

64. Monica Marks, "Islamic Feminism Can Work in Tunisia," *Dallas Morning News*, October 27, 2011, www.dallasnews.com/opinion/latest-columns/20111027-monica-marks-islamic-feminism-can-work-in-tunisia.ece.

65. Interview with Mayy ElHayawi, professor of literary studies, quality coordinator, and ESL course manager, Department of English, University of 'Ayn Shams, faculty of al-Alsun, Egypt, November 23, 2011, Cairo. She is also a certified English language teacher for adults by the University of Cambridge and certified basic trainer by the International Board of Certified Trainers (IBCT). Her main research interests include postcolonial and gender studies, eco-criticism, diaspora literature, and Middle East women's writings.

66. Ibid.

67. For more information on this, see "Salem Express," www.shipwrecksofegypt .com/images/shippages/salemexpress.html.

68. Ibid.

69. Ibid.

70. Central Intelligence Agency.

71. International Telecommunications Union, "ICT Statistics Newslog—Iran Subscriber Growth Still Going Strong but Signs of a Slowdown," July 27, 2009, www .itu.int/ITU-D/ict/newslog/Iran+Subscriber+Growth+Still+Going+Strong+But +Signs+Of+A+Slowdown.aspx.

72. See the reactions to Darrell West, "The Two Faces of Twitter: Revolution in a Digital Age," *Huffington Post*, June 22, 2009, by Nicola Colbran, "Twitter and YouTube: Positive Developments for Human Rights Protection?"; Shareen Hertel, "Protest, Iranian Style: A Two-Way Conversation?"; and Anja Mihr, "Iran: Who Is Quicker—The Hacker or the Twitter?," *Human Rights and Human Welfare*, August 2009, www.du.edu /korbel/hrhw/news/index.html.

73. Robin Wright, "Fighting Back," *Time*, August 10, 2009, 43.

74. Nasrin Alavi, "Iran's Resilient Rebellion," *Open Democracy*, February 18, 2011, www.opendemocracy.net/nasrin-alavi/irans-resilient-rebellion.

75. Kevin Cross, "Why Iran's Green Movement Faltered: The Limits of Information Technology in a Rentier State," *SAIS Review* 30, no. 2 (Summer–Fall 2010): 183–184.

76. Ibid., 177–180.

77. Mahmood Monshipouri, *Muslims in Global Politics: Identities, Interests, and Human Rights* (Philadelphia: University of Pennsylvania Press, 2009), 85.

78. Raymond William Baker, *Islam Without Fear: Egypt and the New Islamists* (Cambridge, MA: Harvard University Press, 2003), 3.

79. Carnegie's Guide to Egypt's Elections, "The Egyptian Movement for Change (Kifaya)," http://egyptelections.carnegieendowment.org/2010/09/22/the -egyptian-movement-for-change-kifaya.

80. Manar Shourbagy, "The Egyptian Movement for Change—Kefaya: Redefining Politics in Egypt," *Political Culture*, http://publicculture.org/articles/view/19/1/the -egyptian-movement-for-change-kefaya-redefin.

81. David Wolman, "All Posts Tagged Ahmed Maher: Did Egypt Detain a Top Facebook Activist?" *Wired*, February 2, 2011, www.wired.com/dangerroom/tag/ahmed -maher/.

82. Dina Shebata, "The Fall of the Pharaoh: How Hosni Mubarak's Reign Came to an End," *Foreign Affairs* 90, no. 3 (May/June 2011): 28.

83. Wael Ghonim, *Revolution 2.0: The Power of the People Is Greater Than the People in Power, A Memoir* (Boston: Houghton Mifflin Harcourt, 2012), 36.

84. Tina Rosenberg, "Revolution U," in Lynch, Glasser, and Hounshell, *Revolution in the Arab World*, 127–129.

85. Ibid., 141.

86. Maryam Ishani, "The Hopeful Network," in Lynch, Glasser, and Hounshell, *Revolution in the Arab World*, 143–148.

87. Ibid., 148.

88. Ghonim, 80.

89. Ibid., 85.

90. Shebata, 29.

91. Ghonim, 134.

92. Xiaolin Zhuo, Barry Wellman, and Justine Yu, "Egypt: The First Internet Revolt?" *Peace Magazine*, http://peacemagazine.org/archive/v27n3p06.htm.

93. Ibid.

94. Jina Morre, "The Revolution Will Be Blogged," *Christian Science Monitor*, July 4, 2011, 28.

95. David DeGraw, "Analysis of the Global Insurrection Against Neo-Liberal Economic Domination and the Coming American Rebellion—We Are Egypt [Revolution Roundup #3]," http://daviddegraw.org/2011/03/analysis-of-the-global-insurrection -against-neo-liberal-economic-domination-and-the-coming-american-rebellion-we -are-egypt-revolution-roundup-3/.

96. Ursula Lindsey, "Art in Egypt's Revolutionary Square," *Middle East Report*, January 2012, www.merip.org/mero/interventions/art-egypts-revolutionary-square.

97. Wright, *Rock the Casbah*, 215.

98. Ibid., 127.

99. Lara Dotson Renta, "Hip-Hop & Diaspora: Connecting the Arab Spring," *Arab Media and Society* 13 (Summer 2011), www.arabmediasociety.com/?article=777.

100. Ibid.

101. Ibid.

102. Wright, *Rock the Casbah*, 116.

103. Ibid., 116–117.

104. Ibid., 118.

105. Rose Hackman, "Hip-Hop the Soundtrack of Arab Spring," *Thedailynewsegypt .com*, January 12, 2012, http://thedailynewsegypt.com/music/hip-hop-the-soundtrack -of-the-arab-spring.html.

106. Wright, *Rock the Casbah*, 128–132.

107. Andrew Linklater, *Critical Theory and World Politics: Citizenship, Sovereignty, and Humanity* (New York: Routledge, 2007), 189.

108. Andrew Linklater, "Historical Sociology," in *Theories of International Relations*, 4th ed., eds. Scott Burchill et al. (New York: Palgrave-Macmillan, 2009), 151.

109. Ibid., 188.

110. Ibid., 182–183. See also Richard Devetak, "Critical Theory," in Burchill et al. *Theories of International Relations*, 176.

111. Linklater, 183.

112. Laura Sjoberg, "Emotion, Risk, and Feminist Research in IR," *International Studies Review* 13, no. 4 (December 2011): 702–703.

113. For more on Edmund Burke's emphasis on emotional and rational phenomena, see Lauren Hall, "Rights and the Heart: Emotions and Rights Claims in the Political Theory of Edmund Burke," *The Review of Politics* 73, no. 4 (Fall 2011): 617–618.

114. Hicham Safieddine, "The Arab Uprisings One Year On: Beyond Bouazizi," *Alakhbar English*, December 20, 2011, http://english.al-akhbar.com/content/arab -uprisings-one-year-beyond-bouazizi.

115. Kurt Anderson, "The Protesters," *Time*, December 26, 2011, 82.

116. Ghonim, 140.

117. Ibid., 139.

118. Ibid., 141.

119. Marc Lynch, "The Big Think Behind the Arab Spring," *Foreign Policy*, December 2011, www.foreignpolicy.com/articles/2011/11/28/the_big_think.

120. Steve Coll, "The Second Tunisian Revolution: A New Model of Change for a New Generation," US/ME Policy Brief, July 18, 2011, www.usmep.us/usmep/wp-content/uploads/2011-18-USMEPolicy-Brief1.pdf.

121. Cecelia Lynch, "'Kony 2012': If Only Helping Africa Were So Simple," *Christian Science Monitor*, April 9, 2012, 36.

122. Ibid.

Chapter 5

1. Anthony Tirado Chase, *Human Rights, Revolution, and Reform in the Muslim World* (Boulder: Lynne Rienner Publishers, 2012), 121.

2. David P. Forsythe, *The Politics of Prisoner Abuse: The United States and Enemy Prisoners after 9/11* (New York: Cambridge University Press, 2011), 24.

3. For more on this subject, see Mahmood Monshipouri, "US-Iran Relations" in *Iran Today: An Encyclopedia of Life in the Islamic Republic*, Vol. 2, eds. Mehran Kamrava and Manochehr Dorraj (Westport, CT: Greenwood Press, 2008), 491–499.

4. Stephen Kinzer, *Overthrow: America's Century of Regime Change from Hawaii to Iraq* (New York: Times Books, 2006), 118.

5. Ibid., 201.

6. James A. Bill, *The Eagle and the Lion: The Tragedy of American-Iranian Relations* (New Haven: Yale University Press, 1988), 172.

7. Mahmood Monshipouri, *Islamism, Secularism, and Human Rights in the Middle East* (Boulder: Lynne Rienner Publishers, 1988), 172.

8. Ibid.

9. Charles Hauss, *Comparative Politics: Domestic Responses to Global Challenges*, 5th ed. (Belmont, CA: Thomson Wadsworth, 2006), 395.

10. Rouhollah Ramazani, *Revolutionary Iran: Challenge and Response in the Middle East* (Baltimore: Johns Hopkins University Press, 1986), 126.

11. Melvin Friedlander, *Conviction and Credence: U.S. Policymaking in the Middle East* (Boulder: Lynne Rienner Publishers, 1991), 79.

12. John L. Esposito, *The Islamic Threat: Myth or Reality?* 3rd ed. (New York: Oxford University Press, 1999), 124.

13. Judith S. Yaphe, "U.S.-Iran Relations: Normalization in the Future?" *Strategic Forum* 188 (Washington, DC: Institute for National Strategic Studies, National Defense University, 2002).

14. Shahram Chubin, *Iran's Nuclear Ambitions* (Washington, DC: Carnegie Endowment for International Peace, 2006).

15. This section is based on Mahmood Monshipouri, "Nuclear Program," in Kamrava and Dorraj, *Iran Today*, 356–362.

16. Ali M. Ansari, *Confronting Iran: The Failure of American Foreign Policy and the Next Great Crisis in the Middle East* (New York: Basic Books, 2006).

17. Mahmood Monshipouri, "Iran's Nuclear Program: What Does the Current Impasse Mean?" *Muslim Public Affairs Journal*, January 2006, 9–13.

18. Ibid.

19. Peter Jenkins, "Where Are the Iran Talks Heading after Moscow?" *Lobelog Foreign Policy*, June 24, 2012, www.lobelog.com/where-are-the-iran-talks-heading-after-moscow/.

20. Vali Nasr, "For Iran Breakthrough, Coalition Cannot Break Down," *Bloomberg.com*, May 17, 2012, www.bloomberg.com/news/2012-05-17/for-iran-breakthrough-coalition-cannot-break-down.html.

21. Tony Karan, "In Nuclear Talks, Iran and the West Agree to Disagree—and Keep Talking," *Time.com*, May 24, 2012, http://news.yahoo.com/breakdown-breakthrough-iran-nuclear-talks-hit-snag-075407041.html.

22. Daniel Levy, "Iran Nuclear Talks Succeed Just by Continuing," *The Guardian*, May 31, 2012, www.guardian.co.uk/commentisfree/2012/may/31/iran-nuclear-talks-succeed-by-continuing.

23. Ali Abdullah-Khani, "What Happens after Baghdad Talks: Scenarios and Solutions," *Iran Review*, June 3, 2012, www.iranreview.org/content/Documents/What_Happens_after_Baghdad_Talks_Scenarios_and_Solutions.htm.

24. Abolqasem Qasemzadeh, "From Baghdad to Moscow," *Iran Review*, June 2, 2012, www.iranreview.org/content/Documents/From_Baghdad_to_Moscow.htm.

25. Hooman Majd, *The Ayatollahs' Democracy: An Iranian Challenge* (New York: W. W. Norton, 2010), 30.

26. Charles Kurzman, "Cultural Jiu-Jitsu and the Iranian Greens," in *The People Reloaded: The Green Movement and the Struggle for Iran's Future*, eds. Nader Hashemi and Danny Postel (Brooklyn: Melville House, 2010), 8.

27. Nikolay A. Kozhanov, "US Economic Sanctions Against Iran: Undermined by External Factors," *Middle East Policy* XVIII, no. 3 (Fall 2011): 155–156.

28. Ibid., 156.

29. Ibid.

30. Amir Taheri, *The Persian Night: Iran Under the Khomeinist Revolution* (New York: New Material, 2010), 196–197.

31. Roland Flamini, "Turmoil in the Arab World," in *Global Issues*, 2011 ed., CQ Researcher (Washington, DC: CQ Press, 2012), 187.

32. Chase, 131.

33. "Iranian Opposition Bids to Hold Pro-Egypt Rally," Reuters, February 6, 2011, http://af.reuters.com/article/topNews/idAFJOE7150AX20110206.

34. Scott Peterson, "Iran's Khamenei Praises Egyptian Protesters, Declares 'Islamic Awakening,'" *Christian Science Monitor*, February 4, 2011, www.csmonitor.com/World/Middle-East/2011/0204/Iran-s-Khamenei-praises-Egyptian-protesters-declares-Islamic-awakening.

35. "Larijani: Regional Uprisings Inspired by Iran's Islamic Revolution," Fars News Agency, March 3, 2011, http://english.farsnews.com/newstext.php?nn=8912120642.

36. "Parliament Backs Tunis, Egypt Uprisings," Press TV, January 30, 2011, www.presstv.ir/detail/162695.html.

37. Roshanak Taghavi, "Mideast Unrest Could Boost Iran, but It Faces Upheaval at Home," *Christian Science Monitor*, April 15, 2011, www.csmonitor.com/World/Middle-East/2011/0415/Mideast-unrest-could-boost-Iran-but-it-faces-upheaval-at-home.

38. Charles Kurzman, "The Arab Spring: Ideals of the Iranian Green Movement, Methods of the Iranian Revolution," *International Journal of Middle East Studies* 22 (2012): 163.

39. Ibid.

40. Flamini, 173.

41. Mohammed Ayoob, "Beyond the Democratic Wave in the Arab World: The Middle East's Turko-Persian Future," *Insight Turkey* 13, no. 2 (Spring 2011): 61.

42. John Glaser, "Qatar, Turkey Express Opposition to Unilateral Strike Against Iran," *Antiwar*, March 28, 2012, http://news.antiwar.com/2012/03/28/qatar-turkey -express-opposition-to-unilateral-strike-on-iran/.

43. Ibid., 176.

44. Flamini, 176.

45. Mohammed Ayoob, "Beyond the Democratic Wave in the Arab World: The Middle East's Turko-Persian Future," *Insight Turkey* 13, no. 2 (Spring 2011): 61.

46. Hassan Ahmadian, "Iran and Turkey-Egypt Regional Rivalries," *Iran Review*, September 23, 2011, www.iranreview.org/content/Documents/Iran_and_Turkey _Egypt_Regional_Rivalries.htm.

47. Ayoob, "Beyond the Democratic Wave in the Arab World," 67.

48. Mehdi Khalaji, "Iran on Egypt's Muslim Brotherhood," *The Iran Primer*, USIP, February 25, 2011, http://iranprimer.usip.org/blog/all/Mehdi%20Khalaji.

49. Hany ElWaziry, "Muslim Brotherhood Reformist Wing Rejects Constitutional Amendments," *Al-Masry Al-Youm*, March 18, 2011, www.almasryalyoum.com/en/node /362657.

50. "Who Are the Brotherhood?" *The Middle East* 420 (March 2011): 20–21.

51. Hany ElWaziry, "Muslim Brotherhood Reformist Establishes Political Party," *Al-Masry Al-Youm*, March 23, 2011, www.almasryalyoum.com/en/node/371714.

52. Aaron David Miller, "For America, an Arab Winter," *Wilson Quarterly* XXXV, no. 3 (Summer 2011): 38.

53. See, for example, Landon Thomas Jr., "In Turkey's Example, Some See Map for Egypt," *New York Times*, February 5, 2011, www.nytimes.com/2011/02/06/world /middleeast/06turkey.html. But for a discussion of differences between Turkey and Egypt, including structural differences between the Egyptian Muslim Brotherhood and the AK Party in Turkey, see Ömer Taşpınar, "Egypt and the Turkish Model," The Brookings Institution, February 7, 2011, www.brookings.edu/opinions/2011/0207 _egypt_turkey_taspinar.aspx.

54. Fareed Zakaria, "The Revolution," *Time*, February 14, 2011, 33.

55. Ali Abunimah, "Palestine: Egypt's Uprising and Its Implications for Palestine," *The Electronic Intifada*, January 29, 2011, http://kalamu.posterous.com/palestine -egypts-uprising-and-its-implication.

56. Ibid.

57. Richard Falk, "Post-Mubarak Revolutionary Chances," *AlJazeera English: Opinion*, February 21, 2011, http://english.aljazeera.net/indepth/opinion/2011/02 /201121711284402313.html.

58. Joe Klein, "Road Map for Reform," *Time*, February 21, 2011, 29.

59. For a similar argument, see Arthur Goldschmidt Jr., *A Concise History of the Middle East*, 7th ed. (Boulder: Westview Press, 2002); see chapter 18, "War and the Quest for Peace."

60. Stephen Kinzer, "Diplomacy Is the Best Option for American-Iranian Revolution," in *Is Iran a Threat to Global Security?*, ed. Julia Bauder (New York: Greenhaven Press, 2006), 46–57.

61. Many human rights activists and lawyers have supported this approach. See Pat Lancaster's interview with Shirin Ebadi, "Dr. Shirin Ebadi," *The Middle East* 427 (November 2011): 30.

62. Howard Lafranchi, "The West's Covert War on Iran," *Christian Science Monitor*, January 2 and 9, 2012, 18.

63. Karl Vick, "Was Israel Behind a Deadly Explosion at an Iranian Missile Base?" *Time World*, November 13, 2011, www.time.com/time/world/article/0,8599,2099376,00.html.

64. Scott Shane, "Adversaries of Iran Said to Be Stepping Up Covert Actions," *New York Times*, January 11, 2012, www.nytimes.com/2012/01/12/world/middleeast/iran-adversaries-said-to-step-up-covert-actions.html?pagewanted=all.

65. Roger Cohen, "Don't Do It, Bibi," *New York Times*, January 16, 2012, www.nytimes.com/2012/01/17/opinion/cohen-dont-do-it-bibi.html?_r=2.

66. Trita Parsi, *A Single Roll of the Dice: Obama's Diplomacy with Iran* (New Haven: Yale University Press, 2012).

67. Joe Klein, "Why Tehran Might Be Ready to Talk," *Time*, May 28, 2012, www.time.com/time/magazine/article/0,9171,2115056-1,00.html.

68. Ellen Laipson, "The Arab Spring's Impact on US-Iran Rivalry," *Frontline*, May 19, 2011, www.pbs.org/wgbh/pages/frontline/tehranbureau/2011/05/the-arab-springs-impact-on-us-iran-rivalry.html.

69. Mehdi Mohammadi, "Basic Condition for the Success of Moscow Talks?" *Iran Review*, June 9, 2012, www.iranreview.org/content/Documents/Basic_Condition_for_the_Success_of_Moscow_Talks_.htm.

Chapter 6

1. Amitai Etzioni, "Should We Support Illiberal Religious Democracies?" *The Political Quarterly* 82, no. 4 (October–December 2011): 568.

2. In Iran, for example, the United States and the United Kingdom famously helped to topple the democratically elected Prime Minister Mohammad Mossadeq after he successfully led a popular movement to nationalize Iran's oil industry in the early 1950s. Relying on this history to criticize President Bush's foreign policy toward Iran nearly half a century later, Representative Jim McDermott (D-WA) said on the House floor, "History is worth noting. In 1953, the United States and the United Kingdom launched Operation Ajax, a covert CIA operation to destabilize and remove the democratically elected government of Iran, including Prime Minister Mossadegh. Why? Oil." *Congressional Record* 153, pt. 10 (May 23, 2007): 13725. For a general background on the 1953 coup d'état in Iran and the US response, see Stephen Kinzer, *All the Shah's Men: An American Coup and the Roots of Middle East Terror* (Hoboken, NJ: John Wiley and Sons, 2003).

3. Harry Davidson, "The Economics of War," *The Final Call*, online ed., November 20, 2001.

4. Mai Yamani, *Changed Identities: The Challenge of the New Generation in Saudi Arabia* (London: Royal Institute of International Affairs, 2000).

5. See, for example, Saudi Arabia's recent announcement of sweeping increases in government spending, including a new minimum wage, unemployment benefits, and wage and allowance increases for public employees and university students. Abeer Allam, "Saudi King Disappoints Reformists," *Financial Times*, March 18, 2011, www.ft.com/cms/s/0/c360bf1c-516d-11e0-a9c6-00144feab49a.html#axzz1HdyGSyBx.

6. Fareed Zakaria, "Why It's Different This Time," *Time*, February 28, 2011, 30–31.

7. For a historical analysis of the US foreign policy toward the Middle East and North Africa, see Mahmood Monshipouri and Ali Assareh, "The Middle East and the United States: What to Expect after the Uprisings?" *Insight Turkey* 13, no. 3 (Summer 2011): 121–138.

8. For an examination of the successes and failures of US foreign policy in the Cold War era, including support for repressive regimes and counterinsurgencies, see Campbell Craig and Fredrik Logevall, *America's Cold War: The Politics of Insecurity* (Boston: Harvard University Press, 2009).

9. For a collection of essays on the relationship between human rights considerations and US foreign policy, see generally Natalie Kaufman Hevener, ed., *The Dynamics of Human Rights in the U.S. Foreign Policy* (New York: Transaction Books, 1981).

10. See Mahmood Monshipouri, "The Paradoxes of U.S. Policy in the Middle East," *Middle East Policy* IX, no. 3 (September 2002): 65–84.

11. F. Gregory Gause III, "The Persistence of Monarchies in the Arabian Peninsula: A Comparative Analysis," in *Middle East Monarchies: The Challenge of Modernity*, ed. Joseph Kostiner (Boulder: Lynne Rienner Publishers, 2000), 179–180.

12. Robert S. Litwack, *Détente and the Nixon Doctrine: American Foreign Policy and the Pursuit of Stability, 1969–1976* (New York: Cambridge University Press, 1984), 194–195.

13. John L. Esposito, *The Islamic Threat: Myth or Reality?* 3rd ed. (New York: Oxford University Press, 1999), 73.

14. Monshipouri, "The Paradoxes of U.S. Policy," 65–84.

15. James A. Bill, *The Eagle and the Lion: The Tragedy of American-Iranian Relations* (New Haven: Yale University Press, 1988), 97.

16. Christopher Joyner, "U.S. Foreign Policy, Democracy, and the Islamic World," in *The United States and Human Rights: Looking Inward and Outward*, ed. David P. Forsythe (Lincoln: University of Nebraska Press, 2000), 262.

17. Ibid., 264.

18. Hugh Eakin, "Will Saudi Arabia Ever Change?" *The New York Review of Books*, January 10, 2013, http://www.nybooks.com/articles/archives/2013/jan/10/will-saudi-arabia-ever-change/?pagination=false.

19. Jay Radzinski and Daniel Nisman, "How to Uproot a New Jihadist Foothold in Africa," *Christian Science Monitor*, April 1, 2013, 36.

20. For a stimulating analysis of US foreign policy, see the opinions expressed by Melani McAlister, Stephen Baker, and Richard Ebeling in Josh Burek, "Searching for Foreign Policy Lessons," *Christian Science Monitor*, September 25, 2001, www.csmonitor.com.

21. Noam Chomsky, "United States, Global Bully: Terrorism, Weapon of the Powerful," http://mondediplo.com/2001/12/02terrorism. This is an edited extract of a talk Chomsky gave at the Massachusetts Institute of Technology on October 18, 2001.

22. Michel Chossudovsky, "Who Is Osama Bin Laden?" *Global Dialogue* 3, no. 4 (Autumn 2001): 5.

23. Ibid.

24. See John L. Esposito's comments quoted in Nick Snow, "In the Wake of September 11," *Oil and Gas Investor* 21, no. 11 (November 2001): 60.

25. Stephen Zunes, "Ten Things You Should Know About U.S. Policy in the Middle East," *AlterNet*, September 26, 2001, www.zmag.org.

26. Augustus Richard Norton, "America's Approach to the Middle East: Legacies, Questions, and Possibilities," *Current History*, January 2002, 4.

27. Mahmood Monshipouri, *Terrorism, Security, and Human Rights: Harnessing the Rule of Law* (Boulder: Lynne Rienner Publishers, 2012), 224.

28. Ed Blanche, "Arab Spring and the Mukhabarat Moment," *The Middle East* 427 (November 2011): 32.

29. Michael J. Boyle, "The War on Terror in American Grand Strategy," *International Affairs* 84, no. 2 (March 2008): 209.

30. Ibid.

31. William Crotty, ed., *Democratic Development and Political Terrorism: The Global Perspective* (Boston: Northeastern University Press, 2005), 524.

32. Jenny White, "The Ebbing Power of Turkey's Secularist Elite," *Current History* 106, no. 704 (December 2007): 428.

33. Bulent Gokay, "Neoliberal Western Policies Led to Uprisings," *Public Service Europe*, March 11, 2011, www.publicserviceeurope.com/article/99/neoliberal-western -policies-led-to-uprisings.

34. Karen Pfeifer, "Economic Reform and Privatization in Egypt," in *The Journey to Tahrir: Revolution, Protest, and Social Change in Egypt*, eds. Jeannie Sowers and Chris Toensing (New York: Verso Books, 2012), 206–209.

35. Ibid., 222.

36. Timothy Mitchell, "Dreamland: The Neoliberalism of Your Desires," in Sowers and Toensing, *The Journey to Tahrir*, 233.

37. Barbara Kotschwar et al., *Reengaging Egypt: Options for U.S.-Egypt Economic Relations* (Washington, DC: Peterson Institute for International Economics, 2010), 41.

38. Marion Dixon, "An Arab Spring," *Review of African Political Economy* 38, no. 128 (June 2011): 309.

39. Max Rodenbeck, "Volcano of Rage," *The New York Review of Books*, March 24, 2011, 6.

40. Kristen Chick, "Fruit of Tahrir Tastes Bitter to Some," *Christian Science Monitor*, June 11, 2012, 22–23; also see an editorial piece, "Egypt Lets Its People Go," *Christian Science Monitor*, June 11, 2012, 33.

41. David D. Kirkpatrick, "Islamists Facing Pressure from Old Elite," *New York Times*, June 15, 2012, A1, A16. The Egyptian constitutional court had sought the dissolution of Parliament at least twice before, in 1987 and 1990, for similar reasons.

42. Hamza Hendawi, "Future Is Clouded as Egyptians Go to Polls," *U-T San Diego*, June 17, 2012, A12.

43. David D. Kirkpatrick, "Morsi Is Winner of Egyptian Presidency, *New York Times*, June 24, 2012, www.nytimes.com/2012/06/25/world/middleeast/mohamed -morsi-of-muslim-brotherhood-declared-as-egypts-president.html?emc=na.

44. Dan Murphy, "Is Egypt's Revolution Over?" *Christian Science Monitor*, July 2, 2012, 18–19.

45. "Egypt's New President Vows Unity, but Powers Are Limited," CNN, June 25, 2012, www.cnn.com/2012/06/25/world/africa/egypt-politics/index.html ?hpt=wo_c1.

46. Shadi Mokhtari, "Cairo Optimism: The People Are Now Part of the Equation," *OpenDemocracy*, June 24, 2012, www.opendemocracy.net/shadi-mokhtari/cairo -optimism-people-are-now-part-of-equation.

47. Hamza Hendawi, "Egypt's Morsi Grants Himself Far-Reaching Powers," AP, November 22, 2012, http://m.apnews.com/ap/db_15727/contentdetail.htm ?contentguid=LvOowaFE.

48. Melissa Gray, "Morsi Edict Divides Egypt, but it Unifies Opponents: Critics and Observers Say," *CNN International*, November 26, 2012, www.cnn.com/2012/11/25 /world/meast/egypt-morsy-views/index.html?hpt=wo_c1.

49. David D. Kirkpatrick, "Egypt's Leader Said to Agree to Limit Scope of Judicial Decree," *New York Times*, November 26, 2012, www.nytimes.com/2012/11/27/ world/middleeast/egypts-president-said-to-limit-scope-of-judicial-decree.html ?emc=na.

50. "Muslim Brotherhood's Morsi Declared Egypt's New President," CNN, June 24, 2012, www.cnn.com/2012/06/24/world/africa/egypt-politics/index.html?hpt=hp_t1.

51. "Egypt's New President Vows Unity."

52. Daniel Byman, "Israel's Pessimistic View of the Arab Spring," *Washington Quarterly* 34, no. 3 (Summer 2011): 130.

53. Ibid., 131.

54. Kareen Fahim, "Challenges Multiply for Presidential Winner in Egypt," *New York Times*, June 24, 2012, www.nytimes.com/2012/06/25/world/middleeast/challenges-multiply-for-victor-in-egypt.html?_r=1&ref=world.

55. Rodenbeck, 6.

56. "Transition in Egypt: A Twist," *Christian Science Monitor*, April 23, 2012, 13.

57. For an excellent analysis on this subject, see "The Arab Revolutions and Human Rights," *Human Rights and Human Welfare*, www.du.edu/korbel/hrhw/roundtable/2011/panel-a/01-2011/arabrevolution.html.

58. Fareed Zakaria, "How Democracy Can Work in the Middle East," *Time*, February 3, 2011, www.time.com/time/world/article/0,8599,2045888-4,00.html.

59. Fouad Ajami, "Demise of the Dictators," *Newsweek*, February 14, 2011, 18–27.

60. Richard Falk, "Libya After Qaddafi," *The Nation*, October 26, 2011, www.thenation.com/article/164221/libya-after-qaddafi.

61. Dirk Vandewalle, "Good Riddance, Gaddafi," *Newsweek*, September 5, 2011, 38–40.

62. Nicolas Pelham, "Libya's Restive Revolutionaries," *Middle East Report*, June 1, 2012, www.merip.org/mero.

63. Ibid.

64. Quoted in Mary-Jane Deeb, "The Arab Spring: Libya's Second Revolution," in *The Arab Spring: Change and Resistance in the Middle East*, eds. Mark L. Haas and David W. Lesch (Boulder: Westview Press, 2013), 73.

65. Ibid.

66. Falk.

67. Michelle Dunne, "Libya's Revolution: Do Institutions Matter?" *Current History* 110, no. 740 (December 2011): 370–371.

68. Abigail Hauslohner, "Hope Among the Ruins," *Time*, June 4, 2012, 38–42.

69. Robin Pomeroy, "Analysis: Iran Hopes Gaddafi Domino Will Fall the Right Way," Reuters, August 25, 2011, www.reuters.com/article/2011/08/25/us-libya-iran-idUSTRE77O39V20110825.

70. Reza Sanati, "A Troubling Lesson from Libya: Don't Give Up Nukes," *Christian Science Monitor*, September 5, 2011, 34.

71. Edwin Lane, "After Qaddafi, Libya's Amazigh Demand Recognition," *BBC News Africa*, December 23, 2011, www.bbc.co.uk/news/world-africa-16289543.

72. Ibid.

73. Elizabeth Dickinson, "Arabs Lose Keynote of Unity," *Christian Science Monitor*, April 23, 2012, 19–20.

74. See, for example, "Half of Bahraini Citizens Are Suffering from Poverty and Poor Living Conditions," *Bahrain Center for Human Rights*, September 24, 2004, www.bahrainrights.org/node/199.

75. Michael Hudson, "Crackdown in Bahrain: Notes from the Field," Al-Jazeera, March 21, 2011, http://english.aljazeera.net/indepth/opinion/2011/03/201132111471720661 .html#.

76. Mohammad Khajouei, "National Dialogue Fails in Bahrain," *Iran Review*, July 21, 2011, www.iranreview.org/content/Documents/National_Dialogue_Fails_in _Bahrain.htm.

77. Anthony Shadid, "Bahrain Boils Under the Lid of Repression," *New York Times*, September 15, 2011, www.nytimes.com/2011/09/16/world/middleeast/repression -tears-apart-bahrains-social-fabric.html?_r=1&nl=todaysheadlines&emc=tha22.

78. Ibid.

79. Aaron David Miller, "For America, An Arab Winter," *Wilson Quarterly* XXXV, no. 3 (Summer 2011): 42.

80. Barak Barfi, quoted in Anthony H. Cordesman, Barak Barfi, Bassam Haddad, and Karim Mezran, "The Arab Uprisings and U.S. Policy: What Is the American National Interest?" *Middle East Policy* XVIII, no. 2 (Summer 2011): 10.

81. Elizabeth Dickinson, "Racing to Nowhere," *Christian Science Monitor*, April 23, 2012, 19.

82. Stephen Lendman, "Bahrain: A Case Study in Despotism," *International: Police State and Prisons*, April 1, 2012, www.indybay.org/newsitems/2012/04/01/18710498 .php.

83. Dickinson, "Racing to Nowhere," 19.

84. "UN Condemns Bahrain Verdicts," *Irishtimes.com*, www.irishtimes.com /newspaper/breaking/2011/0930/breaking51.html.

85. Souad Mekhennet, "Bahrain Holds Grand Prix Event, as Protesters Keep a Distance," *New York Times*, April 23, 2012, A6.

86. James L. Gelvin, *The Arab Uprisings: What Everyone Needs to Know* (New York: Oxford University Press, 2012), 114.

87. Ibid., 115.

88. Richard Falk, "Syria: The Tragic Space between the Unacceptable and the Impossible," Al-Jazeera, May 31, 2012, www.aljazeera.com/indepth/opinion/2012 /05/20125318233126386.html.

89. Richard Falk, "A Brief Further Comment on Syria," http://richardfalk .wordpress.com/2012/07/25/a-brief-further-comment-on-syria.

90. Ibid.

91. Gelvin, 112.

92. Falk, "A Brief Further Comment on Syria."

93. David E. Sanger, "Rebel Arms Flow Is Said to Benefit Jihadists in Syria," *New York Times*, October 14, 2012, www.nytimes.com/2012/10/15/world/middleeast /jihadists-receiving-most-arms-sent-to-syrian-rebels.html?nl=todaysheadlines&emc =edit_th_20121015.

94. Ibid.

95. Falk, "A Brief Further Comment on Syria."

96. Anthony Shadid, "Fear of Civil War Mounts in Syria as Crisis Deepens," *New York Times*, January 14, 2012, www.nytimes.com/2012/01/15/world/middleeast/syria -in-deep-crisis-may-be-slipping-out-of-control.html?pagewanted=all.

97. Kyle Almond, "Why the World Isn't Intervening in Syria," CNN, February 23, 2012, www.cnn.com/2012/02/23/world/syria-intervention/index.html.

98. "Lebanese Druze Leader Fears Civil War in Syria," Reuters, January 18, 2012, www.reuters.com/article/2012/01/18/us-syria-jumblatt-idUSTRE80H0N220120118.

99. Fareed Zakaria, "The Case Against Intervention in Syria," *Time*, June 11, 2012, www.time.com/time/magazine/article/0,9171,2116135-1,00.html.

100. Marc Lynch, "Syria," *Economist*, June 3, 2012, www.economist.com/debate /days/view/815.

101. Gelvin, 118.

102. Reza Marashi and Trita Parsi, "The Gift and the Curse: Iran and the Arab Spring," in Haas and Lesch, *The Arab Spring*, 146.

103. Gelvin, 155.

104. Mehdi Mohammadi, "Syria's Developments and Iran's National Security Equation," *Iran Review*, July 22, 2012, www.iranreview.org/iranSpectrum/index.aspx.

105. Francesco Sisci, "China Plays the Middle East Card," *Asian Times*, April 23, 2002.

106. "China Backs Transition in Syria, Opposes Intervention," Reuters, September 5, 2012, http://news.yahoo.com/china-backs-transition-syria-opposes-intervention -055405757.html.

107. Ibid.

108. Daniel Treisman, "Why Russia Supports Syria's Assad," UCLAToday, published on CNN, February 2, 2012, http://today.ucla.edu/portal/ut/PRN-russia-s-support -for-assad-regime-228392.aspx.

109. Andrei Tsygankov, "Why Russia Still Backs Assad," *The Moscow Times* 5002 (October 29, 2012), www.themoscowtimes.com/opinion/article/why-russia-still-backs -assad/470555.html.

110. Ruslan Pukhov, "Why Russia Is Backing Syria," op-ed, *New York Times*, July 6, 2012, www.nytimes.com/2012/07/07/opinion/why-russia-supports-syria.html.

111. Ibid.

112. Mehran Kamrava, "The Arab Spring and the Saudi-Led Counterrevolution," *Orbis* 56, no. 1 (Winter 2012): 96–104.

113. Mark Landler and Neil MacFarquhar, "Heavier Weapons Push Syrian Crisis Toward Civil War," *New York Times*, June 13, 2012, A1 and A12.

114. Christa Case Bryant, Scott Peterson, and Nicholas Blanford, "Obama Faces a Hotter Mideast," *Christian Science Monitor*, March 25, 2013, 18–20.

115. Mohammad Reza Kiani and Maysam Behravesh, "The Syrian Crisis: What Is at Stake for Regional Players?" *Iran Review*, September 4, 2011, www.iranreview.org /content/Documents/The_Syrian_Crisis_What_is_at_Stake_for_Regional_Players .htm.

116. An interview by Hassan Khaled Chatila, "The Revolt in Syria: Its Roots and Prospects," *Links: International Journal of Socialist Renewal*, May 9, 2011, http://links.org .au/node/2322.

117. Ibid.

118. The video can be accessed online at www.youtube.com/watch?v=vQ5ktd YZbbQ&feature=player_embedded. The chants targeting Iran start around the 1:40 mark.

119. Neil MacFarquhar and Hwaida Saad, "Violence in Syria's Capital Even with a Cease-Fire," *New York Times*, April 25, 2012, A6.

120. Nick Cumming-Bruce and Rick Gladstone, "Syria Talks Won't Include the Saudis or Iranians," *New York Times*, June 28, 2012, A10.

121. Ibid.

122. Brock Dahl, "Foreign Military Intervention in Syria?" *Christian Science Monitor*, July 23, 2012, 36.

123. John Hubbel Weiss, "Foreign Military Intervention in Syria?" *Christian Science Monitor*, July 23, 2012, 36.

124. Quoted in Mustafa Akyol, *Islam Without Extremes: A Muslim Case for Liberty* (New York: W. W. Norton, 2011), 241.

125. Ibid.

126. Anthony Shadid, "In the Mideast Riddle, Turkey Offers Itself as an Answer," *New York Times*, September 26, 2011, www.nytimes.com/.

127. Issa Golverdi, "Syria: Convergence of US, Turkey Regional Interests," *Iran Review*, September 17, 2011, www.iranreview.org/content/Documents/Syria_Convergence_of_US_Turkey_Regional_Interests.htm.

128. Alexander Christie-Miller, "Turks Pitch Arabs a Democratic Model," *Christian Science Monitor*, September 26, 2011, 10.

129. Ibid.

130. Hassan Ahmadian, "Iran and Turkey-Egypt Regional Rivalries," *Iran Review*, September 23, 2011, www.iranreview.org/content/Documents/Iran_and_Turkey_Egypt_Regional_Rivalries.htm.

131. Christie-Miller, "Turks Pitch Arabs a Democratic Model."

132. Ali Valigholizadeh, "Iran & NATO Missile Shield in Turkey," *Iran Review*, September 16, 2011, www.iranreview.org/content/Documents/Iran_NATO_Missile_Shield_in_Turkey.htm.

133. Bahram Amir Ahmadian, "Missile Defense Shield: Much Ado for Nothing," *Iran Review*, September 30, 2011, www.iranreview.org/content/Documents/Missile_Defense_Shield_Much_Ado_for_Nothing_.htm.

134. John Hughes, "Turkey's Mideast Potential Marred by Israeli Dispute," *Christian Science Monitor*, October 10, 2011, 37.

135. Golverdi.

136. Fareed Zakaria, "The Storm Before the Calm," *Time*, October 3, 2011, 19.

137. Mark L. Haas, "Turkey and the Arab Spring: Ideological Promotion in a Revolutionary Era," in Haas and Lesch, *The Arab Spring*, 162–164; for this quotation, see especially 164.

138. Ömer Taşpınar, "Turkey: An Interested Party," in *The Arab Awakening: America and the Transformation of the Middle East*, eds. Kenneth M. Pollack et al. (Washington, DC: Brookings Institution Press, 2011), 273.

139. Erol Cebeci and Kadir Ustun, "The Syrian Quagmire: What's Holding Turkey Back?" *Insight Turkey* 14, no. 2 (2012): 18.

140. Ibid., 21.

141. Miller, 42.

142. Richard Phelps, "Islamism Has Lost Its Monopoly on Dissent," *The Guardian*, February 17, 2011, www.guardian.co.uk/commentisfree/belief/2011/feb/17/islamism-dissent-uprisings-middle-east.

143. See the letter to the editor, "Our Condolences, the Muslim Brotherhood Says," *New York Times*, September 14, 2012, A22.

144. Ibid.

145. Marc Santora, "Streets Are Cleared in Cairo; Unrest toward Film Subsides," *New York Times*, September 15, 2012, www.nytimes.com/2012/09/16/world/middleeast/anti-american-protests-subside-in-middle-east.html?ref=world.

146. Bobby Ghosh, "The Agents of Outrage: Flashpoint," *Time*, September 24, 2012, 34.

147. David D. Kirkpatrick, "Cultural Clash Fuels Muslims Raging at Film," *New York Times*, September 16, 2012, www.nytimes.com/2012/09/17/world/middleeast/muslims-rage-over-film-fueled-by-culture-divide.html?_r=1 &pagewanted=all.

148. S. M. Farid Mirbagheri, *War and Peace in Islam: A Critique of Islamic/ist Political Discourses* (New York: Palgrave-Macmillan, 2012), 171.

149. Robin Wright, "The Middle East: They've Arrived," in *The Islamists Are Coming: Who They Really Are*, ed. Robin Wright (Washington, DC: Woodrow Wilson Center Press, US Institute of Peace Press, 2012), 6. Wright has divided the new spectrum of Islamism into classical Islamists (Iran's Ayatollah Khomeini and Egypt's Sayyid Qutb; Salafis are mentioned here as only a small but new fraction of the classical Islamists), neo-Islamists (reform-minded Islamic groups within Egypt's Muslim Brothers and Tunisia's An-Nahda), and post-Islamists (AKP in Turkey). See 8–9.

150. Samer Shehata, "Egypt: The Founders," in Wright, *The Islamists Are Coming*, 28.

151. Quinn Mecham, "The Rise of Islamist Actors: Formulating a Strategy for Sustained Engagement," *Project on Middle East Democracy*, April 27, 2012, 1–6, http://pomed.org/wordpress/wp-content/uploads/2012/04/POMED-Policy-Brief_Mecham.pdf.

152. Thomas Pierret, "Syria: Old-Timers and Newcomers," in Wright, *The Islamists Are Coming*, 78–79.

153. Christopher Alexander, "Tunisia: The Best Bet," in Wright, *The Islamists Are Coming*, 48.

154. See Teddy3inDC, "Islamist Rise After the Arab Spring," *Global Voice Hall*, www.globalvoicehall.com/islamist-rise-after-arab-spring.

155. Michael A. Lange, "After the Arab Spring: Political Islam on the Rise?" *Kas International Reports*, April 2012, 18, www.kas.de/wf/doc/kas_30741-544-2-30.pdf?120416182201.

156. Larbi Sadiki, "The Arab Spring: Voting Islamism," Al-Jazeera, December 7, 2011, www.aljazeera.com/indepth/opinion/2011/12/2011126105646767454.html.

157. Kristen Chick and John Thorne, "How Islamist Are They?" *Christian Science Monitor*, August 20, 2012, 18–20.

158. Lange.

159. Steven Lee Myers, "US Is Near Pact to Cut $1 Billion from Egypt Debt," *New York Times*, September 4, 2012, A1–A7.

160. Annika Folkeson, "Islamist Groups: Parties and Factions," in Wright, *The Islamists Are Coming*, 138.

161. Hisham H. Ahmed, "The Arab Spring, the West, and Political Islam," *Solidarity*, January/February 2012, www.solidarity-us.org/node/3492.

162. Mecham, 3.

163. Ibid., 5.

164. Mirbagheri, 176.

165. Jeremy Pressman, "Same Old Story? Obama and the Arab Uprisings," in Haas and Lesch, *The Arab Spring*, 232.

166. Tony Evans, *Human Rights in the Global Political Economy: Critical Processes* (Boulder: Lynne Rienner Publishers, 2010), 38.

167. Michael Hudson, "Crackdown in Bahrain: Notes from the Field," Al-Jazeera, March 21, 2011, http://english.aljazeera.net/indepth/opinion/2011/03/201132111471720661.html#.

168. Robert Marquand, "Dignity Drives Arab Revolts," *Christian Science Monitor*, March 14, 2011, 10.

169. Pfeifer, 222–223.

170. Kenneth M. Pollack, "The United States: A New American Grand Strategy for the Middle East," in Pollack et al., *The Arab Awakening*, 318.

171. Shadi Hamid, "Islamists and the Brotherhood: Political Islam and the Arab Spring," in Pollack et al., *The Arab Awakening*, 37.

172. Bahey eldin Hassan, *Fractured Walls . . . New Horizons: Human Rights in the Arab Region, Annual Report 2011* (Cairo: Cairo Institute for Human Rights Studies, 2012), 16–17, www.cihrs.org/wp-content/uploads/2012/06/the-report-e.pdf.

173. Ibid., 21.

174. Hamid, 37.

175. Ibid., 38.

176. Marc Lynch, *The Arab Uprising: The Unfinished Revolutions of the New Middle East* (New York: Public Affairs, 2012), 232.

177. Ibid., 231–232.

178. International Crisis Group, "Popular Protest in North Africa and the Middle East (1): Egypt Victorious?" *Crisis Group*, February 24, 2011, www.crisisgroup.org/en /regions/middle-east-north-africa/egypt-syria-lebanon/egypt/101-popular-protest-in -north-africa-and-the-middle-east-i-egypt-victorious.aspx. For a related commentary, see also an editorial piece, "A Check on Fear in the Mideast," *Christian Science Monitor*, June 20, 2011, 32.

179. Eric Denis, "Demographic Surprises Foreshadow Change in Neoliberal Egypt," in Sowers and Toensing, *The Journey to Tahrir*, 235–241.

180. Gönül Tol, "The 'Turkish Model' in the Middle East," *Current History* 111, no. 749 (December 2012): 350–355.

181. Elliot Colla, "The People Want," *Middle East Report, No. 263* 42, no. 2 (Summer 2012): 13.

182. Shadi Mokhtari, "The New Politics of Human Rights in the Middle East," *Foreign Policy*, October 30, 2012, http://mideast.foreignpolicy.com/posts/2012/10/30/ the_new_politics_of_human_rights_in_the_middle_east.

183. Ayman Al-Sayyad, a former adviser to the Egyptian President Mohamed Morsi and currently the editor-in-chief of *Weghat Nazar*, an Egyptian monthly literary magazine, underlined the significance of spontaneity on the street, considering it an advantage for the youth movements that lack the necessary political institutions in place to directly challenge or even shape the government's policies. I interviewed Al-Sayyad on January 8, 2013, in Cairo, Egypt.

184. Nezar Al-Sayyad, "The Virtual Square: Urban Space, Media, and the Egyptian Uprising," *Harvard International Review* 34, no. 1 (Summer 2012).

185. I conducted an interview with Ahmed Maher on January 7, 2013, in Cairo, Egypt. His words and a reasonable degree of optimism in his outlook of things to come in the region lifted my spirit.

186. Ellen Lust, Gamal Soltan, and Jakob Wichmann, "After the Arab Spring: Islamism, Secularism, and Democracy," *Current History* 111, no. 749 (December 2012): 363.

187. I interviewed Professor Omaima Abou Bakr at Cairo University on January 9, 2013.

188. Sheri Berman, "The Promise of the Arab Spring: in Political Development, No Gain Without Pain," *Foreign Affairs* 92, no. 1 (January/February 2013): 66.

REFERENCES

Abdullah, Rasha H. 2007. *The Internet in the Arab World: Egypt and Beyond*. New York: Peter Lang Publishing.

Ajami, Fouad. 2011. "Demise of the Dictators." *Newsweek*, February 14: 18–27.

Akkari, Abelijalil. 2004. "Education in the Middle East and North Africa: The Current Situation and Future Challenges." *International Education Journal* 5, no. 2: 144–153.

Amanat, Abbas. 2011. "Empowered Through Violence: The Reinventing of Islamic Extremism." In *The Age of Terror: America and the West After September 11*, edited by Strobe Talbott and Nayan Chanda, 23–52. New York: Basic Books.

Ansari, Ali M. 2006. *Confronting Iran: The Failure of American Foreign Policy and the Next Great Crisis in the Middle East*. New York: Basic Books.

Ayoob, Mohammed. 2011. "Beyond the Democratic Wave in the Arab World: The Middle East's Turko-Persian Future." *Insight Turkey* 13, no. 2, Spring: 57–70.

Bacevich, Andrew J. 2011. "Last Act in the Mideast." *Newsweek*, April 11: 48–49.

Bahry, Louay Y. 2001. "The New Arab Media Phenomenon: Qatar's Al-Jazeera." *Middle East Policy* VIII, no. 2, June: 88–99.

Baker, Raymond William. 2003. *Islam Without Fear: Egypt and the New Islamists*. Cambridge, MA: Harvard University Press.

Bauder, Julia, ed. 2006. *Is Iran a Threat to Global Security?* New York: Greenhaven Press.

Bayat, Asef. 2011. "Arab Revolts: Islamists Aren't Coming!" *Insight Turkey* 13, no. 2, Spring: 9–14.

Beitz, Charles R. 2009. *The Idea of Human Rights*. New York: Oxford University Press.

Bellin, Eva. 2012. "Reconsidering the Robustness of Authoritarianism in the Middle East: Lessons from the Arab Spring." *Comparative Politics* 44, no. 2, January: 127–149.

Berman, Sheri. 2013. "The Promise of the Arab Spring: In Political Development, No Gain Without Pain." *Foreign Affairs* 92, no. 1, January/February: 64–74.

Bill, James A. 1998. *The Eagle and the Lion: The Tragedy of American-Iranian Relations*. New Haven: Yale University Press.

Blankson, Isaac A., and Patrick D. Murphy, eds. 2007. *Negotiating Democracy: Media Transformations in Emerging Democracies*. Albany: State University of New York Press.

Boyle, Michael J. 2008. "The War on Terror in American Grand Strategy." *International Affairs* 84, no. 2, March: 191–209.

Brysk, Alison. 2009. *Global Good Samaritans: Human Rights as Foreign Policy*. New York: Oxford University Press.

Byman, Daniel. 2011. "Israel's Pessimistic View of the Arab Spring." *Washington Quarterly* 34, no. 3, Summer: 123–136.

Cebeci, Erol, and Kadir Ustun. 2012. "The Syrian Quagmire: What's Holding Turkey Back?" *Insight Turkey* 14, no. 2: 13–21.

Charrad, Mounira M. 2001. *States and Women's Rights: The Making of Postcolonial Tunisia, Algeria, and Morocco*. Berkeley: University of California Press.

Chase, Anthony Tirado. 2012. *Human Rights, Revolution, and Reform in the Muslim World*. Boulder: Lynne Rienner Publishers.

Chick, Kristen. 2011. "Why Tunisia? Why Now?" *Christian Science Monitor*, January 31: 8–10.

Chomiak, Laryssa, and John P. Entelis. 2011. "The Making of North Africa's Intifadas." *Middle East Report, No. 259* 41, no. 2, Summer: 8–15.

Chossudovsky, Michel. 2001. "Who Is Osama Bin Laden?" *Global Dialogue* 3, no. 4, Autumn: 1–7.

Ciezadlo, Annia. 2011. "Eat, Drink, Protest: Stories of the Middle East's Hungry Rumblings." *Foreign Policy* 186, May/June: 76–79.

Cohen, Roger. 2009. "Iran: The Tragedy and the Future." *The New York Review of Books* LVI, no. 13, August 13: 7–10.

Cook, Steven A. 2007. *Ruling but Not Governing: The Military and Political Development in Egypt, Algeria, and Turkey*. Baltimore: John Hopkins University Press.

Cross, Kevin. 2010. "Why Iran's Green Movement Faltered: The Limits of Information Technology in a Rentier State." *SAIS Review* 30, no. 2, Summer–Fall: 169–187.

Crotty, William, ed. 2005. *Democratic Development and Political Terrorism: The Global Perspective*. Boston: Northeastern University Press.

Dahi, Omar S. 2011. "Understanding the Political Economy of the Arab Revolts." *Middle East Report, No. 259* 41, no. 2, Summer: 2–6.

Dickinson, Elizabeth. 2012. "Arabs Lose Keynote of Unity." *Christian Science Monitor*, April 23: 19–20.

Donnelly, Jack. 1998. *International Human Rights*. 2nd ed. Boulder: Westview Press.

Droz-Vincent, Phillippe. 2011. "From Fighting Formal Wars to Maintaining Civil Peace." *International Journal of Middle East Studies* 43, no. 3, August: 392–394.

Dunne, Michelle. 2011. "Libya's Revolution: Do Institutions Matter?" *Current History* 110, no. 740, December: 370–371.

Ebadi, Shirin. 1994. *History and Documentation of Human Rights in Iran*. Tehran: Roshangaran.

Ebadi, Shirin, and Azadeh Moaveni. 2006. *Iran Awakening: A Memoir of Revolution and Hope*. New York: Random House.

Eickelman, Dale F. 2002. "Bin Laden, the Arab Street, and the Middle East's Democracy Deficit." *Current History*, January: 36–39.

El-Nawawy, Mohammed, and Adel Iskandar Farag. 2002. *Al-Jazeera: How the Free Arab News Network Scooped the World and Changed the Middle East*. Boulder: Westview Press.

Esposito, John L. 1999. *The Islamic Threat: Myth or Reality?* 3rd ed. New York: Oxford University Press.

————. 2002. *Unholy War: Terror in the Name of Islam*. New York: Oxford University Press.

Etzioni, Amitai. 2011. "Should We Support Illiberal Religious Democracies?" *The Political Quarterly* 82, no. 4, October–December: 567–573.

Evans, Tony. 2011. *Human Rights in the Global Political Economy: Critical Processes*. Boulder: Lynne Rienner Publishers.

Falk, Richard. 2011. "Post-Mubarak Revolutionary Chances." *AlJazeera English: Opinion*. http://english.aljazeera.net/indepth/opinion/2011/02/201121711284402313.html.

Feiler, Bruce. 2011. *Generation Freedom: The Middle East Uprisings and the Remaking of the Modern World*. New York: HarperCollins.

Flamini, Roland. 2012. "Turmoil in the Arab World." *Global Issues*, 2011 ed. CQ Researcher, 165–194. Washington, DC: CQ Press.

Forsythe, David P., ed. 2000. *The United States and Human Rights: Looking Inward and Outward*. Lincoln: University of Nebraska Press.

————. 2011a. *The Politics of Prisoner Abuse: The United States and Enemy Prisoners after 9/11*. New York: Cambridge University Press.

————. 2011b. "US Foreign Policy and Human Rights: Situating Obama." Paper presented at the International Studies Association, Montreal, Canada.

Friedlander, Melvin. 1991. *Conviction and Credence: U.S. Policymaking in the Middle East*. Boulder: Lynne Rienner Publishers.

Friedman, Thomas L. 2012. "Defendant No. 34 Has Her Say." *New York Times*, April 25: A21.

Fuller, Graham E. 2002. "The Future of Political Islam." *Foreign Affairs* 81, no. 2, March/April: 48–60.

Gause, F. Gregory, III. 2011. "Why Middle East Studies Missed the Arab Spring: The Myth of Authoritarian Stability." *Foreign Affairs* 90, no. 4, July/August: 81–90.

Gelvin, James L. 2012. *The Arab Uprisings: What Everyone Needs to Know*. New York: Oxford University Press.

Ghonim, Wael. 2012. *Revolution 2.0: The Power of People Is Greater Than the People in Power: A Memoir*. Boston: Houghton Mifflin Harcourt.

Goldstein, Eric. 2011. "A Middle-Class Revolution." In *Revolution in the Arab World: Tunisia, Egypt, and the Unmaking of an Era*, edited by Marc Lynch, Susan B. Glasser, and Blake Hounshell, 66–69. Washington, DC: Foreign Policy.

Goldstone, Jack A. 2010. "The New Population Bomb: The Four Megatrends That Will Change the World." *Foreign Affairs* 98, no. 1, January/February: 31–43.

Haas, Mark L., and David W. Lesch, eds. 2013. *The Arab Spring: Change and Resistance in the Middle East*. Boulder: Westview Press.

Hashemi, Nader. 2011. "The Arab Revolution of 2011: Reflections on Religion and Politics." *Insight Turkey* 13, no. 2, Spring: 15–21.

Hashemi, Nader, and Danny Postel, eds. 2010. *The People Reloaded: The Green Movement and the Struggle for Iran's Future*. Brooklyn: Melville House.

Hassan, Bahey eldin. 2012. *Fractured Walls … New Horizons: Human Rights in the Arab Region, Annual Report 2011*. Cairo: Cairo Institute for Human Rights Studies, 16–17. www.cihrs.org/wp-content/uploads/2012/06/the-report-e.pdf.

Hatem, Mervat. 2011. "Gender and Revolution in Egypt." *Middle East Report, No. 261* 41, no. 4 (Winter): 38–41.

Hen-Tov, Elliot, and Nathan Gonzalez. 2011. "The Militarization of Post-Khomeini Iran: Praetorianism 2.0." *The Washington Quarterly* 34, no. 1, Winter: 45–59.

Hounshell, Blake. 2011. "The Revolution Will Be Tweeted: Life in the Vanguard of the New Twitter Proletariat." *Foreign Policy* 187, July/August: 20–21.

Howard, Philip N. 2011. *The Digital Origins of Dictatorship and Democracy: Information Technology and Political Islam.* New York: Oxford University Press

Huntington, Samuel P. 1991. *The Third Wave: Democratization in the Late Twentieth Century.* Norman: University of Oklahoma Press.

Kandeel, Amal A. 2011. "Egypt at a Crossroads." *Middle East Policy* XVIII, no. 2, Summer: 37–45.

Karawan, Ibrahim A. 2011. "Politics and the Army in Egypt." *Survival* 53, no. 2, April–May: 43–50.

Karr, Mehranghiz. 1999. *Eliminating Discrimination Against Women: A Comparison of the Convention on Elimination of All Forms of Discrimination Against Women with Iran's Domestic Laws.* Tehran: Parvin.

Khouri, Rami G. 2011. "The Long Revolt." *Wilson Quarterly* XXXV, no. 3, Summer: 43–46.

Kinzer, Stephen. 2006. *Overthrow: America's Century of Regime Change from Hawaii to Iraq.* New York: Times Books.

Knickmeyer, Ellen. 2011. "The Arab World's Youth Army." In *Revolution in the Arab World: Tunisia, Egypt, and the Unmaking of an Era,* edited by Marc Lynch, Susan B. Glasser, and Blake Hounshell, 122–126. Washington, DC: Foreign Policy.

Kozhanov, Nikolay A. 2011. "US Economic Sanctions Against Iran: Undermined by External Factors." *Middle East Policy* XVIII, no. 3, Fall: 144–160.

Kurzman, Charles. 2010. "Cultural Jiu-Jitsu and the Iranian Greens." In *The People Reloaded: The Green Movement and the Struggle for Iran's Future,* edited by Nader Hashemi and Danny Postel, 7–17. Brooklyn: Melville House.

Linklater, Andrew. 2007. *Critical Theory and World Politics: Citizenship, Sovereignty, and Humanity.* New York: Routledge.

Lust, Ellen, Gamal Soltan, and Jakob Wichmann. 2012. "After the Arab Spring: Islamism, Secularism, and Democracy." *Current History* 111, no. 749, December: 362–364.

Lynch, Cecelia. 2012. "'Kony 2012': If Only Helping Africa Were So Simple." *Christian Science Monitor,* April 9: 36.

Lynch, Marc. 2011. "After Egypt: The Limits and Promise of Online Challenges to the Authoritarian Arab State." *Perspectives on Politics* 9, no. 2 (June): 301–310.

———. 2012. *The Arab Uprising: The Unfinished Revolutions of the New Middle East.* New York: Public Affairs.

Lynch, Marc, Susan B. Glasser, and Blake Hounshell, eds. 2011. *Revolution in the Arab World: Tunisia, Egypt, and the Unmaking of an Era.* Washington, DC: Foreign Policy.

Mahdi, Ali Akbar, ed. 2003. *Teen Life in the Middle East.* Westport, CT: Greenwood Press.

Majd, Homan. 2010. *The Ayatollah's Democracy: An Iranian Challenge.* New York: W. W. Norton.

———. 2011. "The Green Movement Is a Viable Civil Rights Movement." In *Iran,* edited by Debra A. Miller. Detroit: Greenhaven Press.

Marquand, Robert. 2011. "Dignity Drives Arab Revolts." *Christian Science Monitor,* March 14: 10.

Marzouki, Nadia. 2011. "From People to Citizens in Tunisia." *Middle East Report, No. 259* 42, no. 2, Summer: 16–19.

Miller, Aaron David. 2011. "For America, an Arab Winter." *Wilson Quarterly* XXXV, no. 3, Summer: 36–42.

Mokhtari, Shadi, 2012. "Cairo Optimism: The People Are Now Part of the Equation." *OpenDemocracy*, June 24. www.opendemocracy.net/shadi-mokhtari/cairo -optimism-people-are-now-part-of-equation.

Mollahosseini, Ali. 2008. "Gender and Employment in Iran." *Indian Journal of Gender Studies* 15, no. 1: 159–162.

Monshipouri, Mahmood. 1988. *Islamism, Secularism, and Human Rights in the Middle East.* Boulder: Lynne Rienner Publishers.

———. 2002. "The Paradoxes of U.S. Policy in the Middle East." *Middle East Policy* IX, no. 3, September: 65–84.

———. 2004. "The Road to Globalization Runs through Women's Struggle: Iran and the Impact of Nobel Peace Prize." *World Affairs* 167, no. 1, Summer: 3–14.

———. 2009. *Muslims in Global Politics: Identities, Interests, and Human Rights.* Philadelphia: University of Pennsylvania Press.

———. 2012. *Terrorism, Security, and Human Rights: Harnessing the Rule of Law.* Boulder: Lynne Rienner Publishers.

Monshipouri, Mahmood, and Ali Assareh. 2009. "The Islamic Republic and the 'Green Movement': Coming Full Circle." *Middle East Policy* XVI, no. 4, Winter: 27–46.

Murphy, Dan, Nicholas Seeley, and Kristen Chick. 2012. "Arab Upheaval Begins to Settle." *Christian Science Monitor*, February 6: 12–13.

Nickiporuk, Brian. 2000. *The Security Dynamics of Demographic Factors.* Santa Monica, CA: Rand.

Norton, Augustus Richard. 2012. "Arab Revolts Upend Old Assumptions." *Current History* 111, no. 741, January: 14–18.

Norton, Augustus Richard, and Ashraf El-Sherif. 2011. "North Africa's Epochal Year of Freedom." *Current History* 110, no. 736, May: 201–203.

Osman, Tarek. 2010. *Egypt on the Brink: From Nasser to Mubarak.* New Haven: Yale University Press.

Parsi, Trita. 2012. *A Single Roll of the Dice: Obama's Diplomacy with Iran.* New Haven: Yale University Press.

Peterson, Scott. 2010. *Let the Swords Encircle Me: Iran—A Journey Behind the Headlines.* New York: Simon and Schuster.

Petras, James. 2011. *The Arab Revolt and the Imperialist Counterattack.* Atlanta: Clarity Press.

Pollack, Kenneth M. 2011. "America's Second Chance and the Arab Spring." *Foreign Policy*, December 5, www.foreignpolicy.com/articles/2011/12/05/americas _second_chance.

Pollack, Kenneth M., et al. 2011. *The Arab Awakening: America and the Transformation of the Middle East.* Washington, DC: Brookings Institution Press.

Ramazani, Rouhollah. 1986. *Revolutionary Iran: Challenge and Response in the Middle East.* Baltimore: Johns Hopkins University Press.

Rodenbeck, Max. 2011. "Volcano of Rage." *The New York Review of Books*, March 24: 4–7.

Rogan, Eugene. 2011. "The Arab Wave." *The National Interest* 113, May/June: 48–56.

Rosenberg, Tina. 2011. "Revolution U." In *Revolution in the Arab World: Tunisia, Egypt, and the Unmaking of an Era*, edited by Marc Lynch, Susan B. Glasser, and Blake Hounshell, 127–142. Washington, DC: Foreign Policy.

Sallam, Hesham. 2011. "Striking Back at Egyptian Workers." *Middle East Report, No. 259* 41, no. 2, Summer: 20–25.

Shebata, Dina. 2011. "The Fall of the Pharaoh: How Hosni Mubarak's Reign Came to an End." *Foreign Affairs* 90, no. 3, May/June: 26–32.

Shadid, Anthony. 2012. "Libya Struggles to Curb Militias as Chaos Grows." *New York Times*, February 9: A1–A6.

Shokr, Ahmad. 2011. "The 18 Days of Tahrir." *Middle East Report, No. 258* 41, no.1, Spring: 14–19.

Simonsen, Jorgen Baek, ed. 2005. *Youth and Youth Culture in the Contemporary Middle East*. Aarhus, Denmark: Aarhus University Press.

Sjoberg, Laura. 2011. "Emotion, Risk, and Feminist Research in IR." *International Studies Review* 13, no. 4, December: 699–703.

Smith, Pamela Ann, and Peter Feuilherade. 2011. "Now, the Media Revolution." *The Middle East* 427, November 21: 35–38.

Sorenson, David S. 2011. "Transitions in the Arab World: Spring or Fall?" *Strategic Studies Quarterly*, Fall: 22–49.

Sowers, Jeannie, and Chris Toensing, eds. 2012. *The Journey to Tahrir: Revolution, Protest, and Social Change in Egypt*. New York: Verso Books.

Taheri, Amir. 2010. *The Persian Night: Iran Under the Khomeinist Revolution*. New York: New Material.

United Nations Development Program, Regional Bureau for Arab States. 2009. *Arab Human Development Report 2009: Challenges to Human Security in the Arab Countries*. New York: UNDP.

———. 2010. *Human Development Report 2010*. New York: UNDP.

Valigholizadeh, Ali. 2011. "Iran & NATO Missile Shield in Turkey." *Iran Review*, September 16, 2011, www.iranreview.org/content/Documents/Iran_NATO_Missile _Shield_in_Turkey.htm.

Vandewalle, Dirk. 2011. "Good Riddance, Gaddafi." *Newsweek*, September 5: 38–40.

White, Jenny. 2007. "The Ebbing Power of Turkey's Secularist Elite." *Current History* 106, no. 704, December: 427–433.

Woodberry, J. Dudley. 2002. "Terrorism, Islam, and Mission: Reflections of a Guest in Muslim Lands." *International Bulletin of Missionary Research*, January: 2–7.

Wright, Robin. 2011. *Rock the Casbah: Rage and Rebellion Across the Islamic World*. New York: Simon and Schuster.

Yamani, Mai. 2000. *Changed Identities: The Challenge of the New Generation in Saudi Arabia*. London: Royal Institute of International Affairs.

Zairmaran, Mohammad, and Shirin Ebadi. 1996. *Modernity and Tradition in the Iranian Legal System*. Tehran: Gangedanesh.

Zakaria, Fareed. 2011a. "The Revolution." *Time*, February 14, 26–33.

———. 2011b. "Why It's Different This Time." *Time*, February 28, 30–31.

Zunes, Stephen. 2001. "Ten Things You Should Know About U.S. Policy in the Middle East." *AlterNet*, September 26, 2001. www.zmag.org.

INDEX

Abdel Nasser, Gamal, 64
Abdullah (king of Saudi Arabia), 135
Abdullah II (king of Jordan), 29, 42
Abou-Bakr, Omaima, 181
Abu Ghraib, 102, 137, 168
Agha Soltan, Neda, 74
Ahmadinejad, Mahmoud,
    72, 80, 110, 116
Al Arabiya, 19
Alawite, 2, 162
Al-Azhar, 81
Albright, Madeleine, 108
Al Jazeera, 8–9, 19, 67
Al-Katiba Military Base, 52
Al-Mahalla Textiles, 89
Al-Nahda Party, 37, 83, 147,
    167–168, 169, 182
Al-Nour Party, 41–42, 82
Al-Qaeda, 2, 110, 127, 128;
    radical Islamists in Syrian,
    156; terror network, 173
Al Wifaq, 153–154
Amazigh (Berbers), 151–152
Anglo-Iranian Oil Company, 134
Annan, Kofi, 159, 162–163
April 6 Youth Movement, 71, 89–90
Arab hip-hop, 92–95
Arabization, 39
Arab League, 157
Arab Monetary Fund (AMF), 4
Arab Spring, 1, 10, 42, 83, 98, 101–102,
    117, 119–120; Arab identity and,
    142; economics and, 132; Egyptian

experience of, 143; Iran and,
    117–120; Islamist dilemma and,
    175; Islamist groups in Libya and,
    152; Libyan fallout of, 149–152;
    regional implications of, 131; role
    of women in, 81–85; Saudi king
    Abdullah and, 135; Turkey and
    the new Middle East, 163–167;
    US foreign policy and, 134, 152
Arafat, Yasser, 136
Assad, Bashar al-, 2, 157, 158,
    159, 162, 163, 164, 166
Assembly of Experts (Majles-
    e-Khobregan), 78

Bagram Air Force Base, 102
Bahrain Centre for Human
    Rights (BCHR), 152, 154
Bakhtiar, Shahpur, 105
Bayat, Asef, 65
Bazargan, Mahdi, 105, 106
BBC, 15
Belaid, Chokri, 182
Ben Ali, Zine El Abidine, 35,
    51, 83, 140, 172, 182
Benghazi, 47, 152
Berlin Wall, 39, 50
Bin Laden, Osama, 136
Bishara, Marwan, 5
Borai, Negad el, 39
Bouazizi, Mohamed, 4, 34, 48, 51, 91,
    96; self-immolation of, 34–35, 48
Bourguiba, Habib, 32, 51, 55, 83

ABOUT THE AUTHOR

Mahmood Monshipouri, PhD, is professor in the Department of International Relations at San Francisco State University and a visiting associate professor at the University of California at Berkeley. He specializes in human rights, identity construction, and globalization in the Muslim world. He is author of *Muslims in Global Politics: Identity, Interests, and Human Rights* (Philadelphia: University of Pennsylvania Press, 2009). His most recent books are *Human Rights in the Middle East: Frameworks, Goals, and Strategies* (New York: Palgrave-Macmillan, 2011) and *Terrorism, Security, and Human Rights: Harnessing the Rule of Law* (Boulder: Lynne Rienner Publishers, 2012).

CPSIA information can be obtained
at www.ICGtesting.com
Printed in the USA
FSOW04n0652280915
11607FS

9 781612 051352